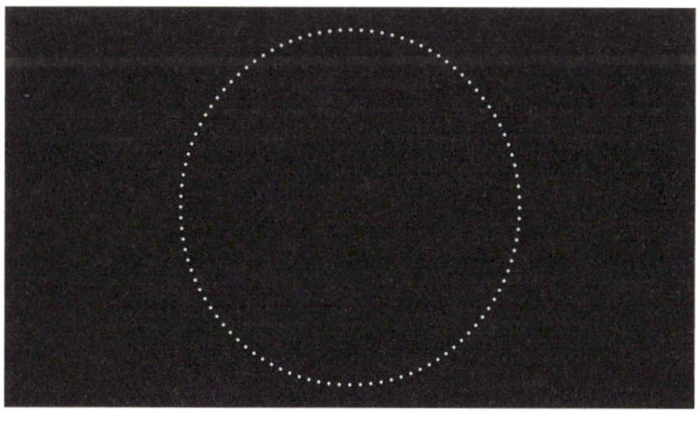

T-I-T-E-L

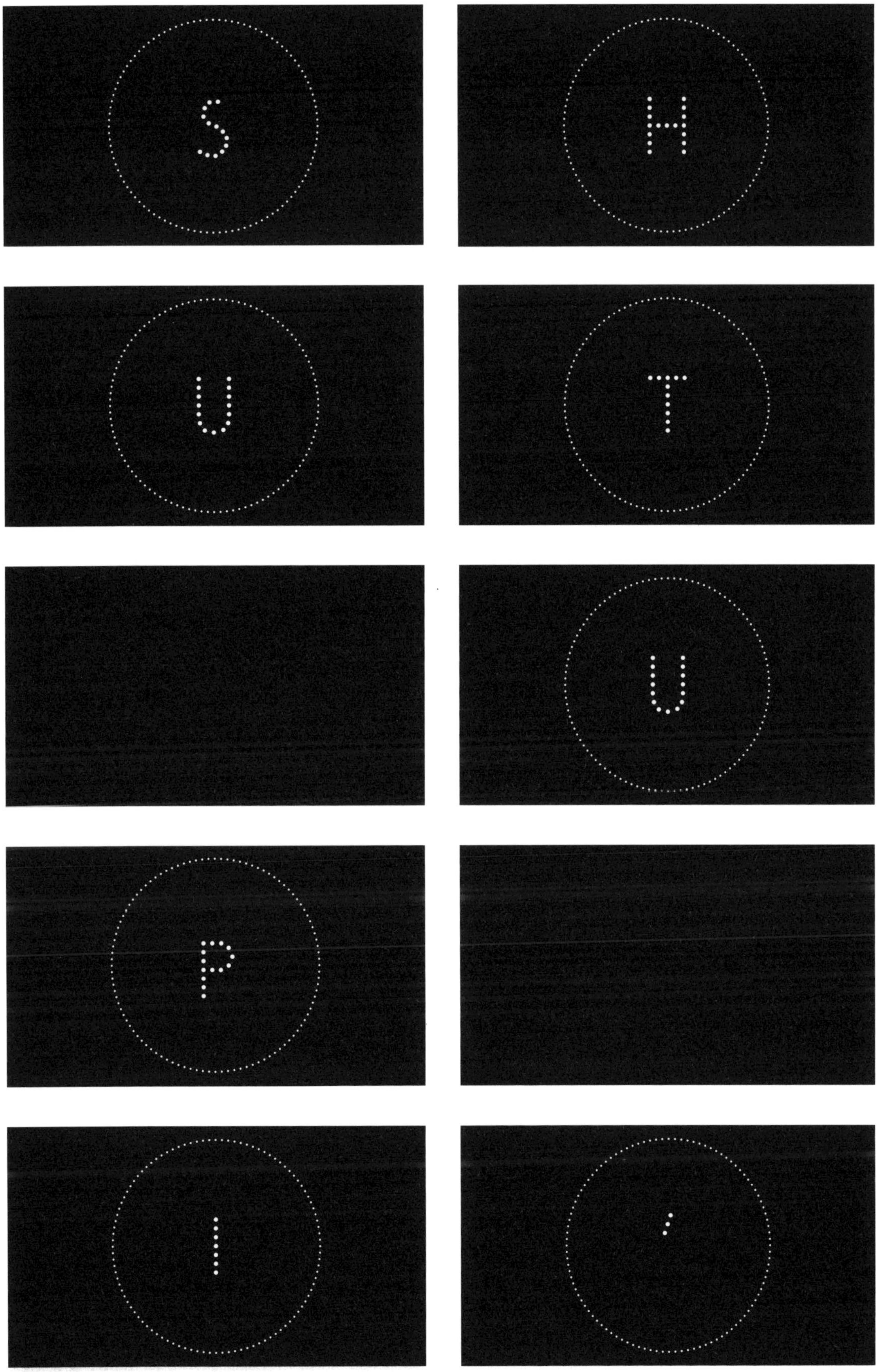

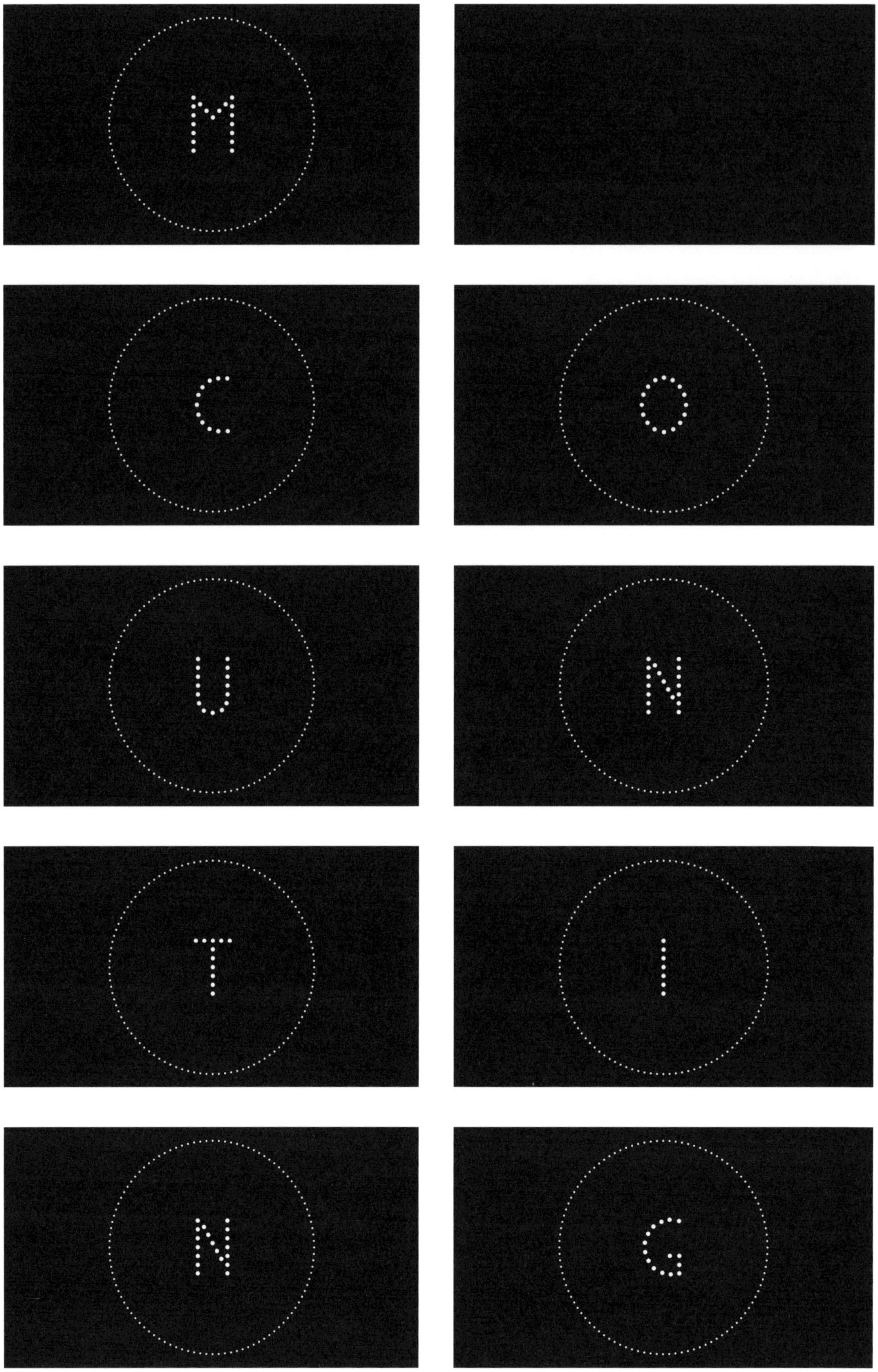
M
C
O
U
N
T
I
N
G

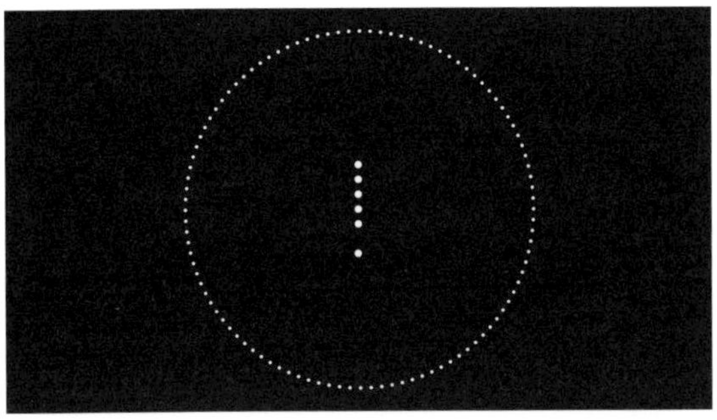

a

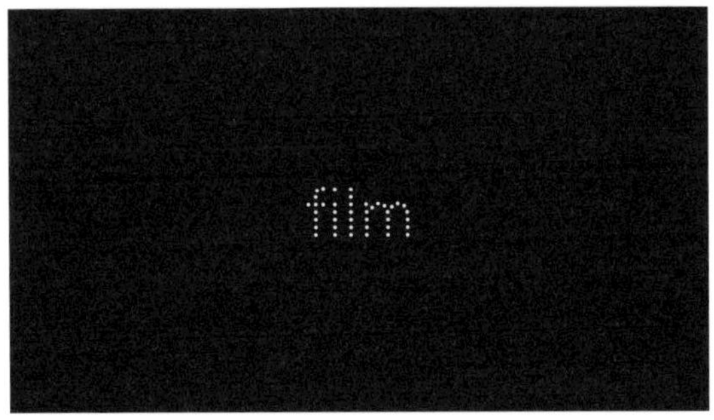
film

written,

directed,

produced

by

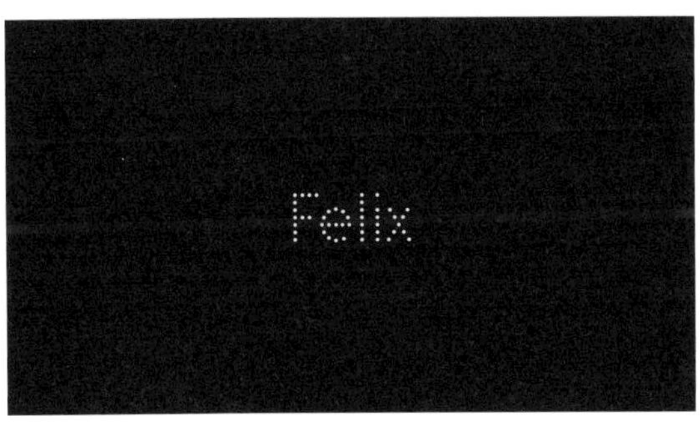
Felix

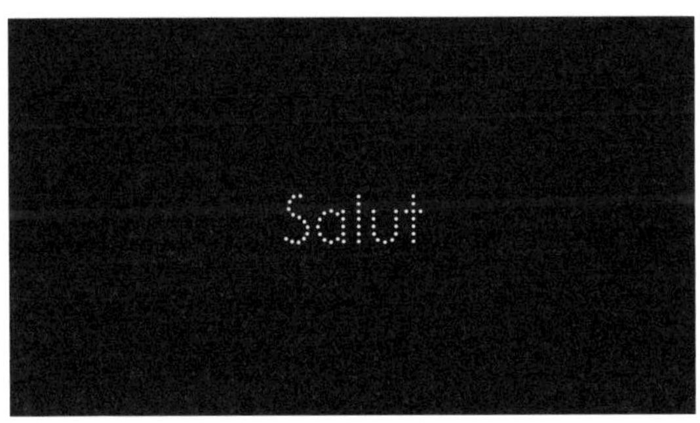
Salut

A-C-T-O-R-S

TARA

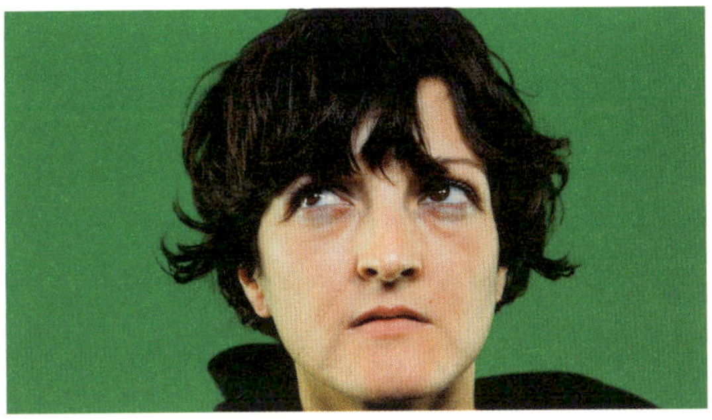

Tara Khan

OHIO

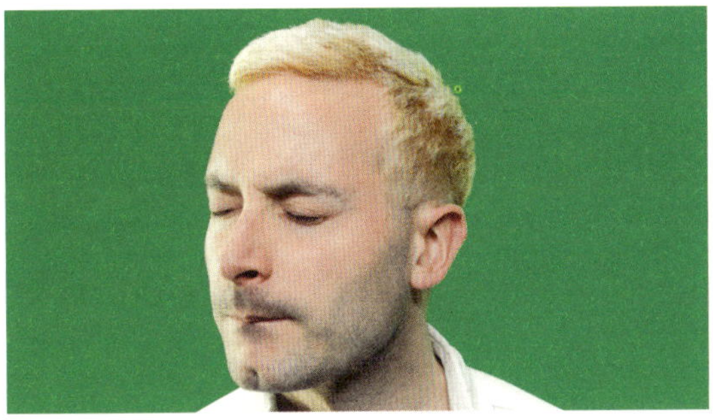

Matthew Lutz-Kinoy

ORACLE

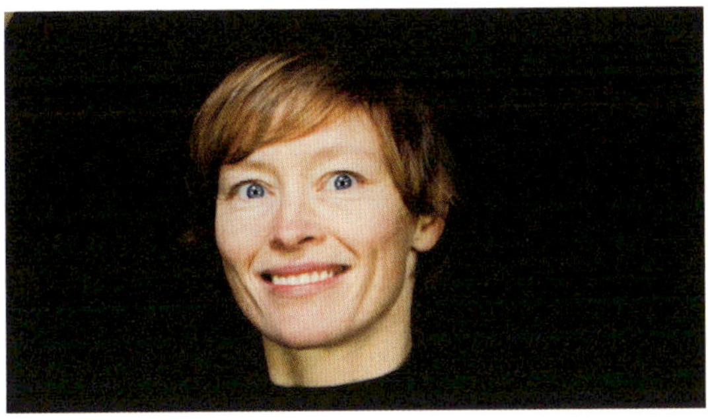

Karen Røise Kielland

MAGIC CHILD

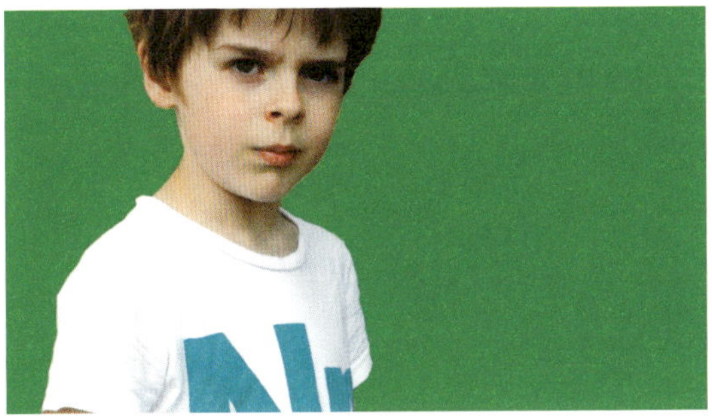

Noah Weigand

DOT

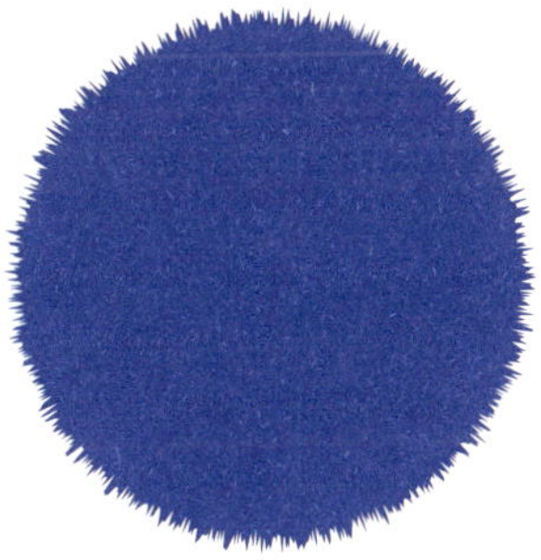

animated by Simon Krahl

VOICE

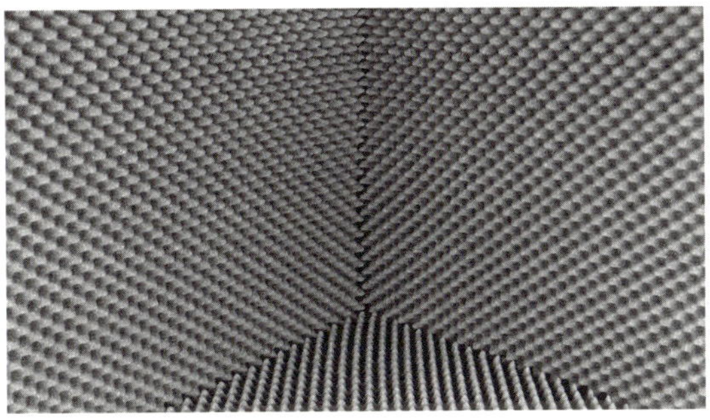

Wendy Taylor

S-C-E-N-E I

Close-up of the Oracle's face. Her eyes are following the movement of something moving from left to right and right to left.

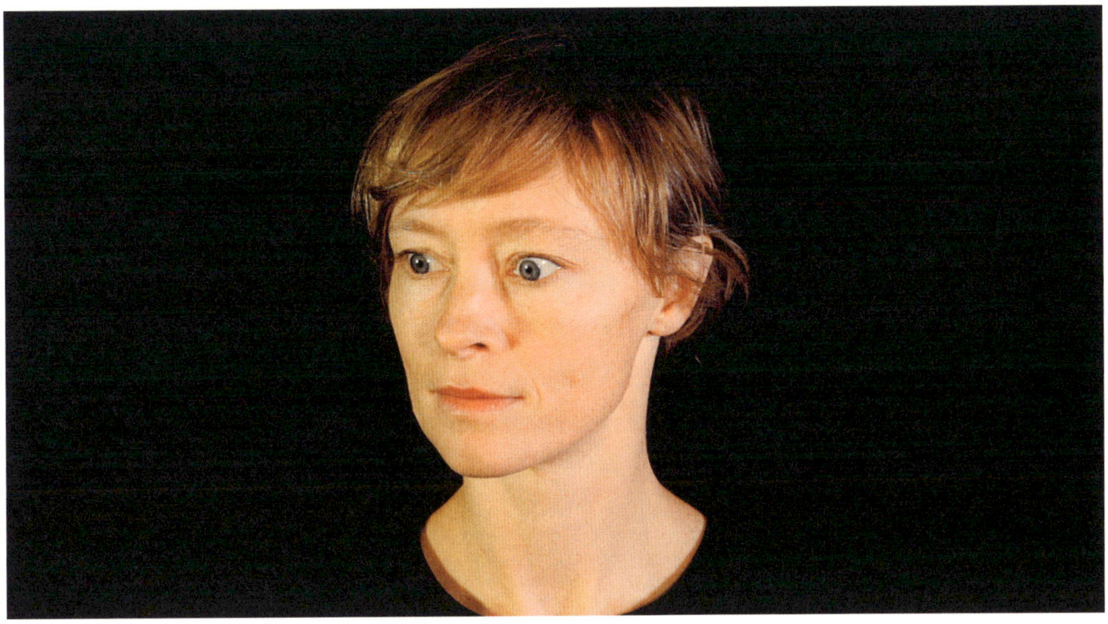

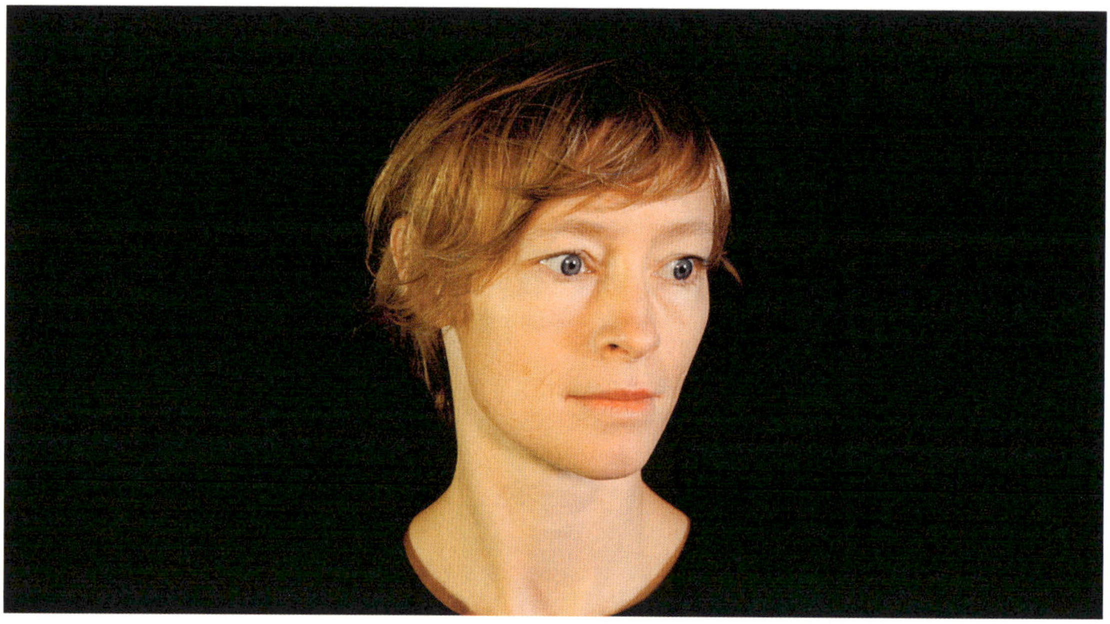

S-C-E-N-E 2

The Dot as speaking clock.

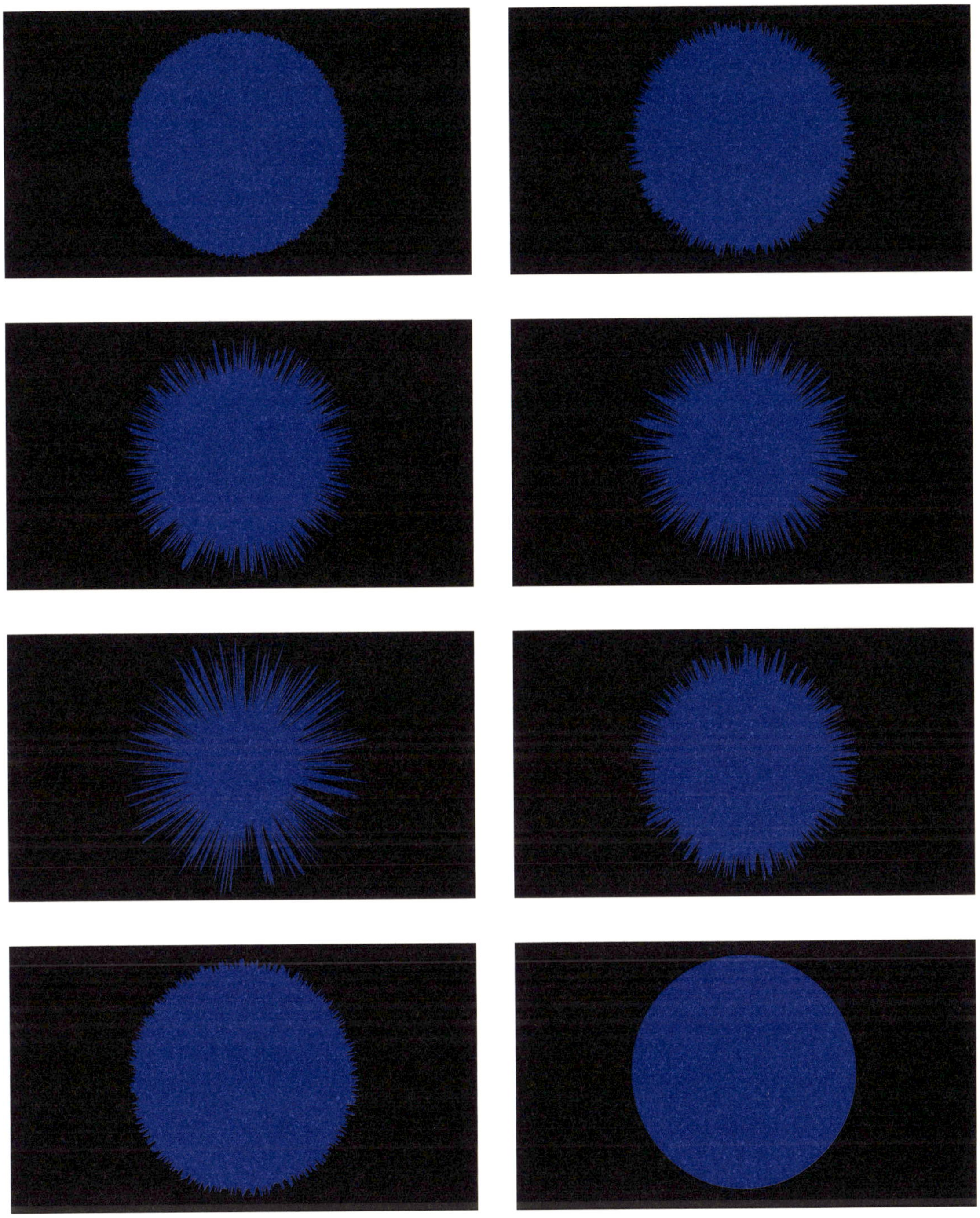

Dot:

At the third stroke it will be 10:28 and 40 seconds ... At the third stroke it will be 10:28 and 55 seconds ... At the third stroke it will be 10:29 and 10 seconds ...

S-C-E-N-E 3

Tara looks at a universe of round objects on a Persian carpet. From time to time she touches an object with her fingers. She holds it in her hands and studies it from different angles. Sometimes – if the object fits a certain criterium – she keeps it in her hand for a little while. Ohio stares into the other direction while he keeps counting. Tara picks up an object and shows it to Ohio.

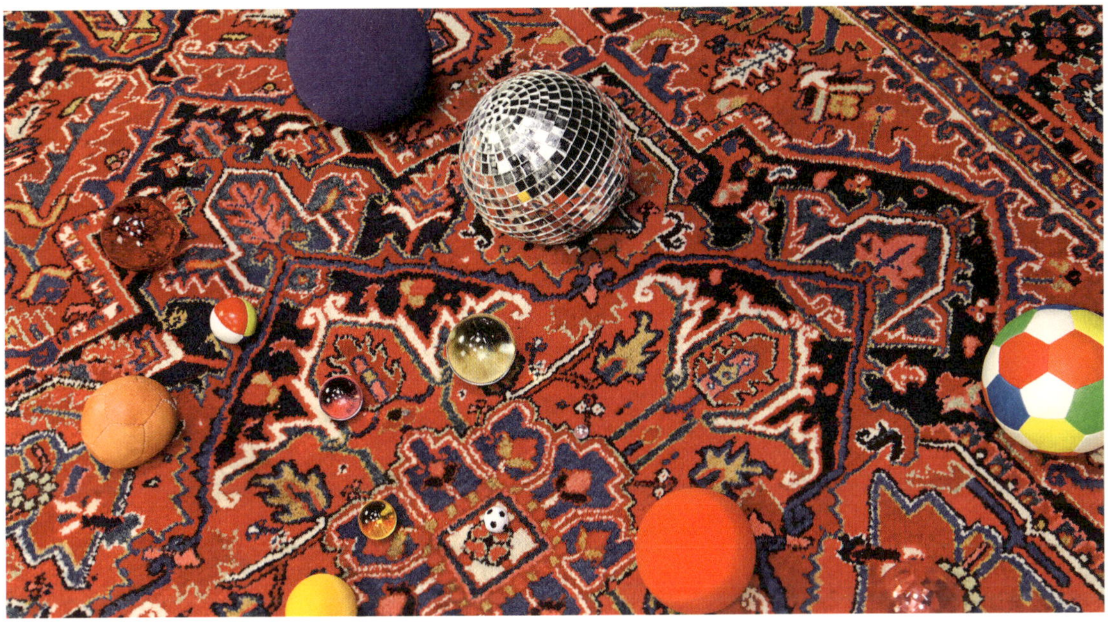

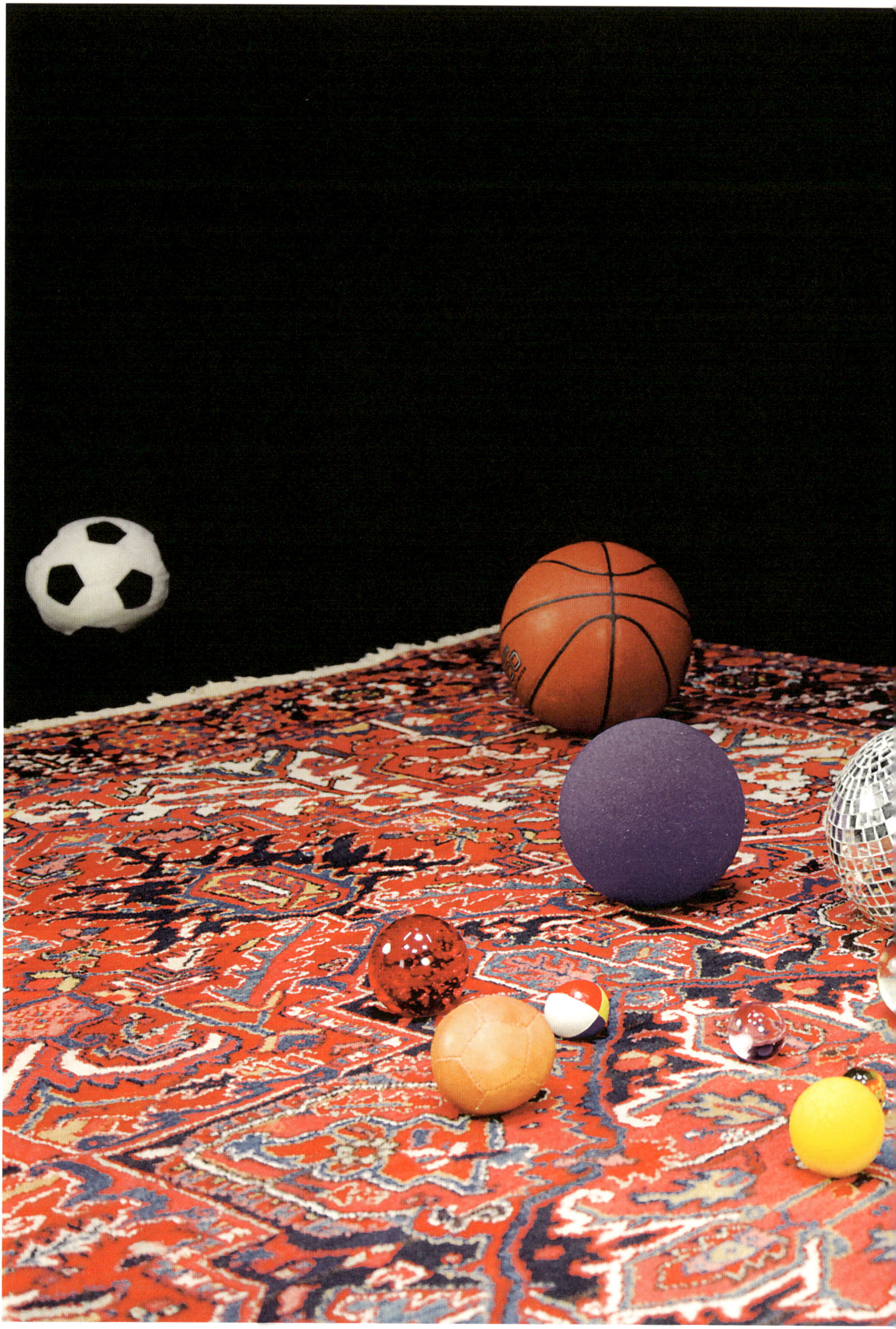

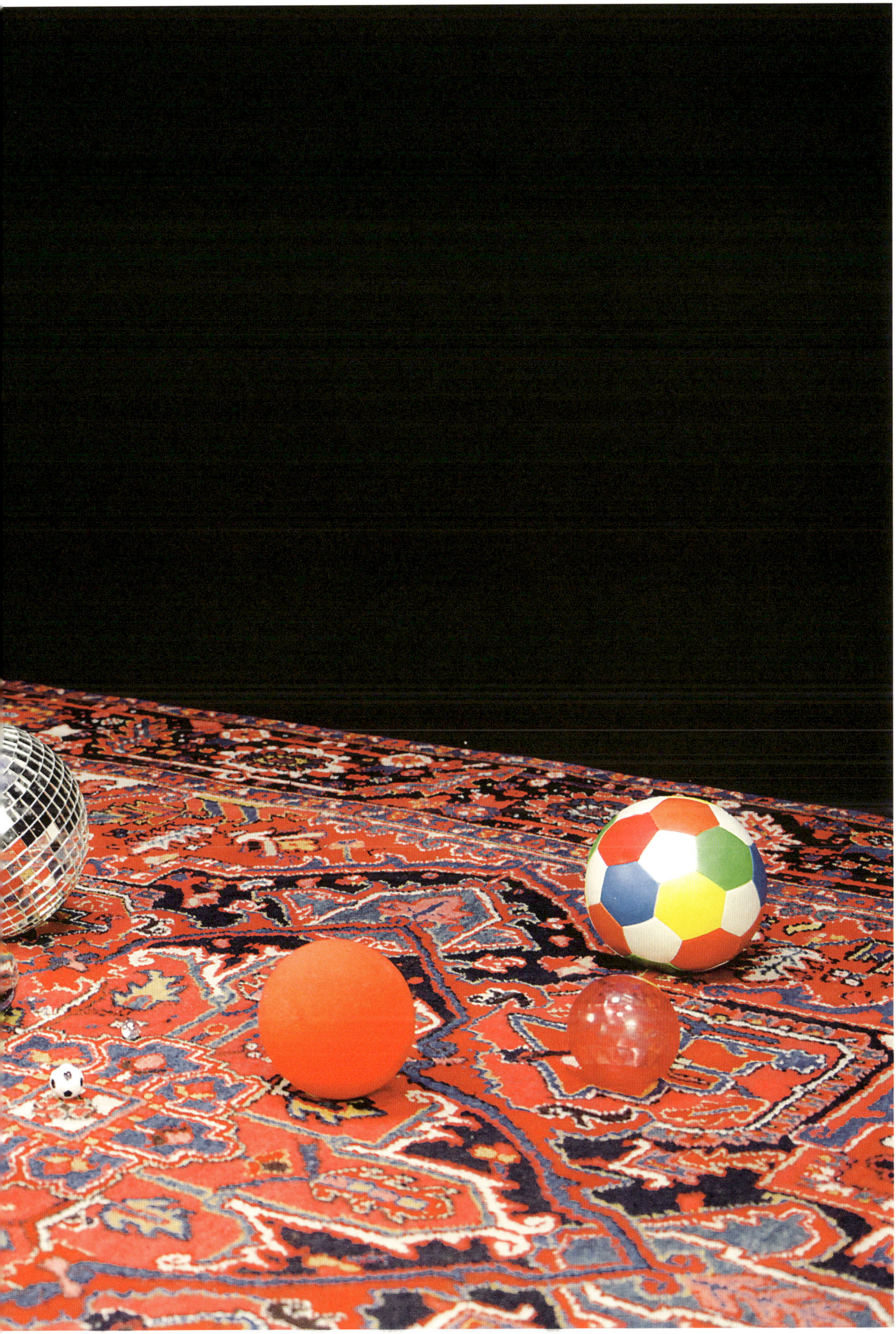

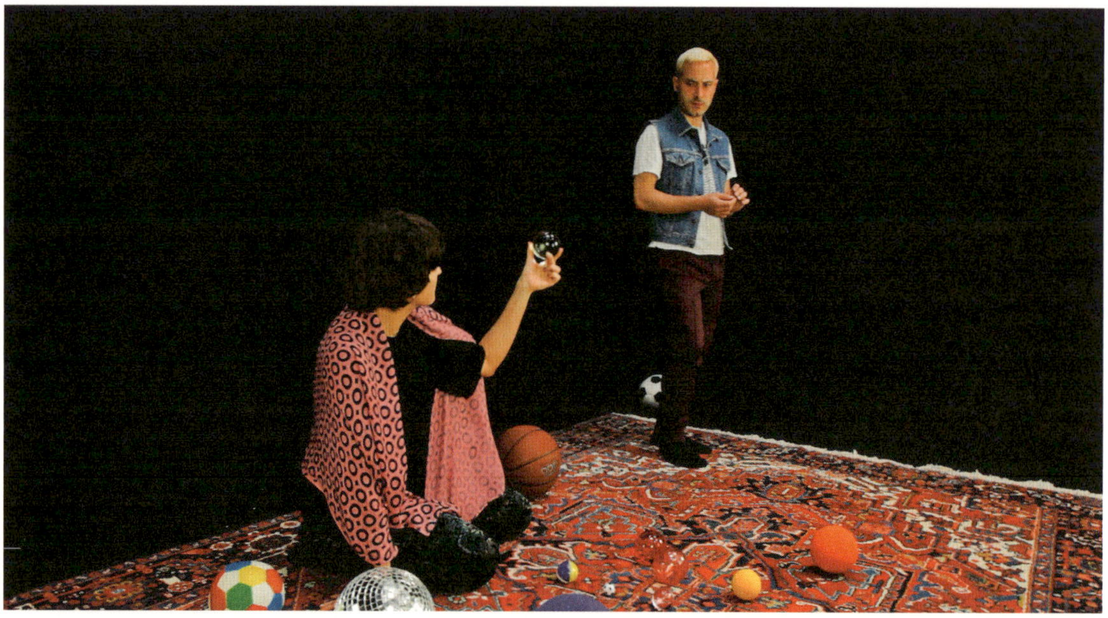

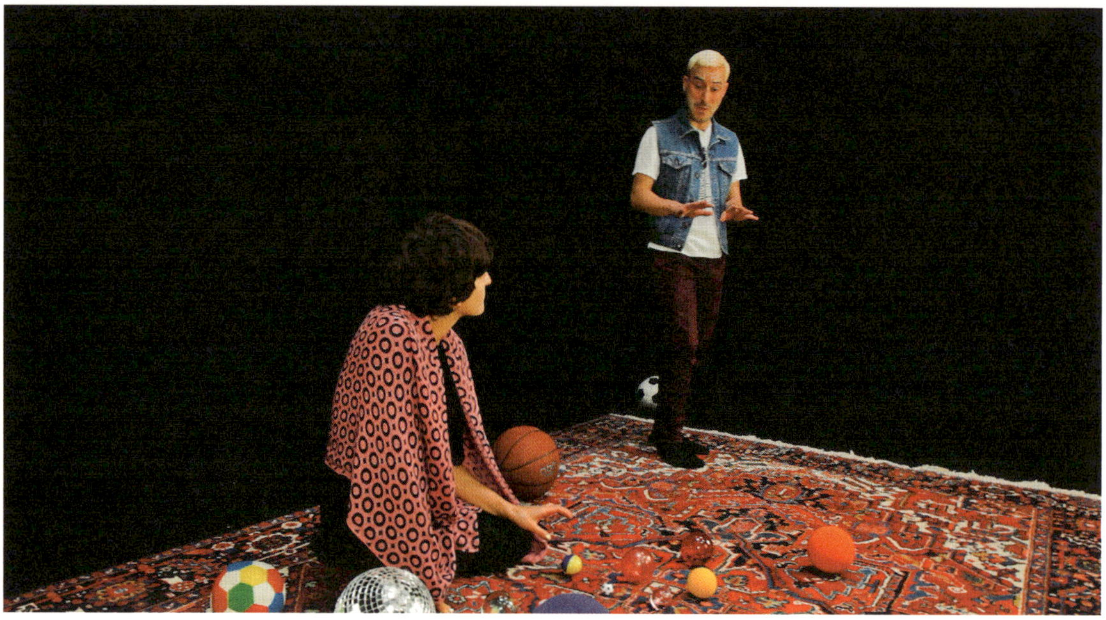

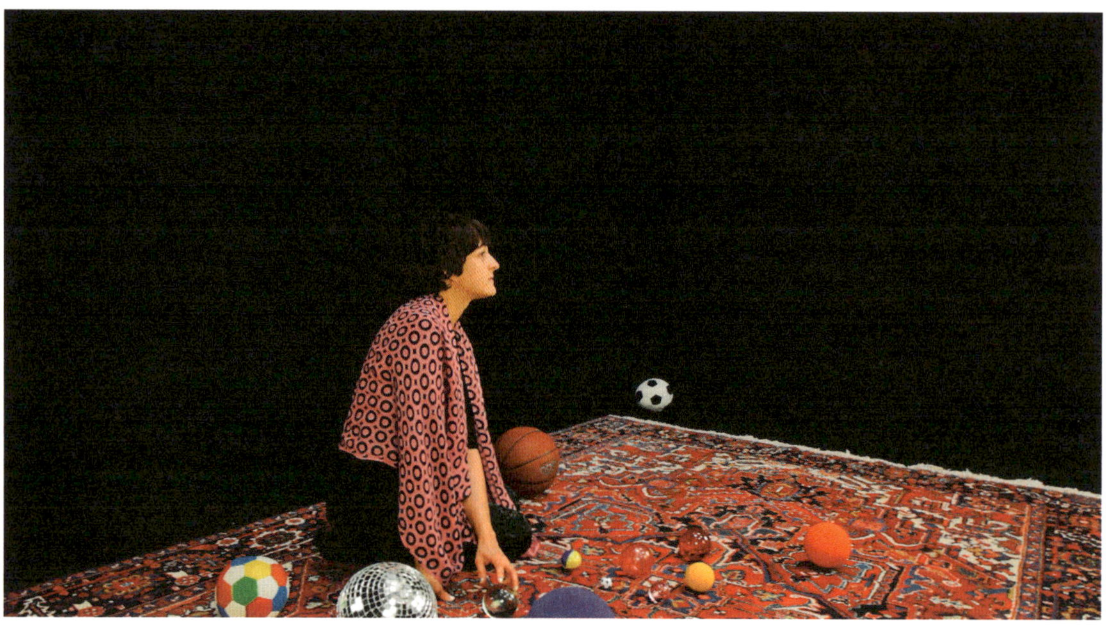

Tara:

What do you think this is? You think this is an “O”?

Ohio:

5, 8, 13. I’m not sure, Tara. I really don’t know. It could be a “Zero” too.

Tara:

It’s so confusing sometimes. In the beginning I thought there was a system to this.

Ohio:

21, 34, 55. Yes, that’s what I thought. We made terrific progress when we started. I felt we were close to a real breakthrough. But somehow ... 89, 144, 233.

Tara:

Yeah, ...

Ohio:

I don’t know Tara, you see – this here – it’s messed up. We just can’t stick it back together and fix it again. 377, 610, 987.

While he is counting, Ohio leaves the scene. Tara wonders where he went and looks around for him.

Tara:

Ohio? Ohio?

S-C-E-N-E 4

The Oracle performs a word with her arms inside a neon light square.

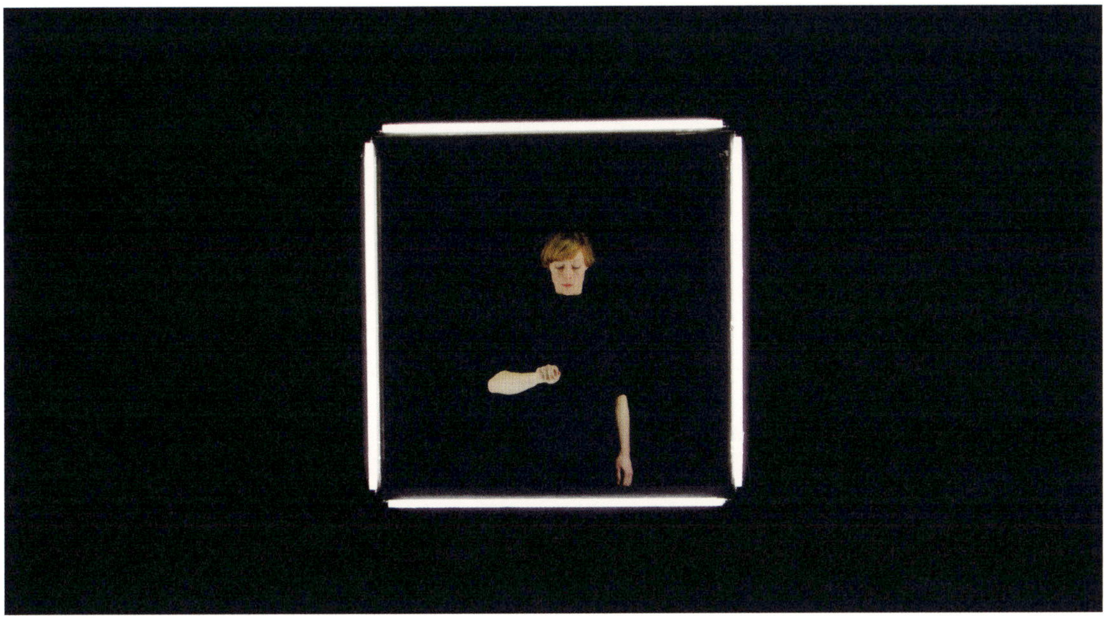

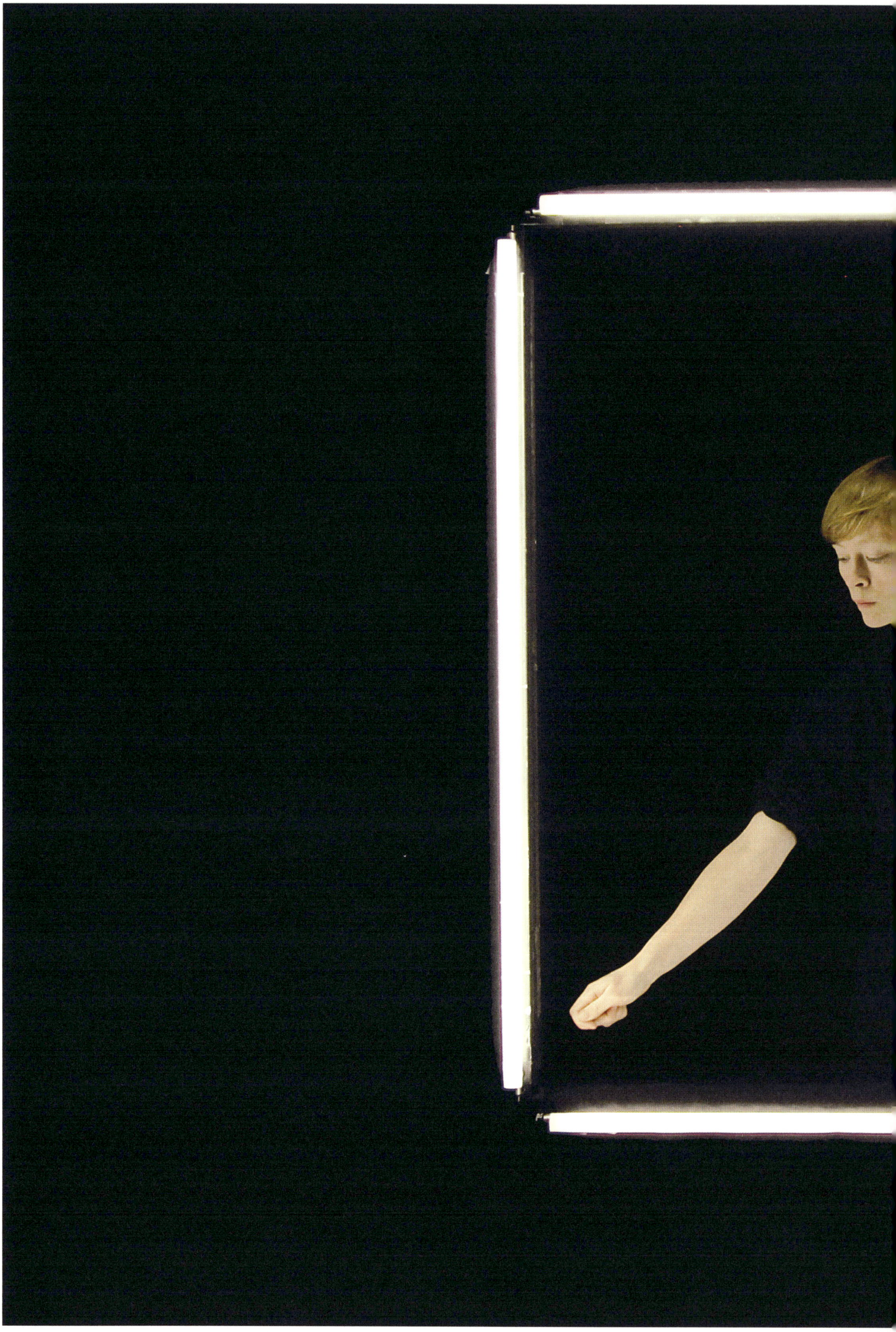

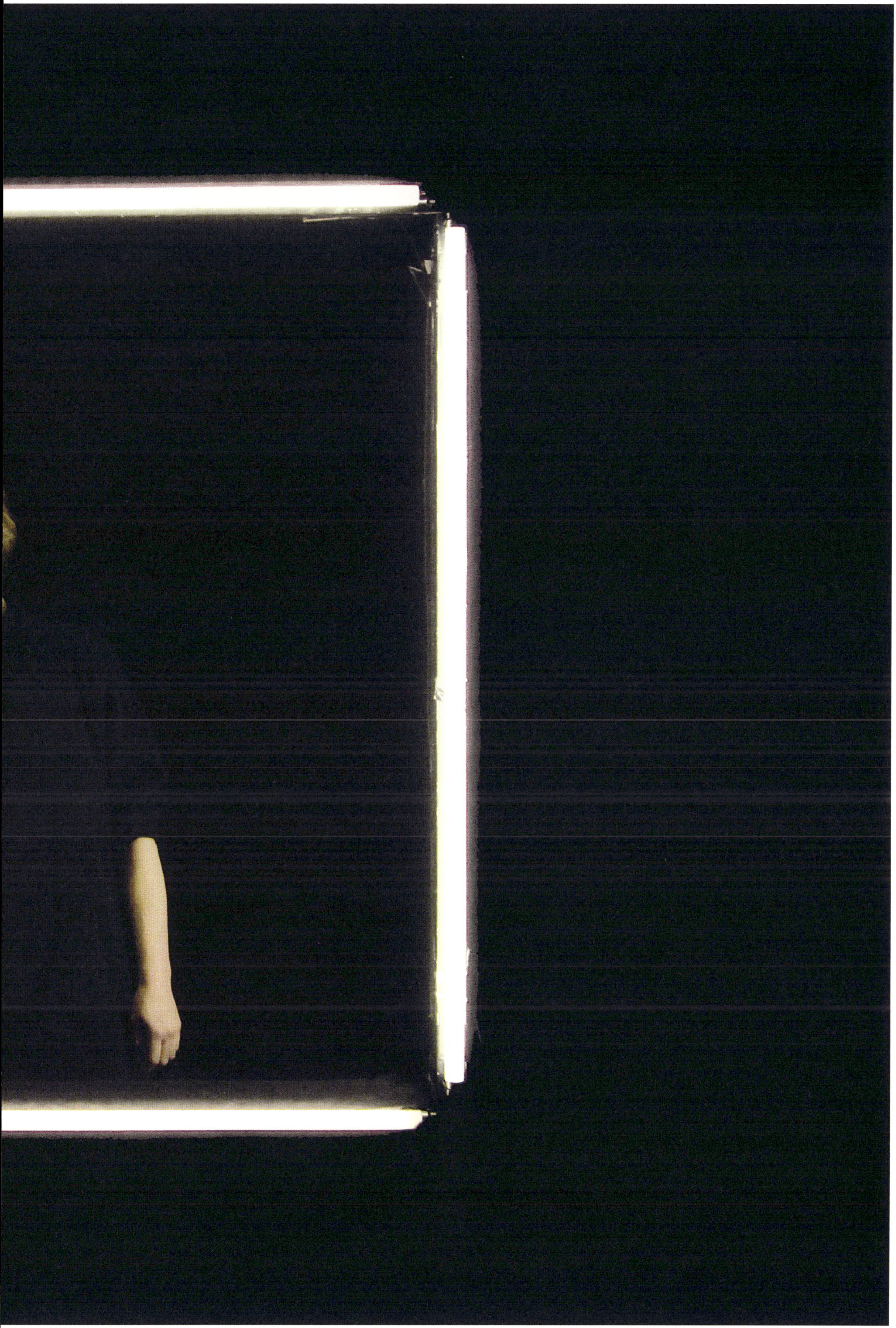

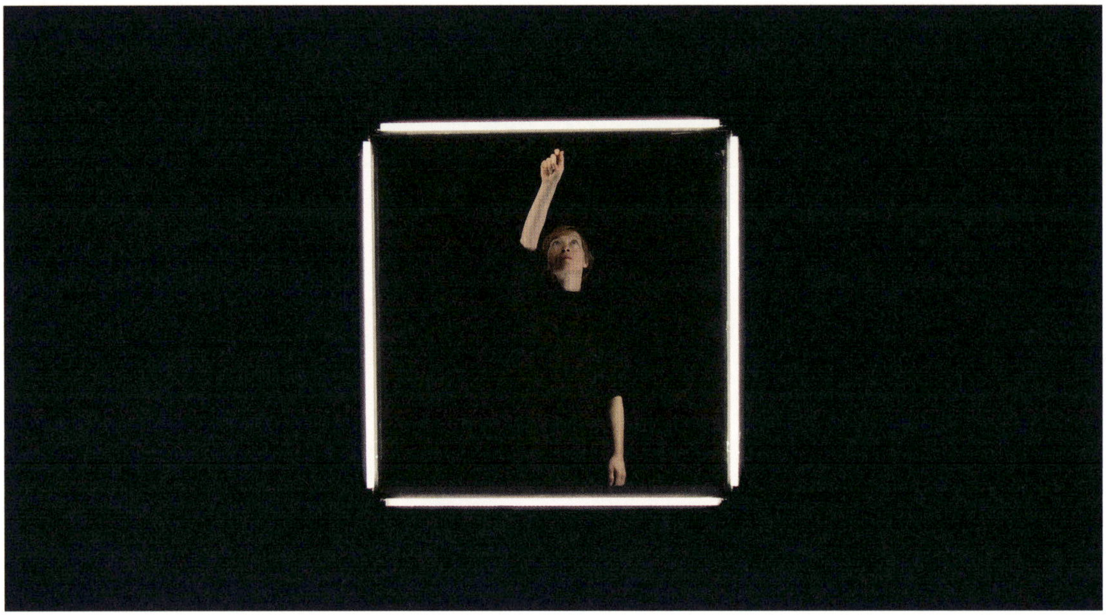

S-C-E-N-E 5

Tara and Ohio are trying to find relaxation in a wellness pyramid. Inside, there is a steam bath with beige marble pannels. Turning from his back onto his stomach, Ohio tries to find a comfortable position. Water gathers from the steam and slowly runs down the pannels. Small drops find each other and form a larger drop. From time to time they drip onto the stone floor and create a sound that becomes part of the environment. At the center of the room, there is a water basin with a marble sphere spinning around its own center. Green, blue and red light dims and fades into each other. Scents, perfumes and slowly rising steam provide a foggy and moist climate. In the background, there is a water dispenser with paper cone cups piled up. The slow dripping of the water on stone and sounds of wind chimes complete the tranquil ambience. All in all an inferno of well-being.

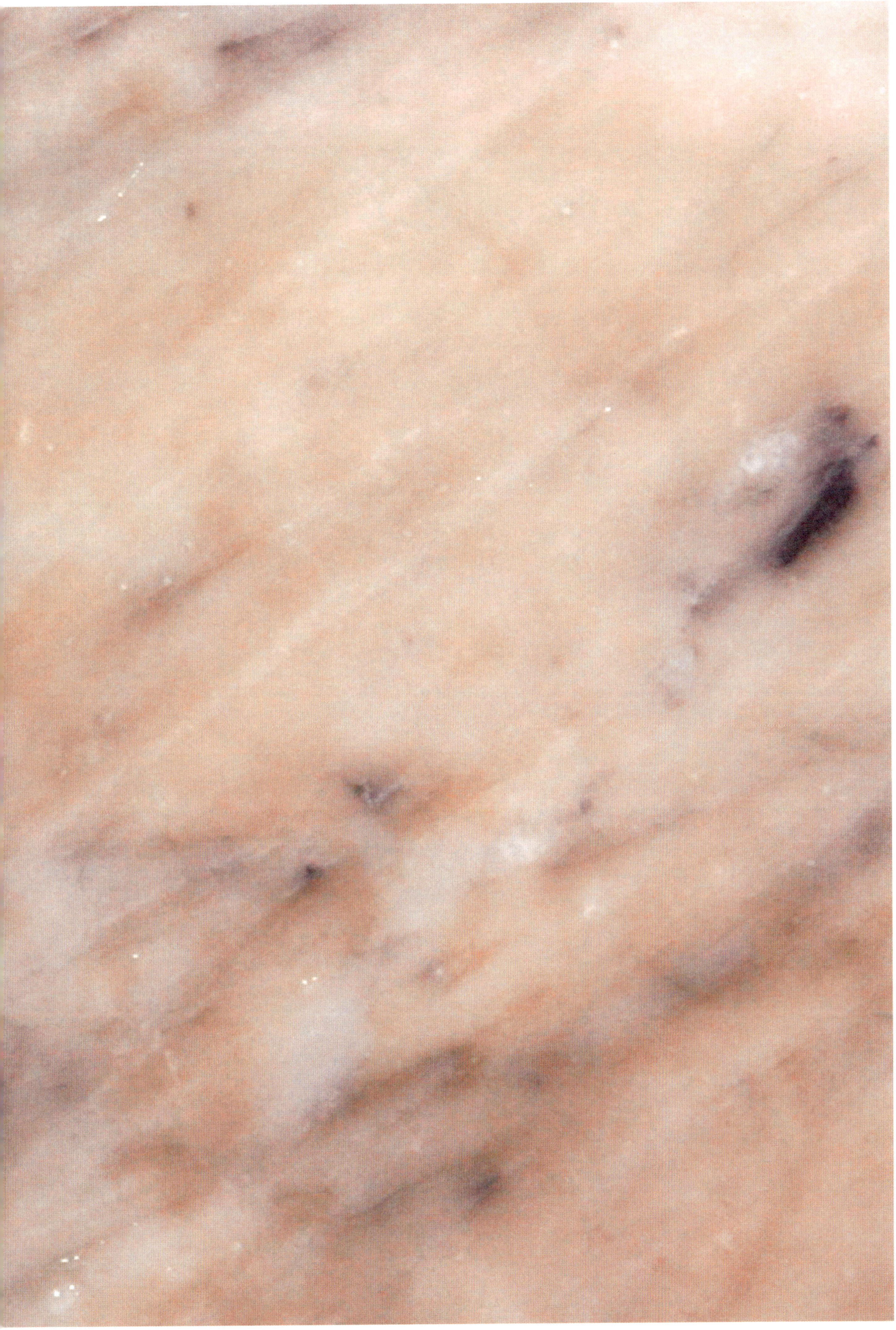

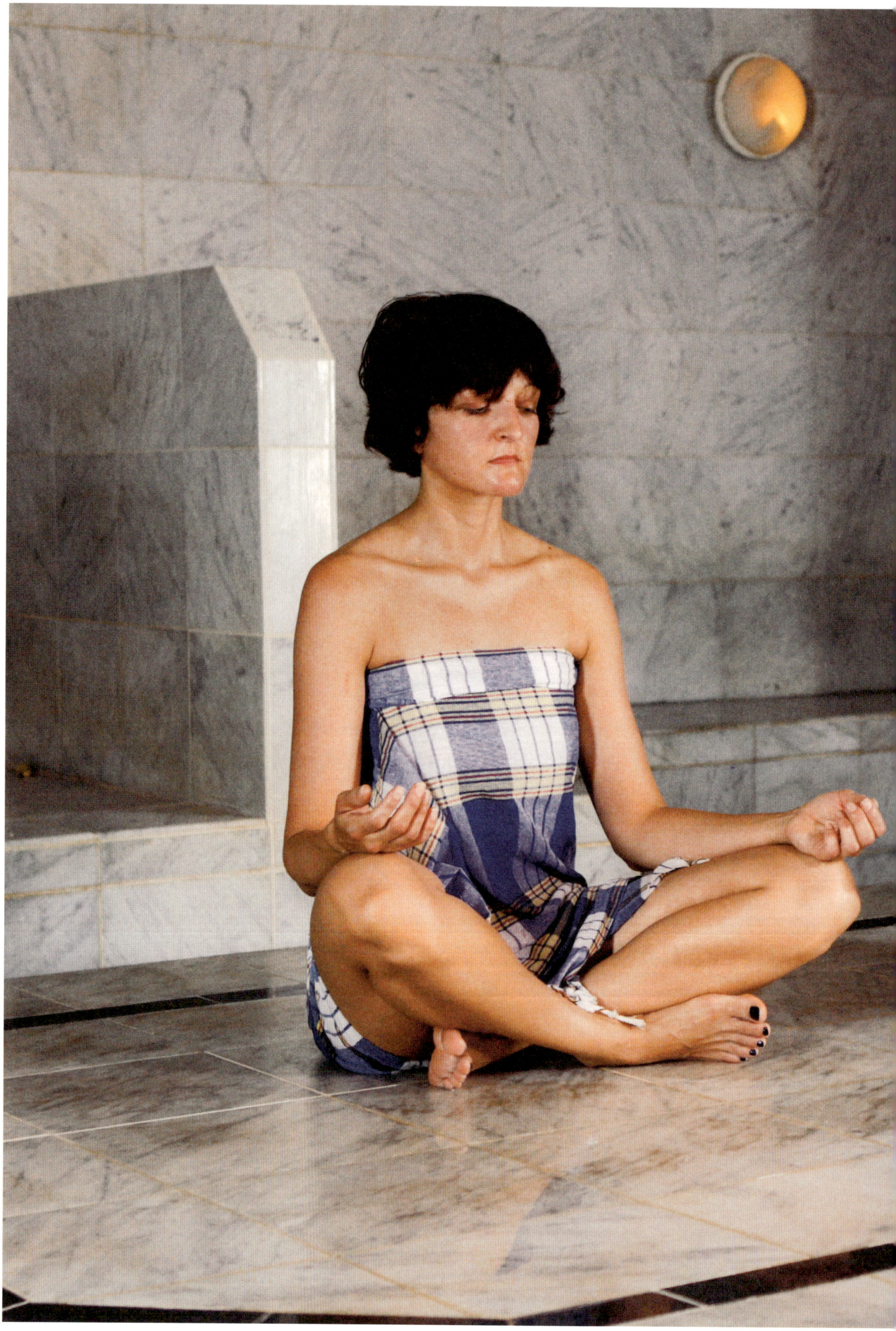

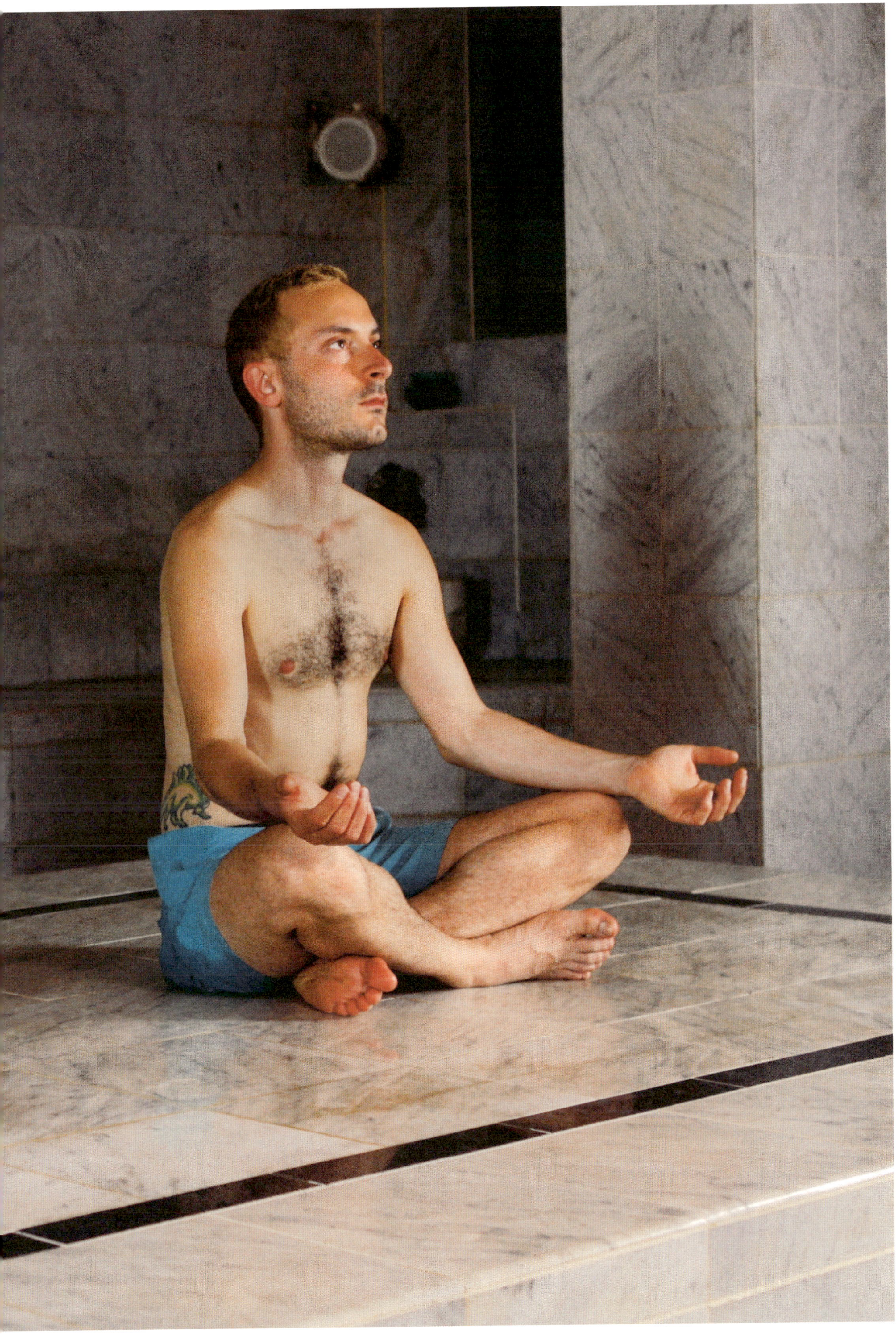

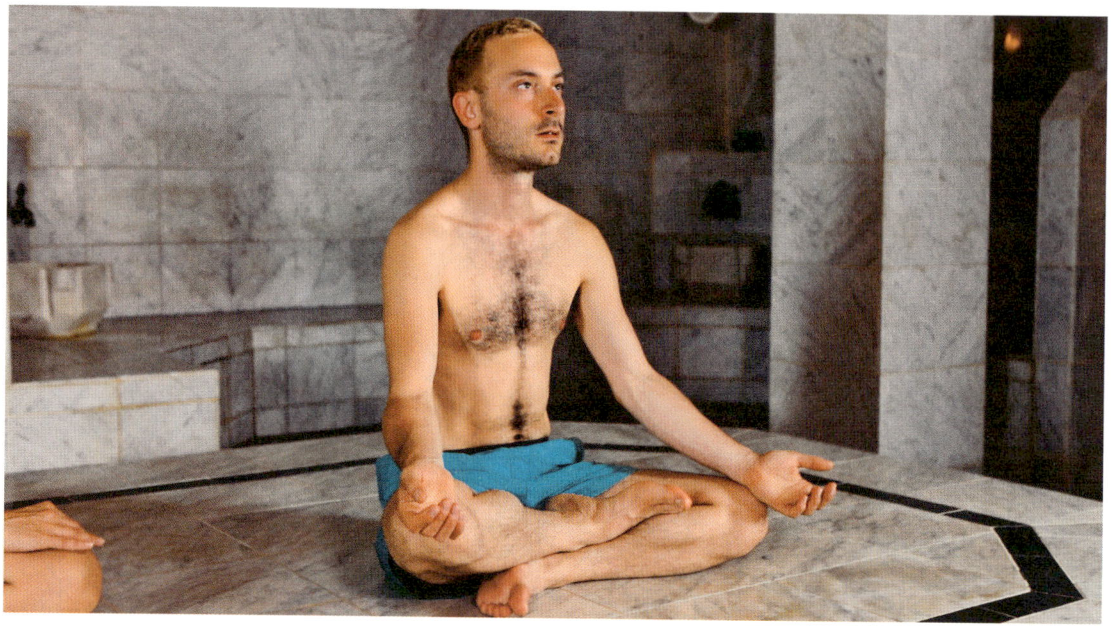

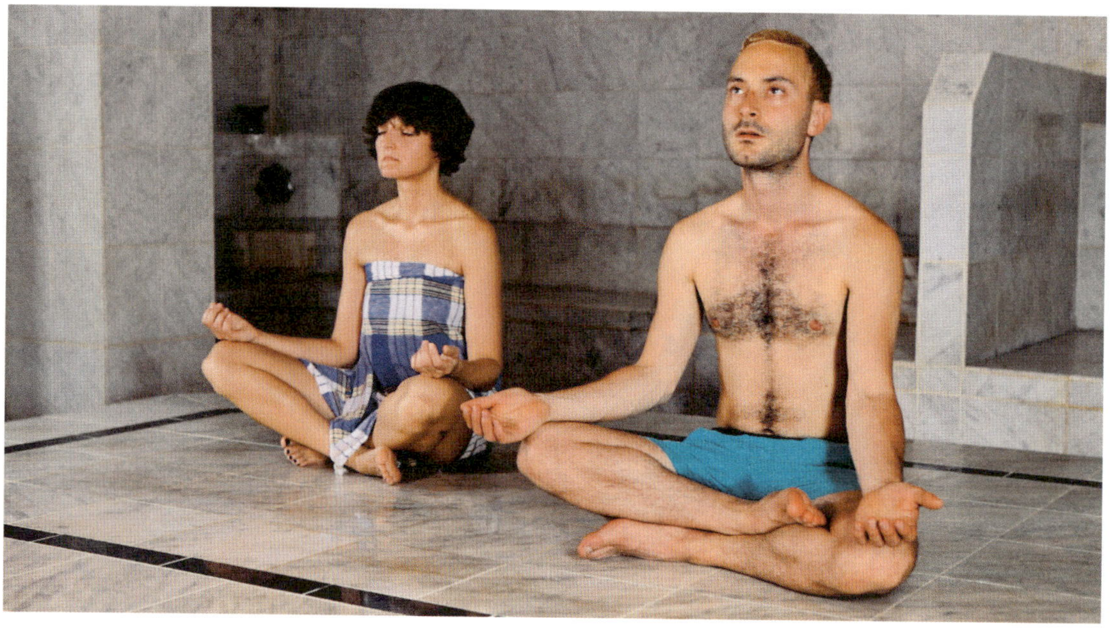

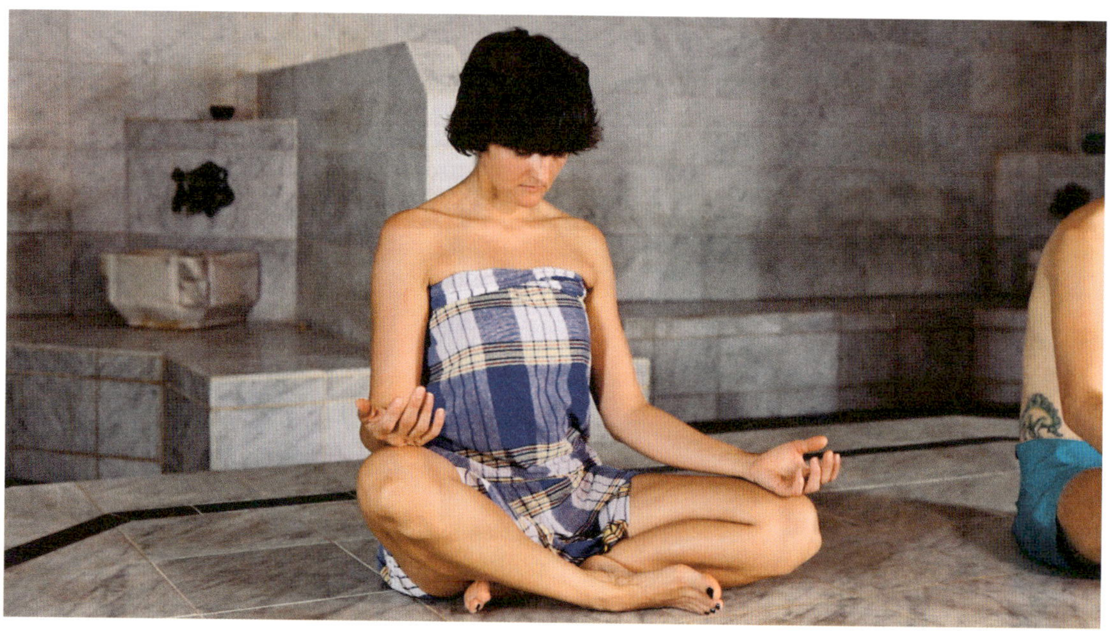

Tara:

Ohio, we have to learn to concentrate. Come here – let's try an exercise. Try this!

Tara und Ohio sit in Lotus position. Tara cramps her face to keep her eyes firmly closed while Ohio concentrates with eyes open. Tara is visualising her center, while Ohio is trying to breathe in and out regulary. A voice comes out of nowhere.

Voice:

Good evening, Tara. Good evening Ohio. I am here for our evening S-E-S-S-I-O-N.

Tara:

Good evening.

Ohio:

Good evening.

Voice:

Welcome to our S-E-S-S-I-O-N. I am so honored to have you on board. How are you today?

Tara:

Thank you, thank you, thank you, for having us, we feel so honored.

Ohio:

Yes, so honored indeed, thank you.

Voice:

Know that this S-E-S-S-I-O-N is absolutely private and that any and all messages you receive through this session are yours to keep. OK. So relax, breathe!

Tara:

OK.

Ohio:

OK.

Voice:

From now on all my messages will be written in UPPER CASE LETTERS, breathe!

Tara:

OK.

Ohio:

OK.

Voice:

THE NEXT 21 DAYS ARE TO BE DEDICATED TO A MAJOR ERADICATION OF OLD BELIEFS, SIGNS, PATTERNS AND STUDIES THAT NO LONGER FIT. WHEREVER YOU WALK, WHOMEVER YOU TALK TO, REMEMBER THIS: I SEE, FEEL, THINK BEYOND LABELS. I RECOGNIZE THE E-X-I-T, THE X, THE WAY OUT.

Tara breathes in. Ohio breathes in.

Voice:

AS I TUNE IN TO THE SPACE, I ASK TO GUIDE US TO THE NECESSARY INFORMATION TO FIND THE E-X-I-T, THE WAY OUT, BREATHE!

S-C-E-N-E 6

The Dot represented by many dots.

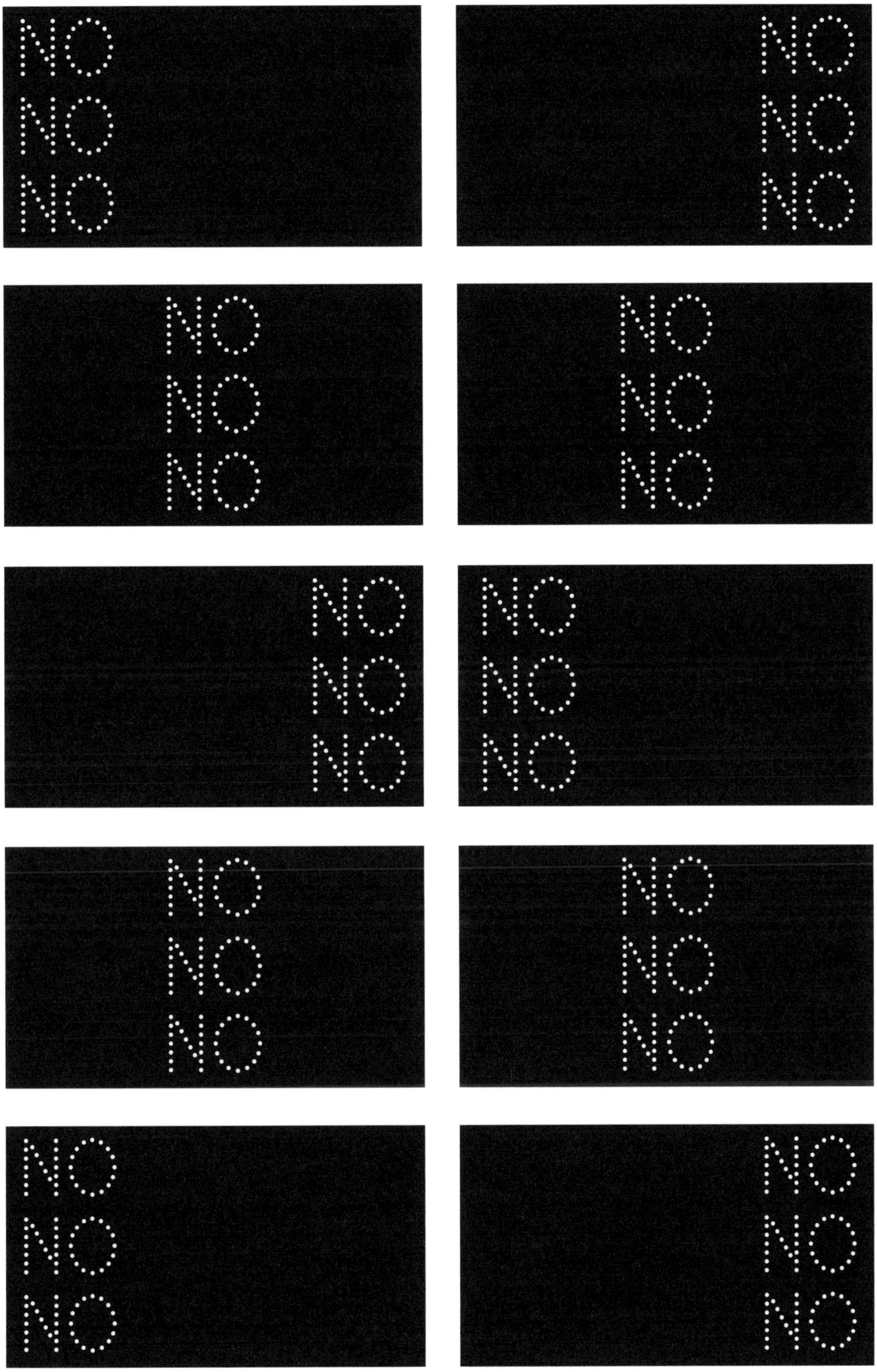

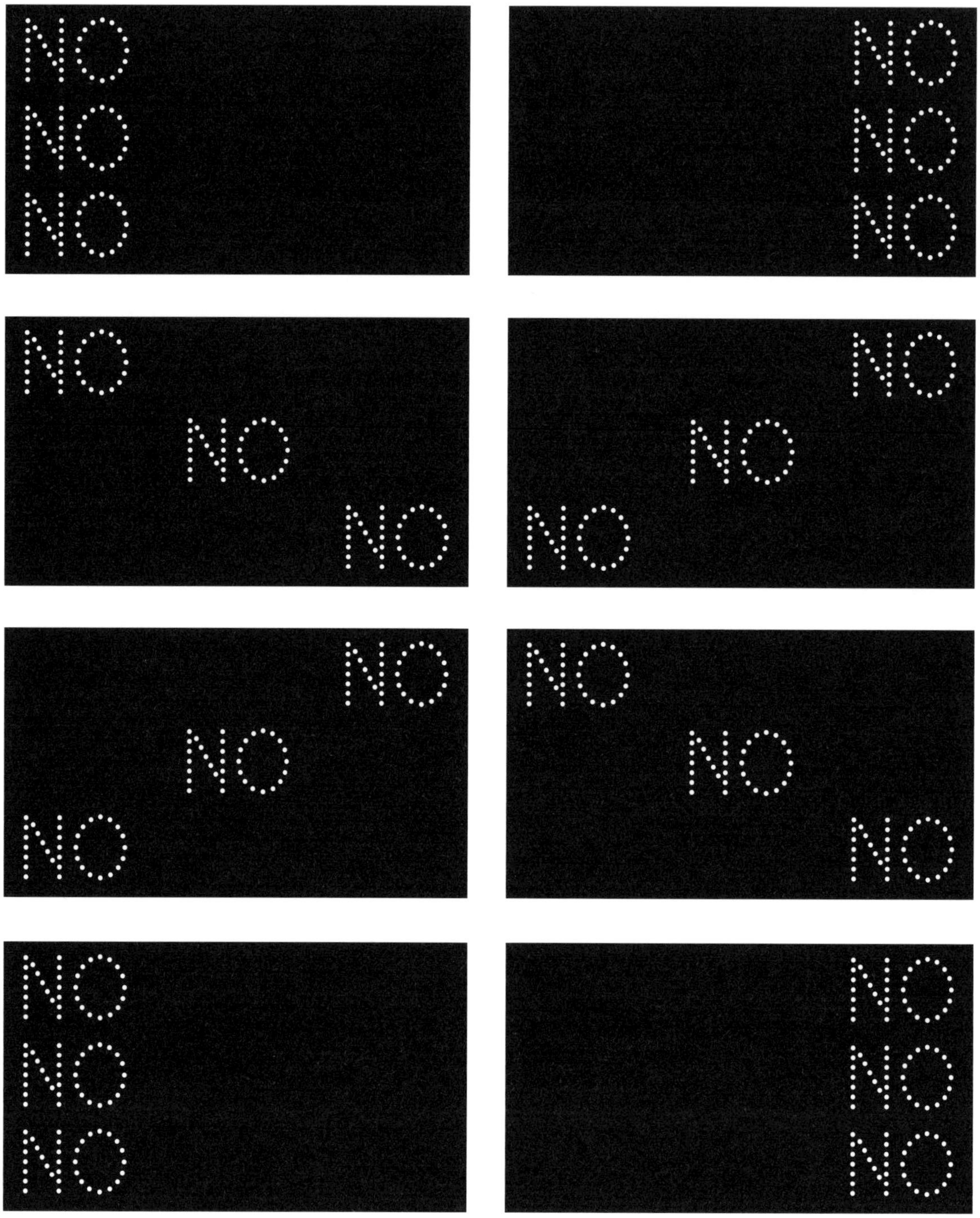
NO NO NO
NO NO NO
NO NO NO
NO NO NO
NO NO NO
NO NO NO
NO NO NO
NO NO NO

S-C-E-N-E 7

A gigantic phone keyboard is painted on the floor. The Oracle is jumping from key to key. There is a sound with every jump. She is spelling a word.

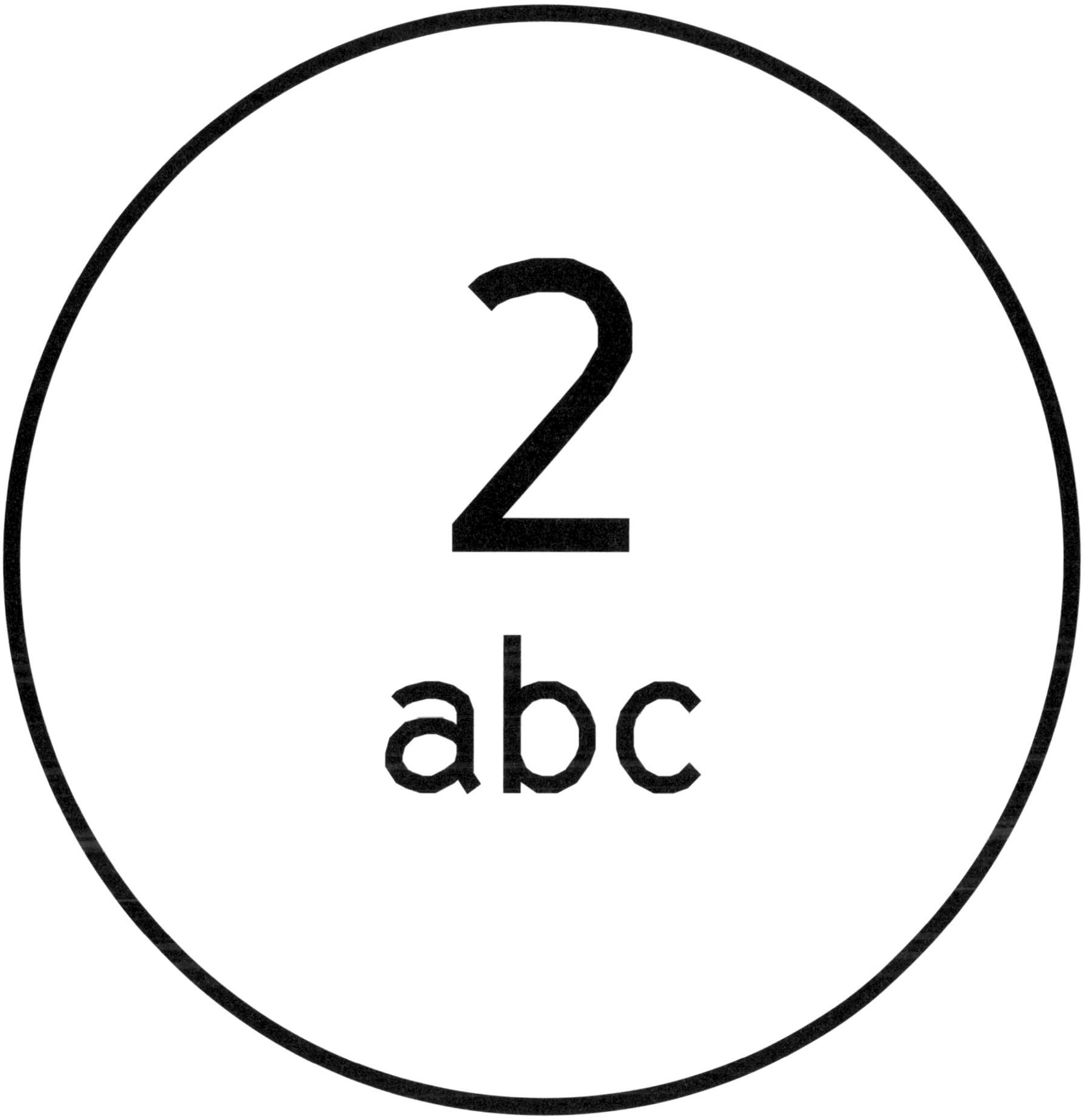

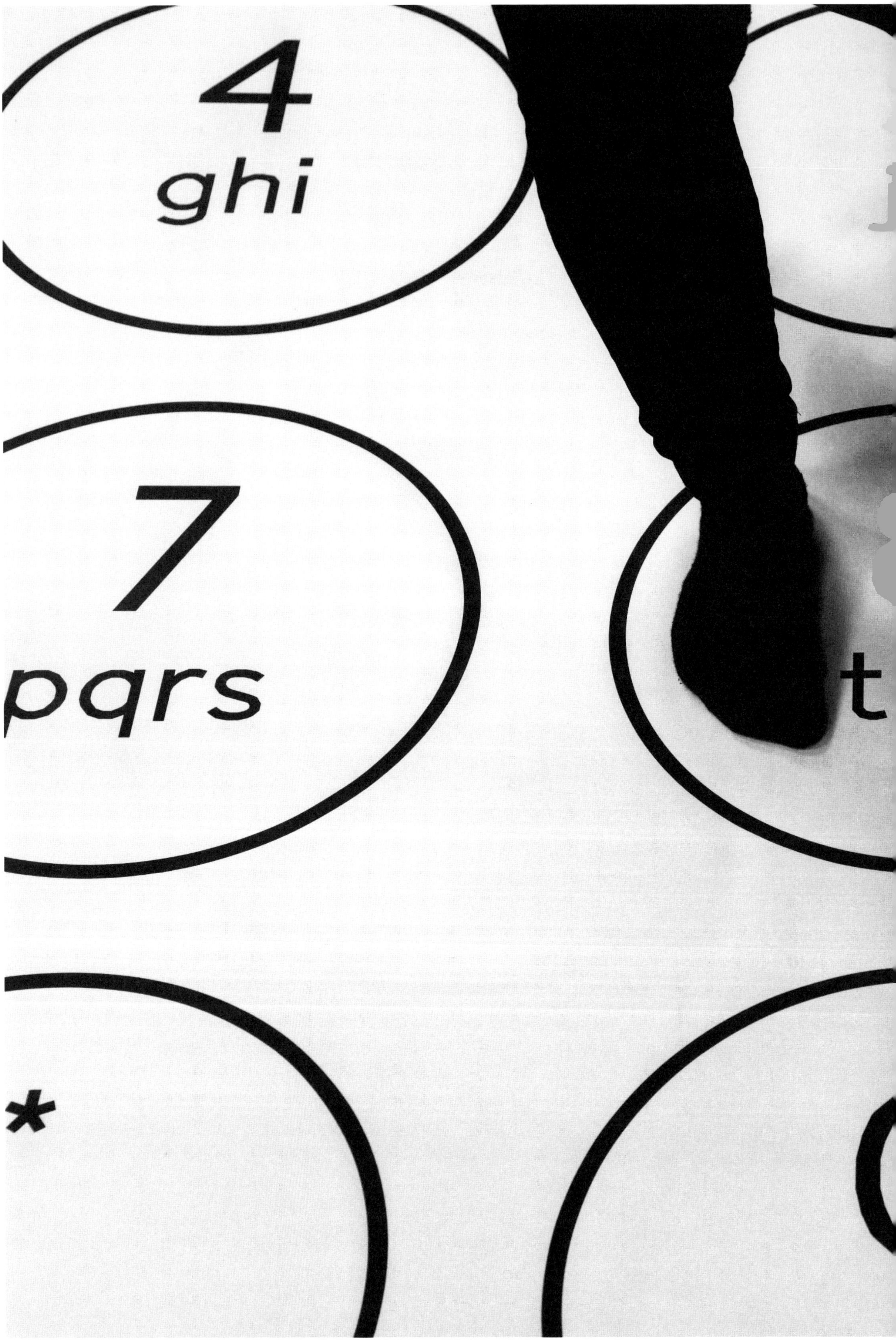
4
ghi
7
pqrs
t
*

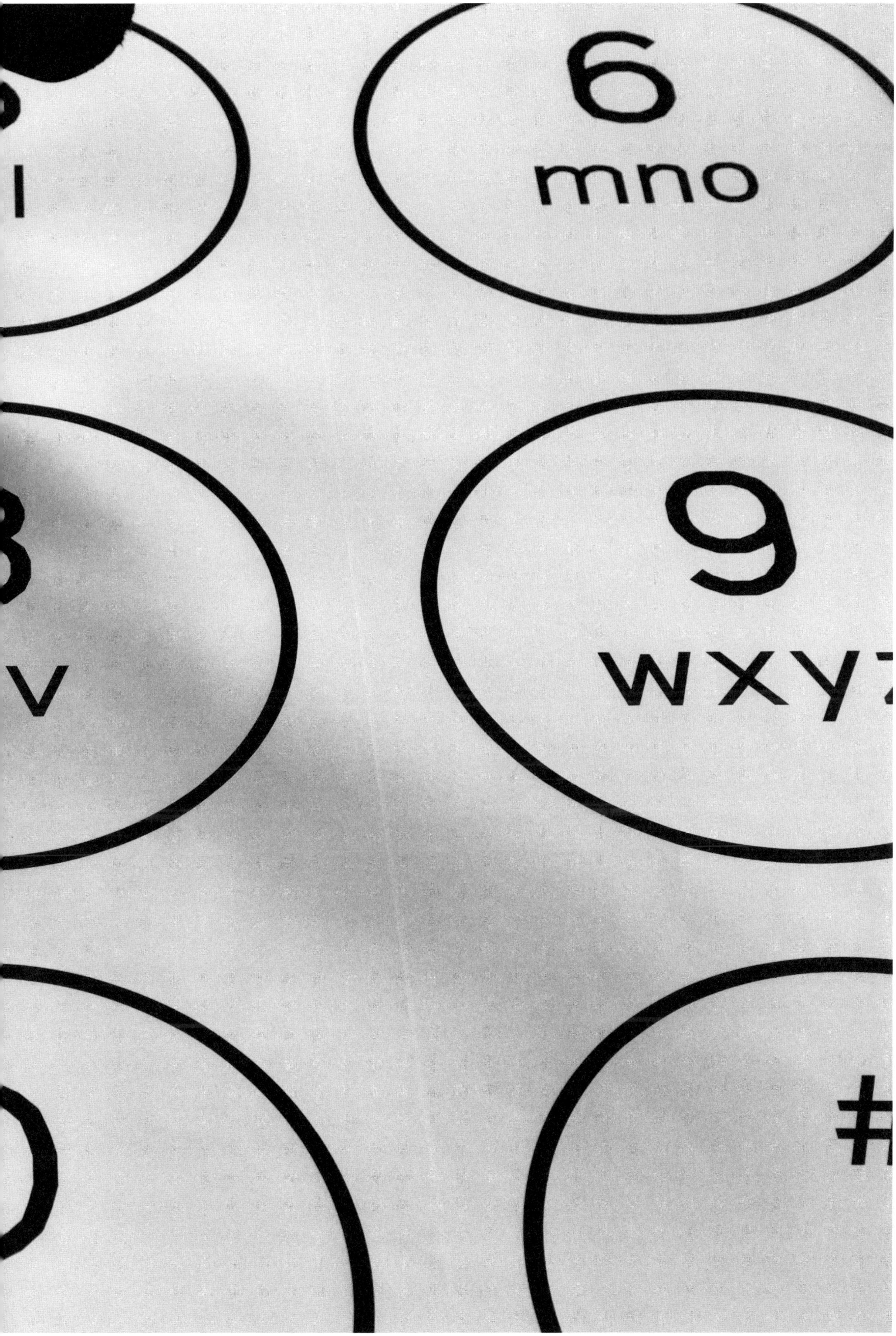
6
mno
9
wxy

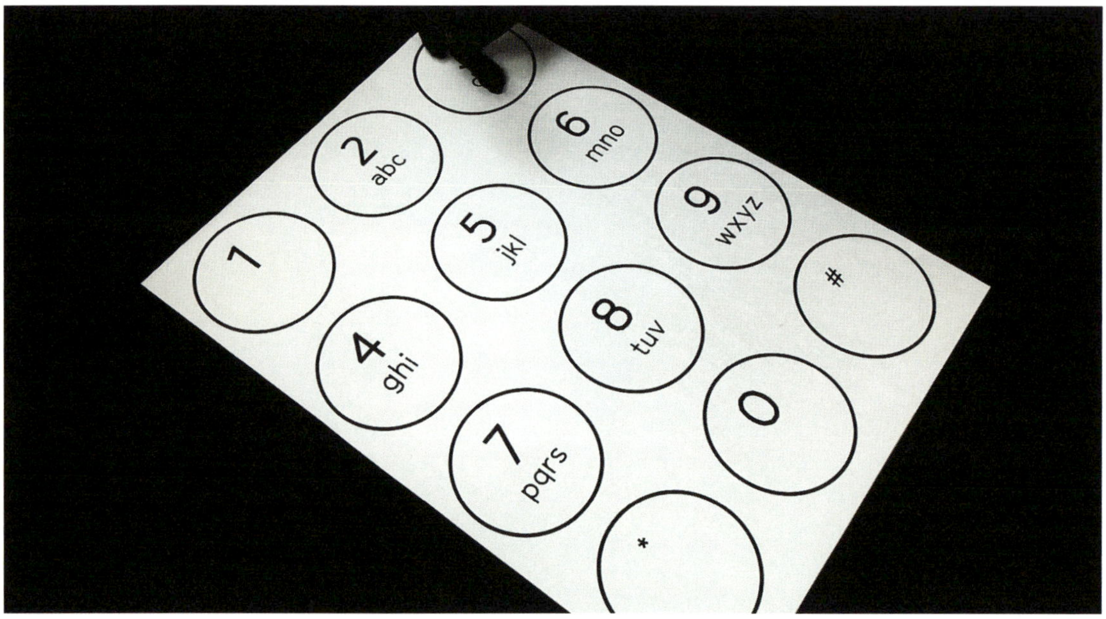
1
2
abc
6
mno
5
jkl
9
wxyz
4
ghi
8
tuv
#
7
pqrs
0
*

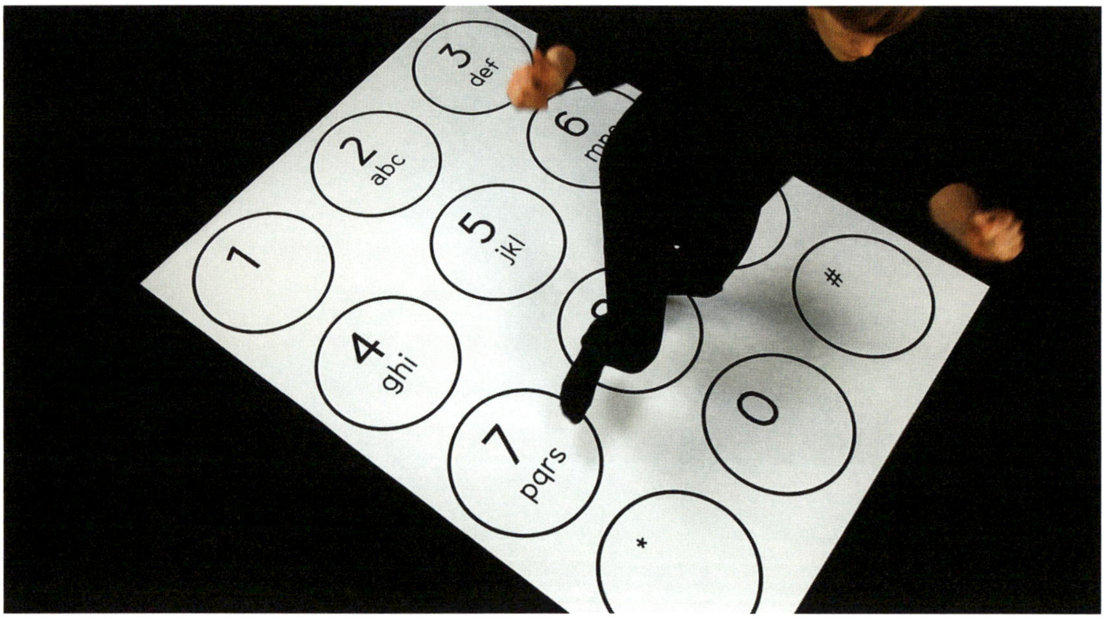
3
def
2
abc
1
5
jkl
#
4
ghi
7
pqrs
0
*

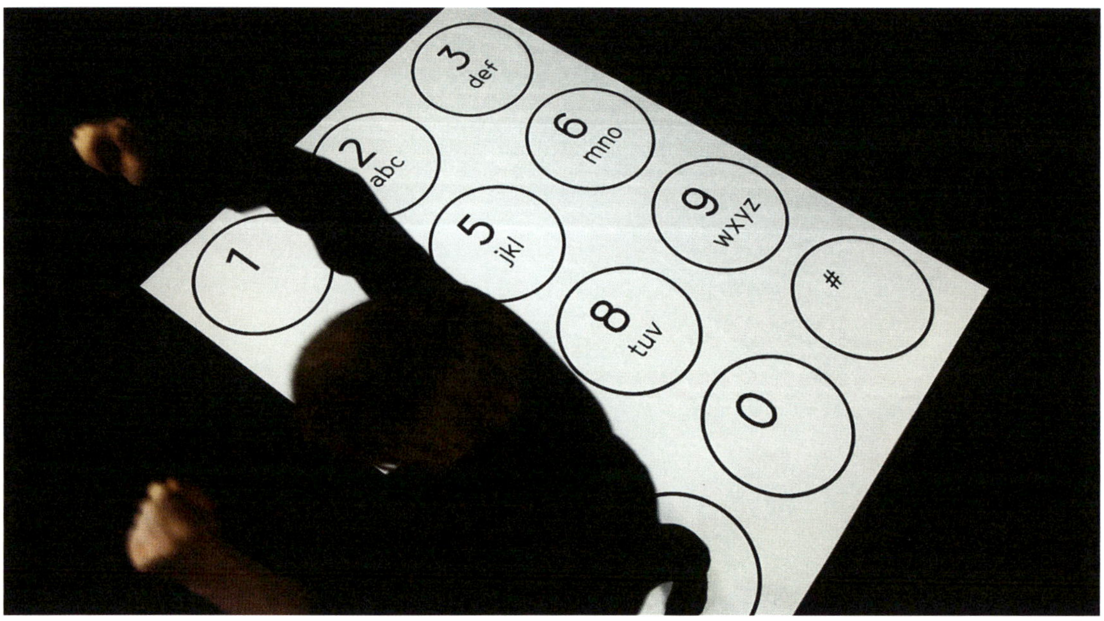
3
def
2
abc
6
mno
5
jkl
9
wxyz
1
8
tuv
#
0

S-C-E-N-E 8

Tara und Ohio enter “The Room of Signs”. Strange mobiles hang from the walls – asterisks, color charts, circles, numbers and intervals, symbols and patterns in different sizes. This room is terribly full of signs.

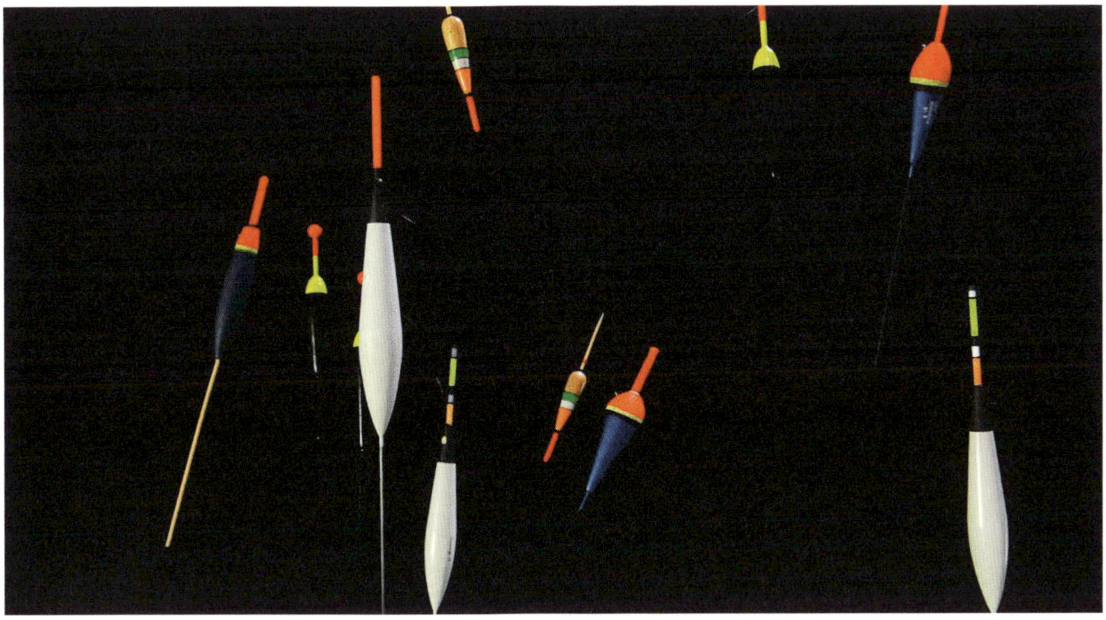

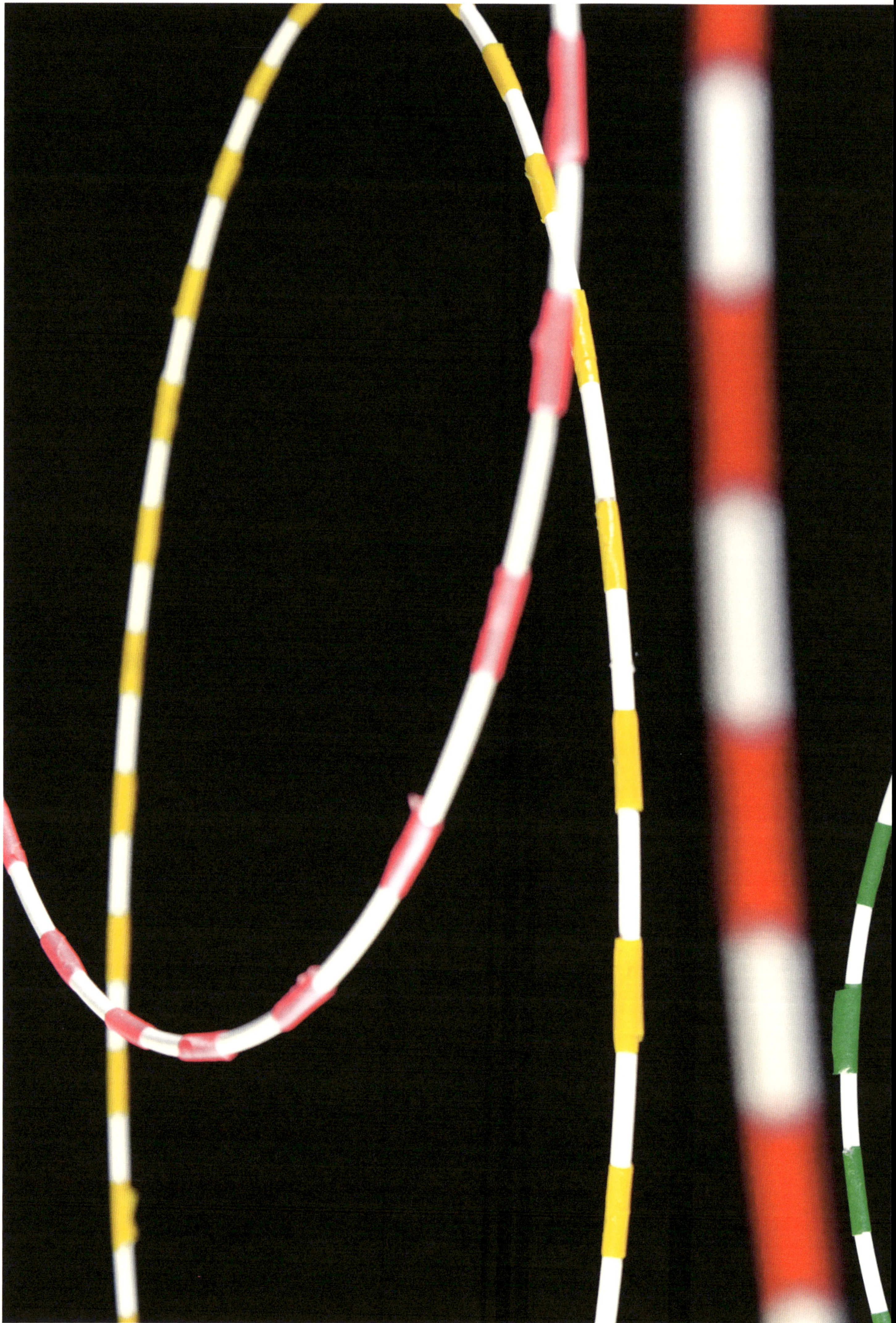

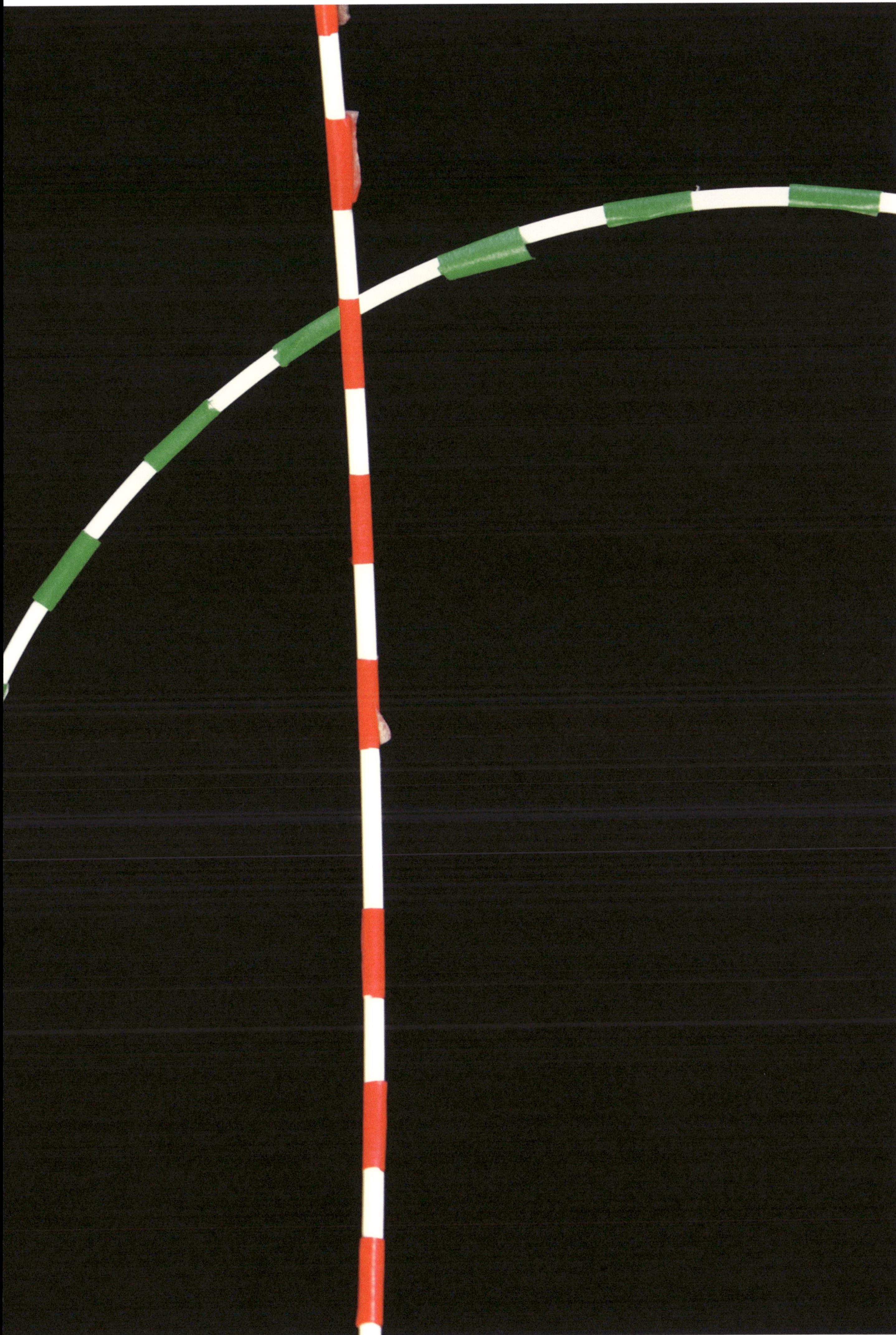

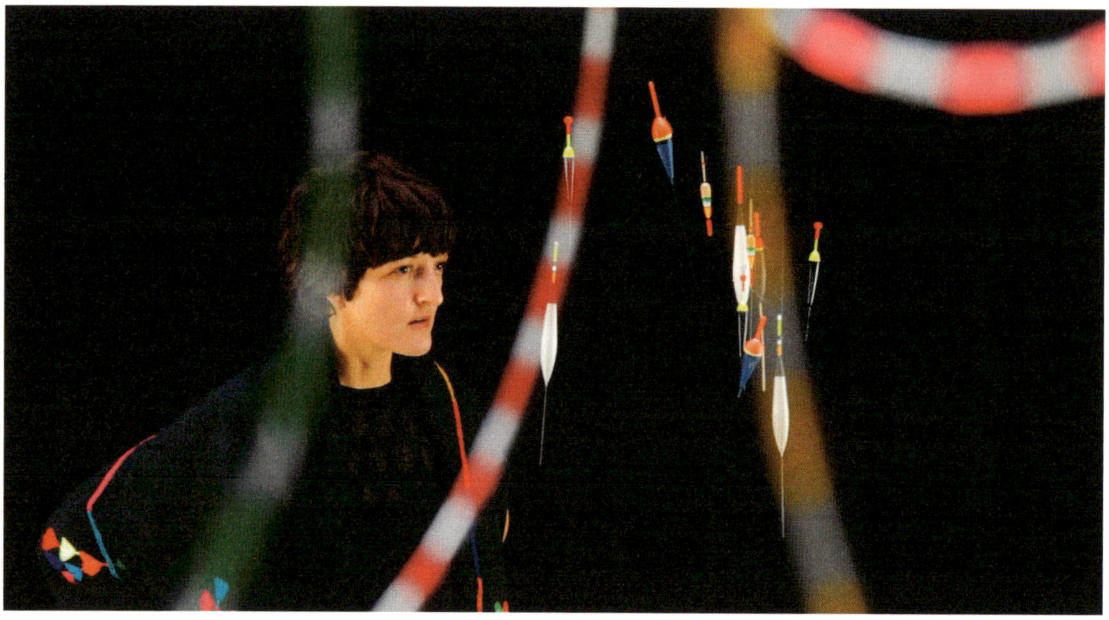

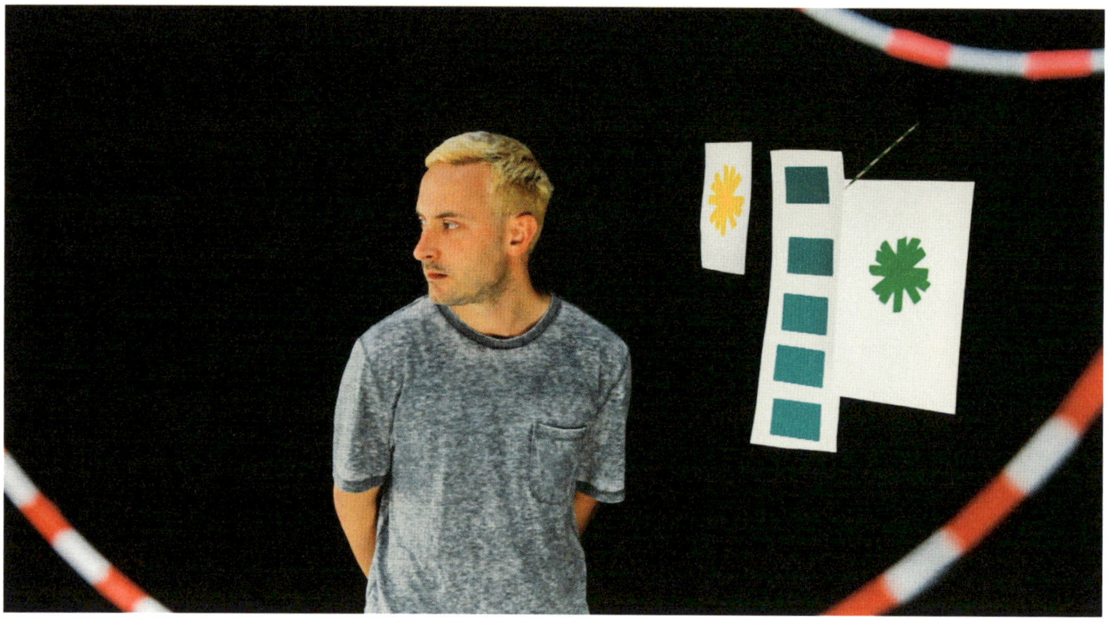

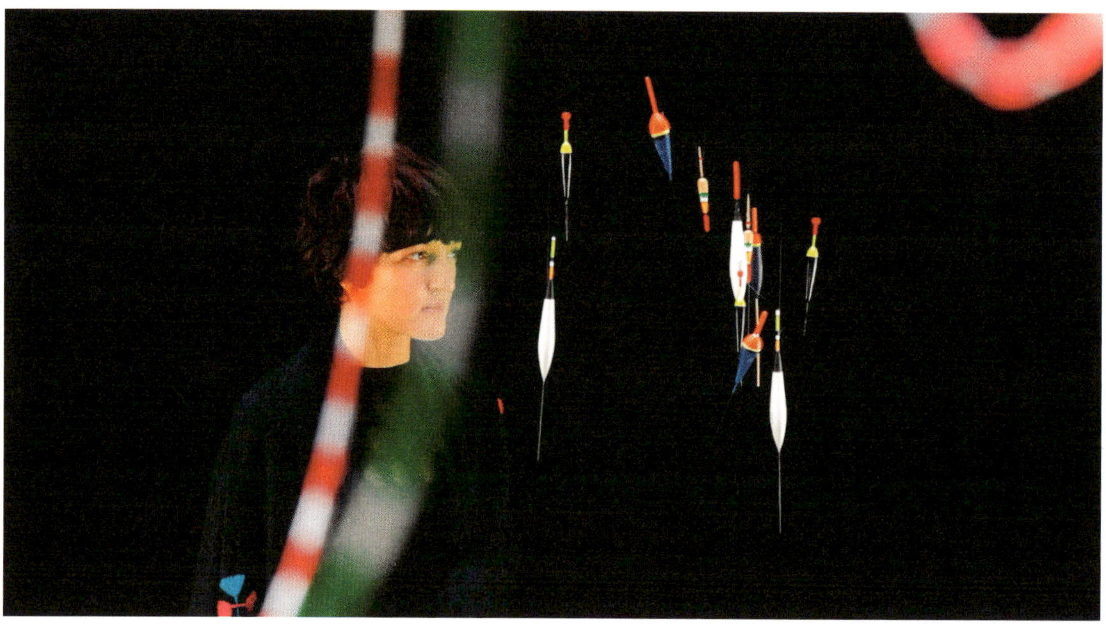

Tara:

Ohio? Where are we?

Ohio:

144, 233, 377 ...

Tara:

And what are we supposed to do here?

Ohio:

Tara, did you not hear what the Oracle said? The next 21 days are dedicated to a major eradication of old signs, patterns and beliefs that no longer fit. Wherever you walk, whomever you talk to, remember this: I see, feel, think beyond labels. I recognize the E-X-I-T, the X, the WAY OUT.

Tara:

Signs, patterns and beliefs that no longer fit. Wherever you walk, whomever you talk to ... the E-X-I-T, the X?

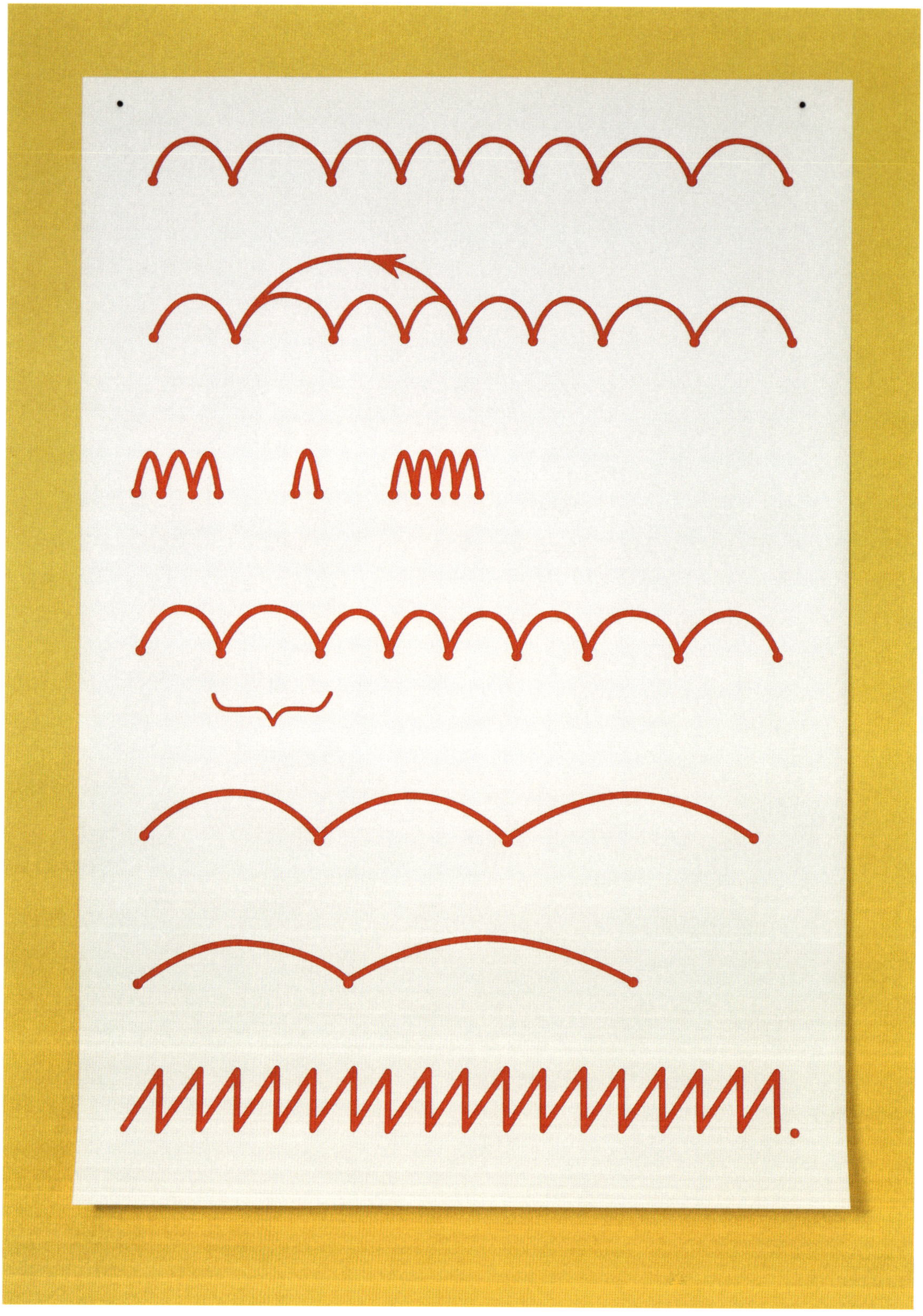

S-C-E-N-E 9

The Dot becomes a digital blackboard.

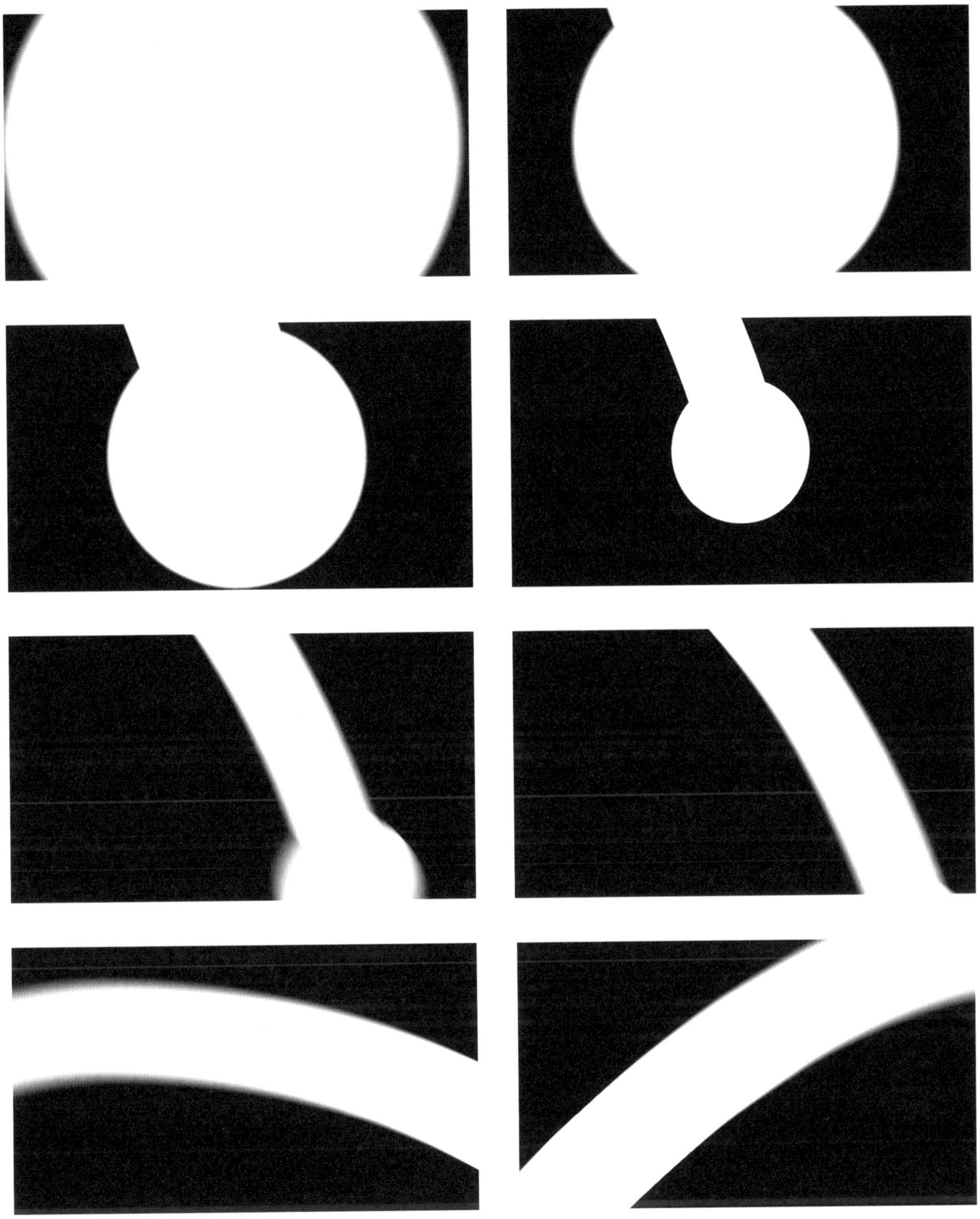

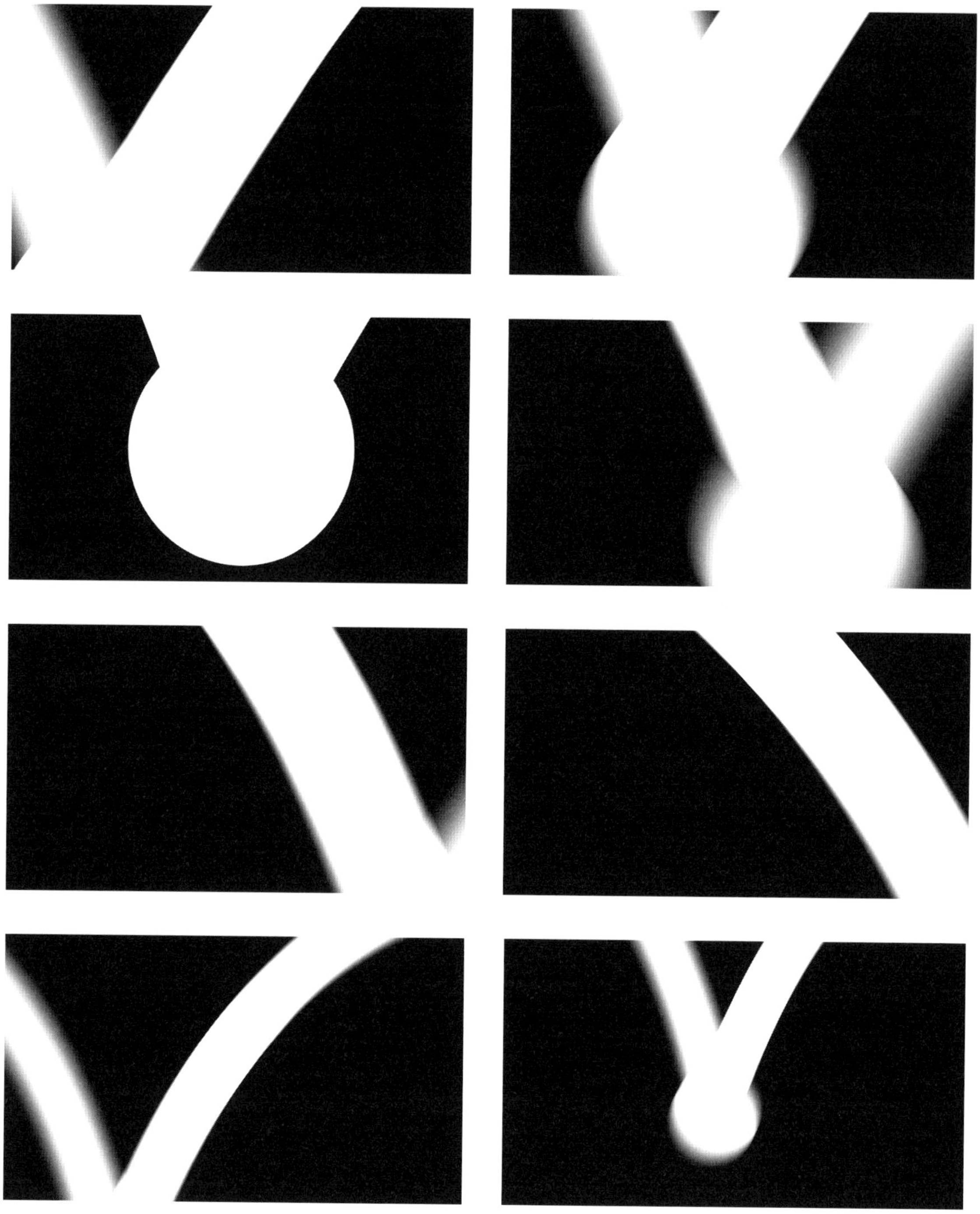

S-C-E-N-E 10

Tara und Ohio are still in the “Room of Signs”. They walk from object to object and study every sign carefully. Sometimes they get closer to an object, study it more carefully and continue to the next.

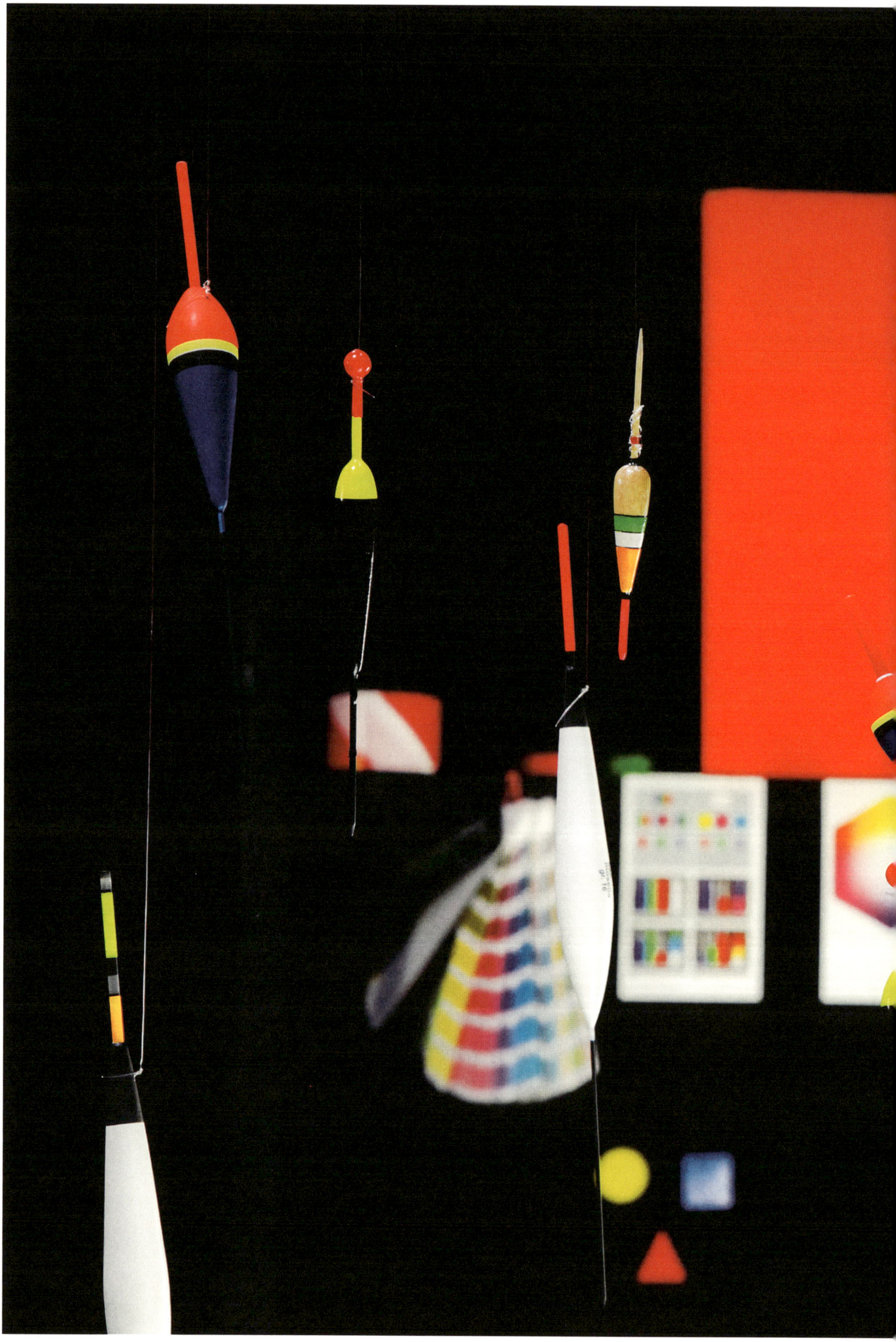

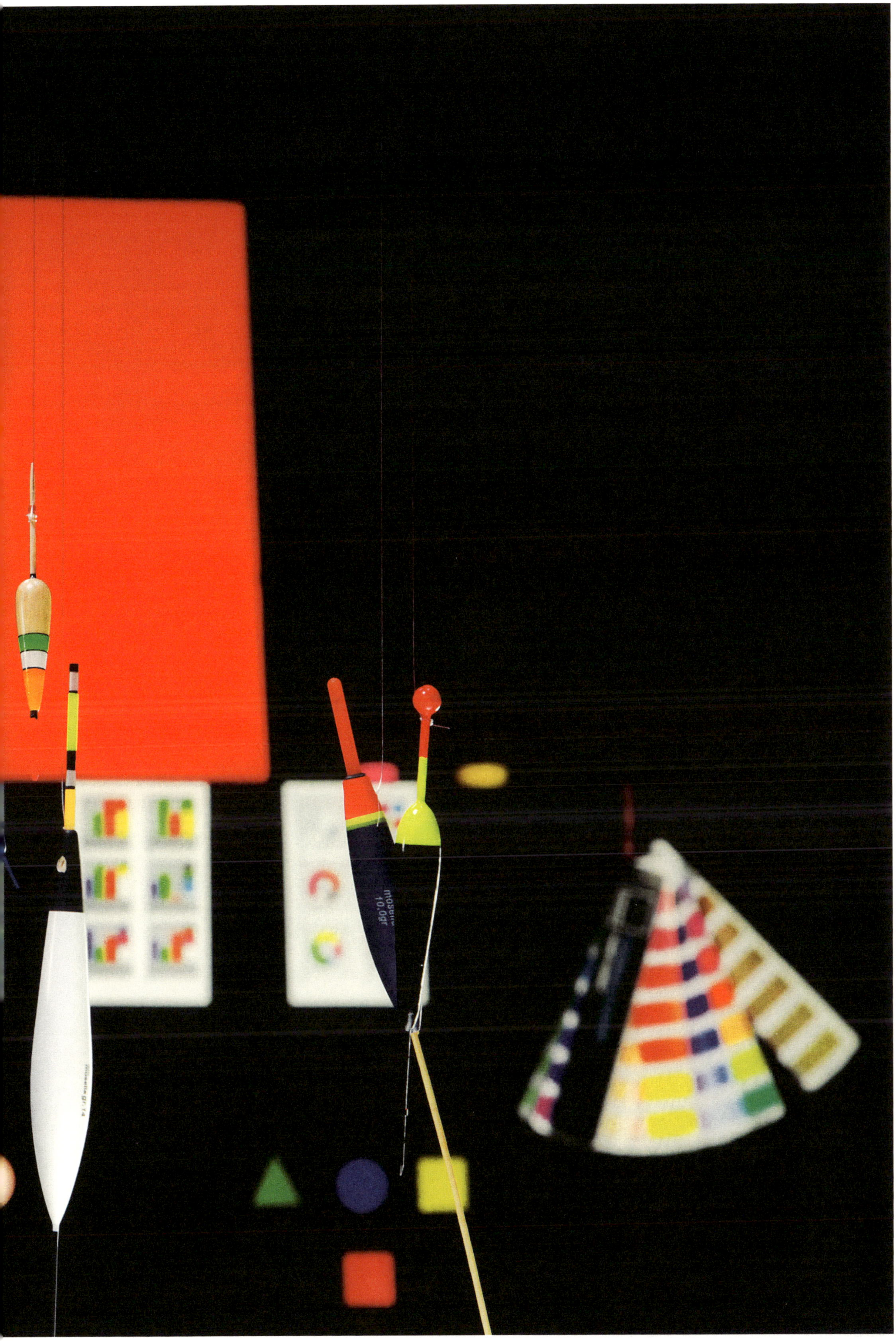

Tara:

There must be a hint somewhere ..., we've been looking for so long now.

Ohio:

Maybe the answer is in a different part of the riddle.

Tara:

Yeah, but what could it be?

Ohio:

I'm not sure, Tara. ... Wherever you walk, whomever you talk to, think this (...) Tara, that's it! The E-X-I-T, the X, the WAY OUT (...) That's the solution. We have to look for an X, that will guide us to the E-X-I-T.

Tara:

Ohio, are you really sure?

Ohio:

Of course I am. What else could it mean?

S-C-E-N-E II

The Oracle, on high heels, walks in and out the camera frame, holding up boards saying “HOME” and “AWAY” with different prices. She keeps walking from left to right, then from right to left, holding up a new board every time she passes the camera frame.

HO
39

ME

9,–

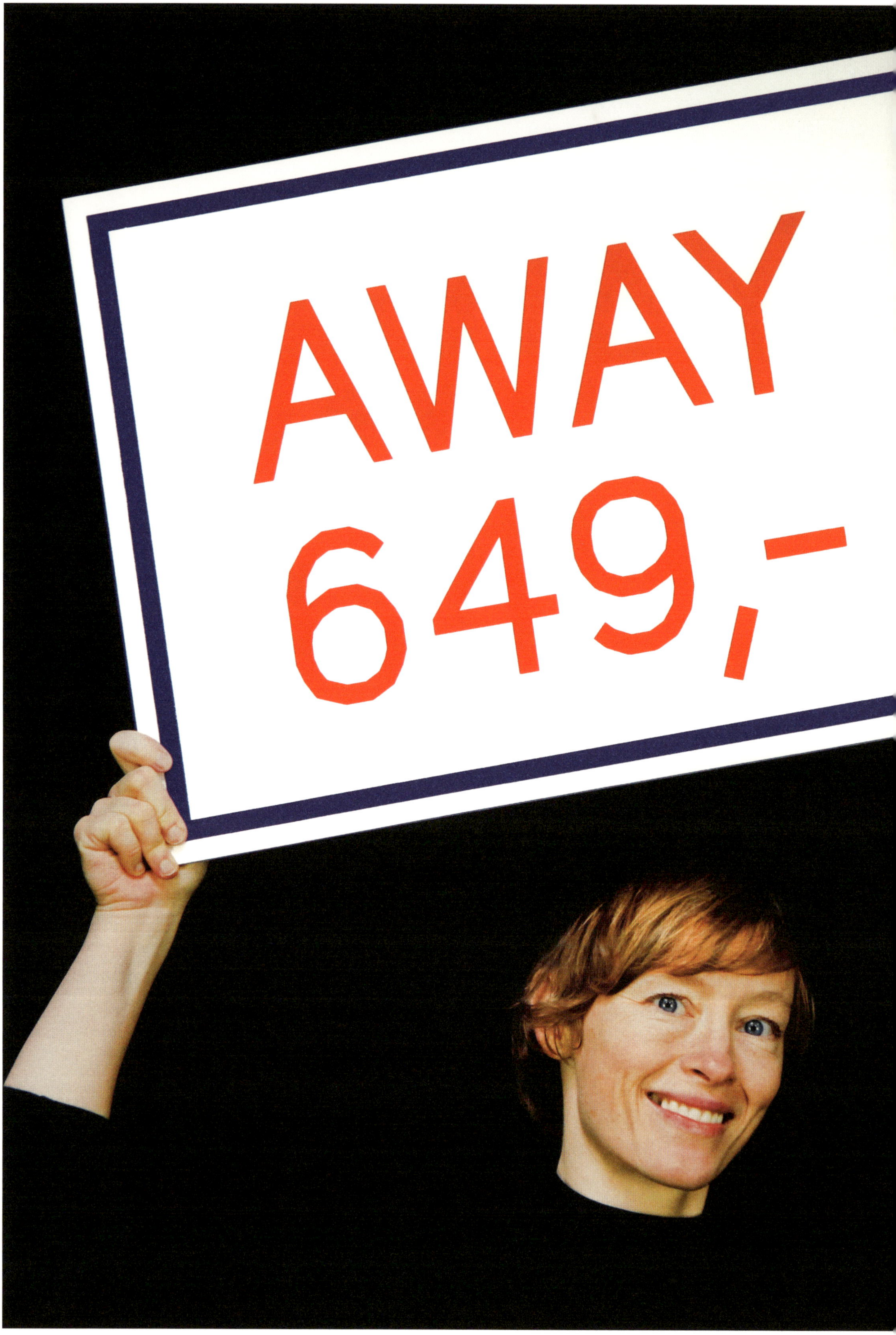
AWAY
649,-

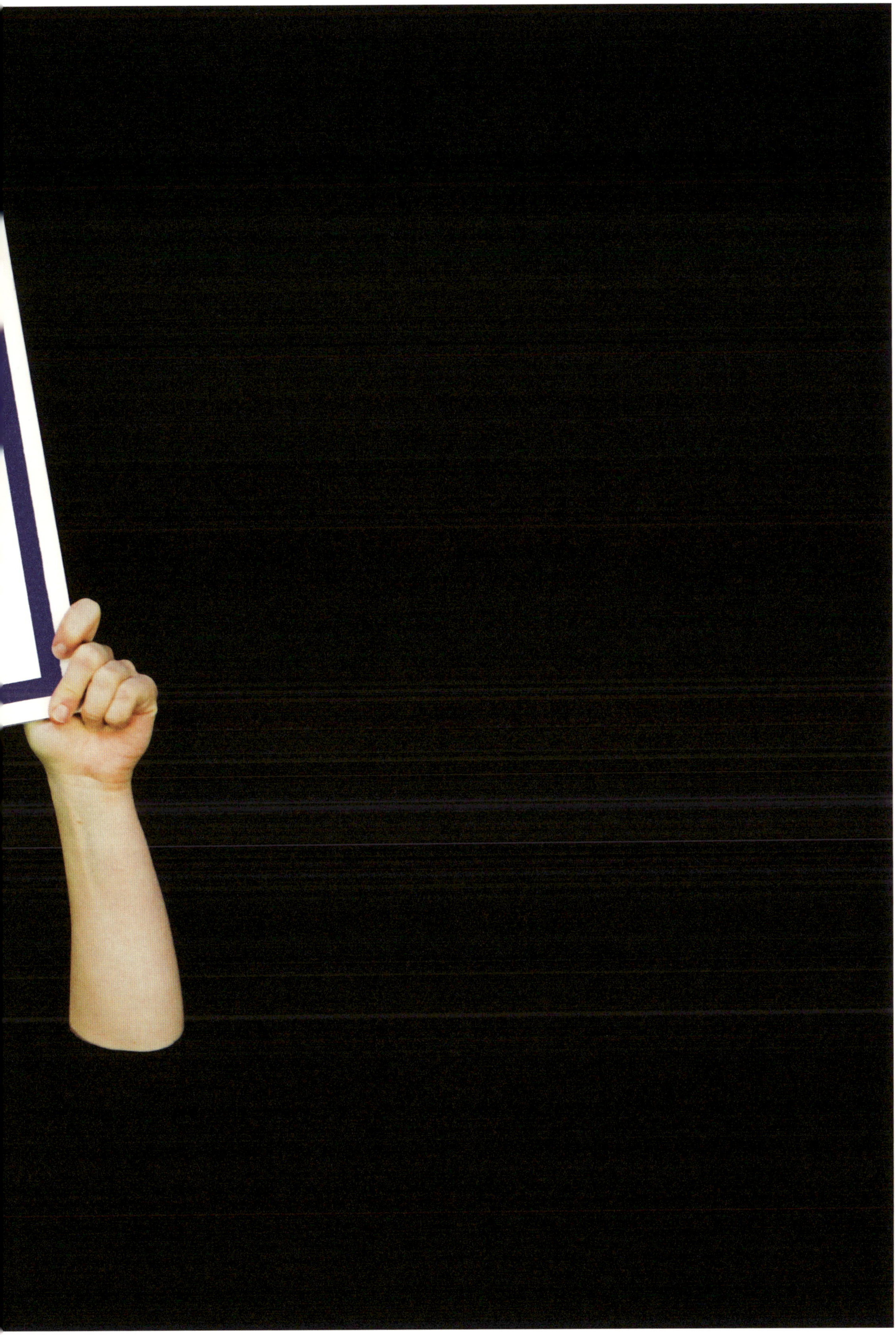

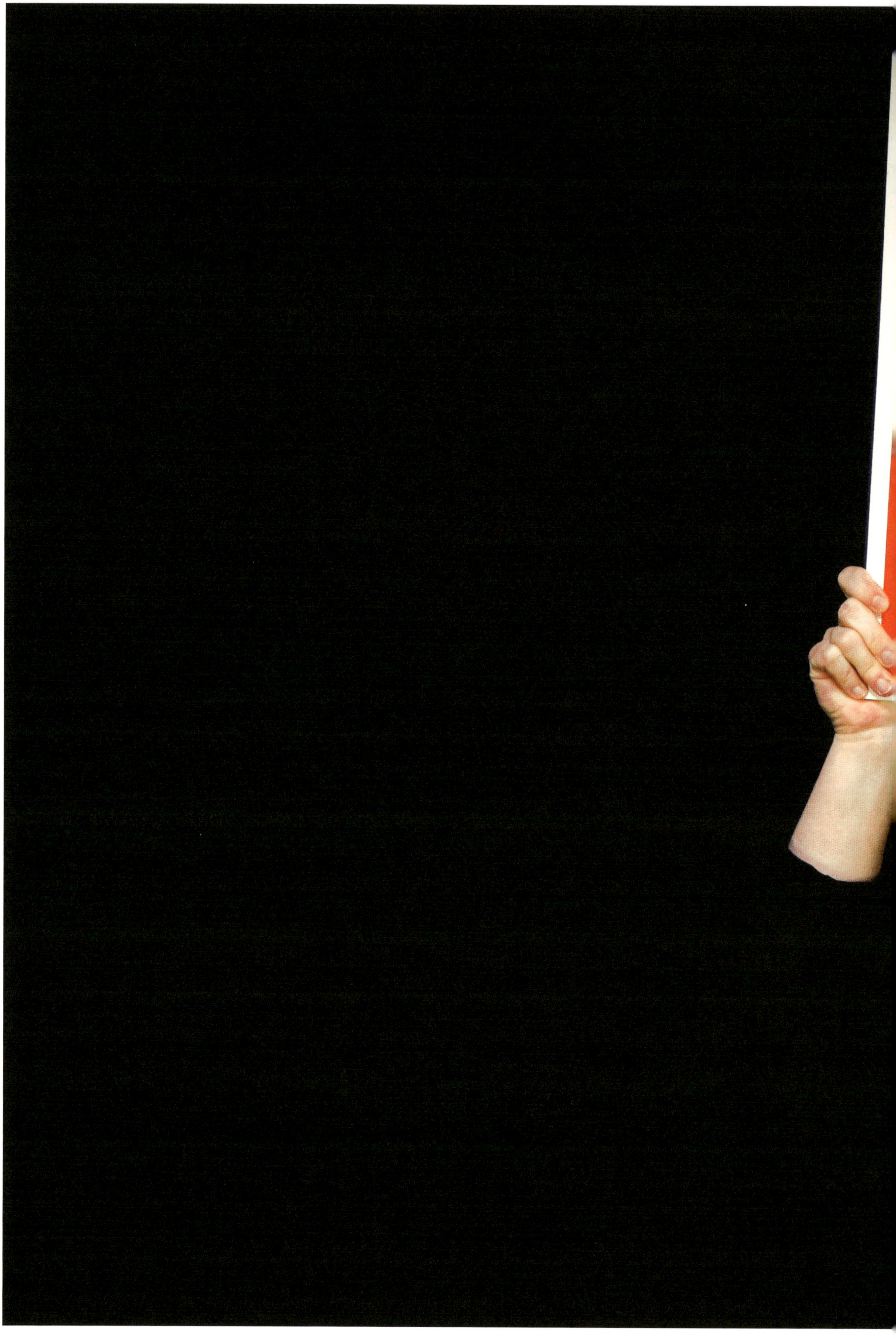

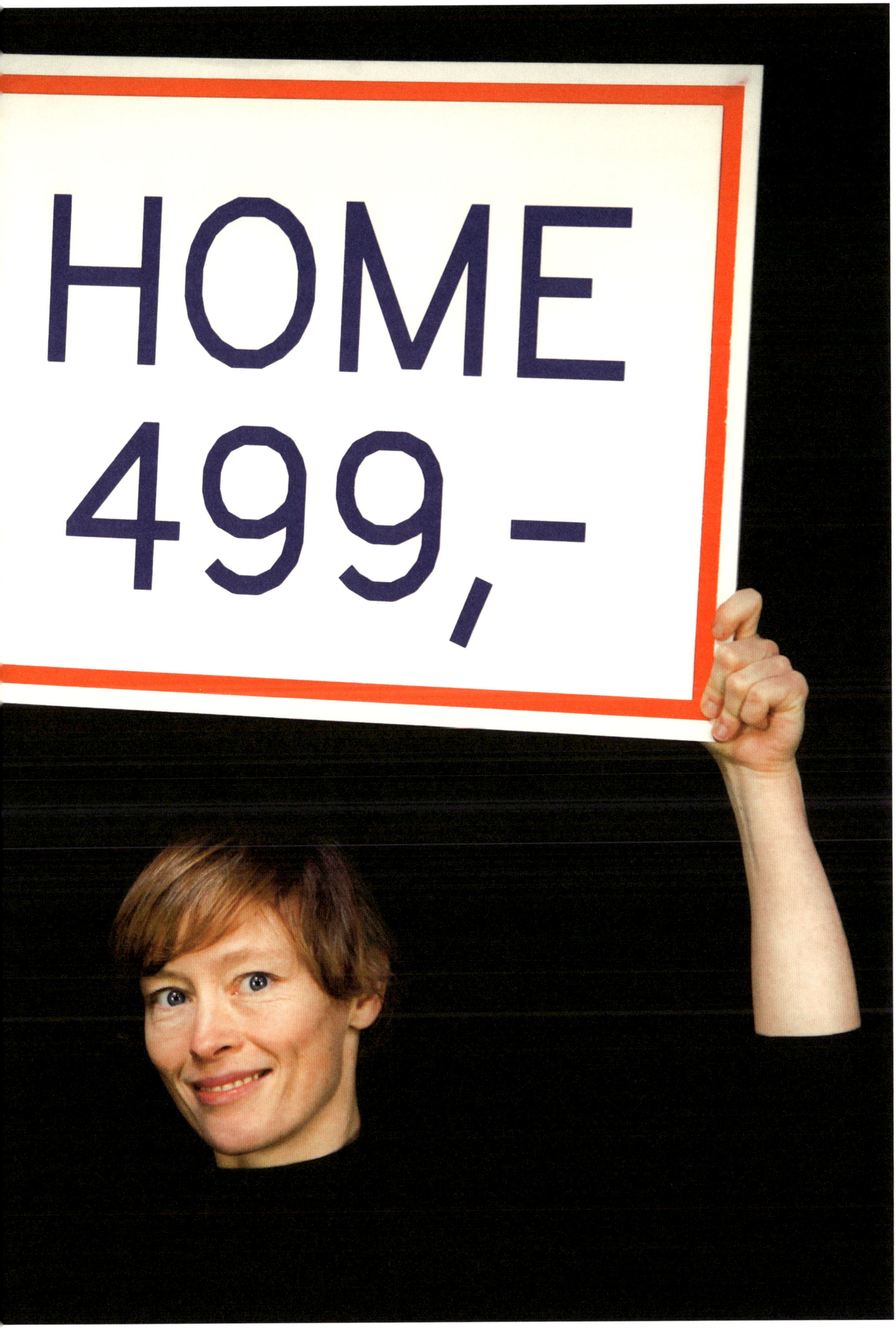
HOME
499,-

AW
89

AY
9,–

S-C-E-N-E 12

Tara and Ohio are still in the "The Room of Signs". A black and white sign game lies on the floor.

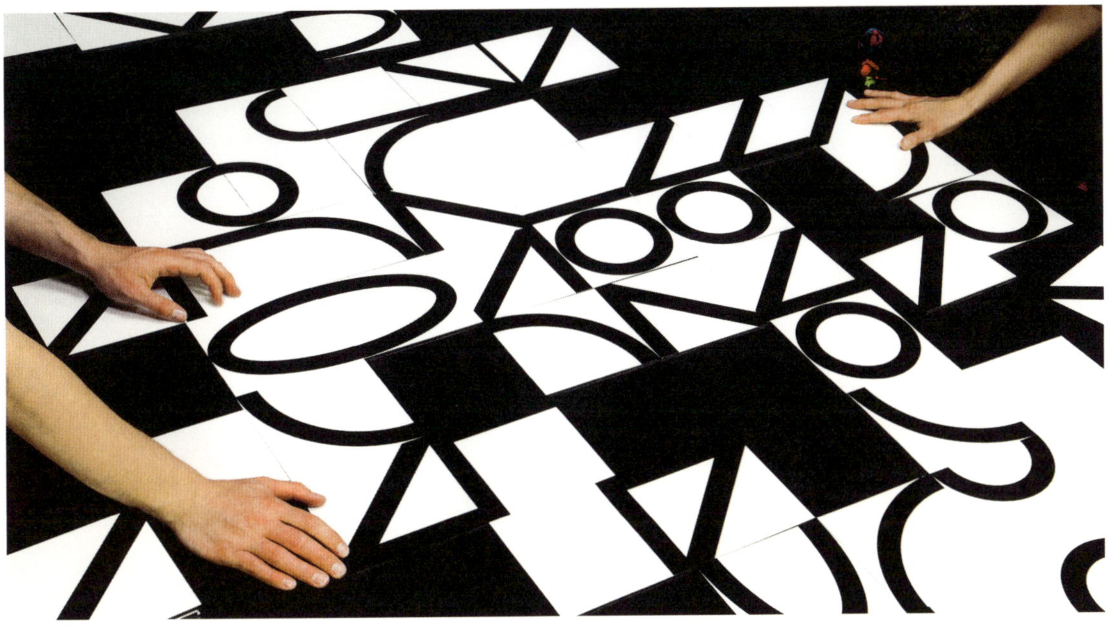

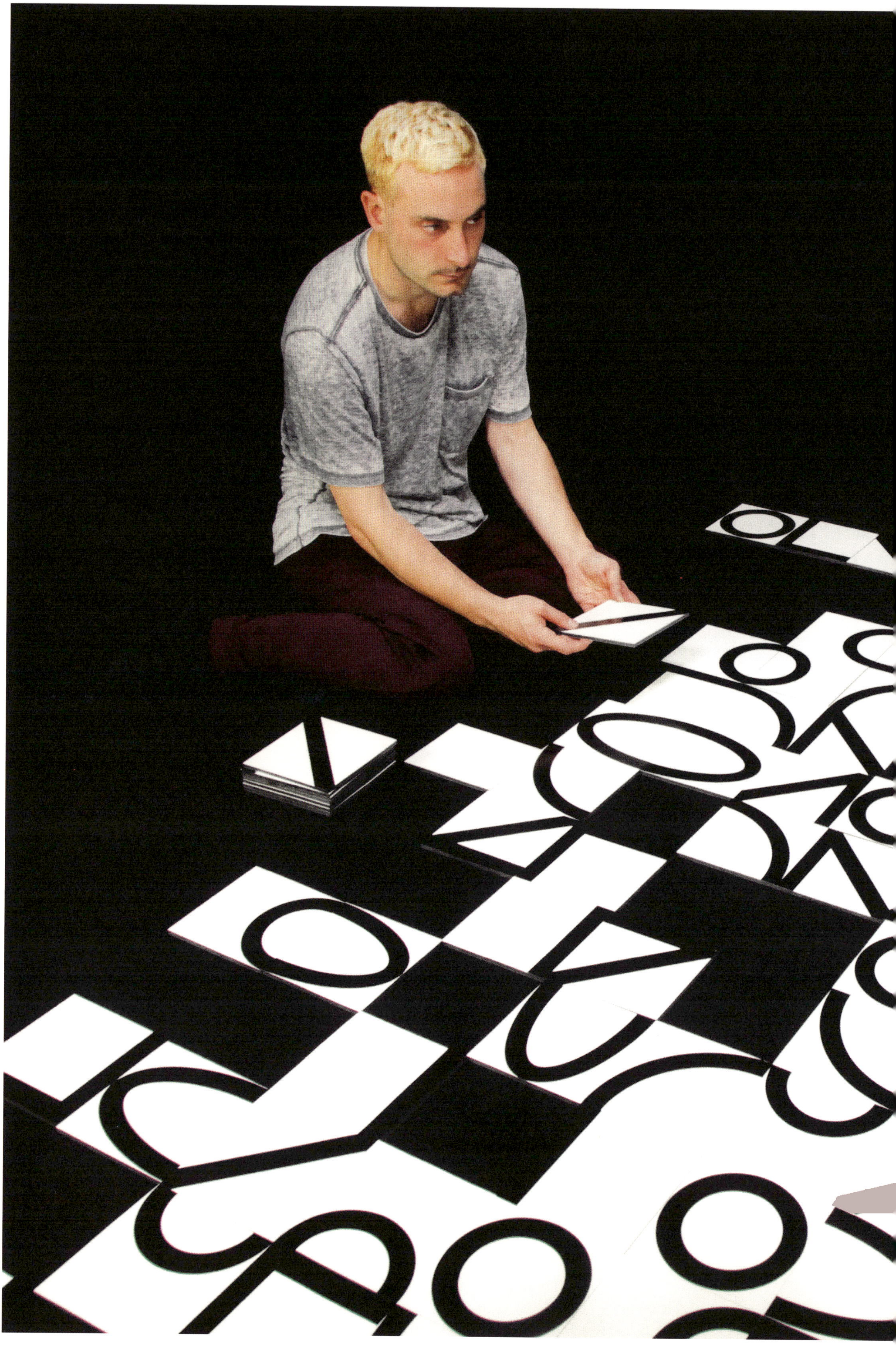

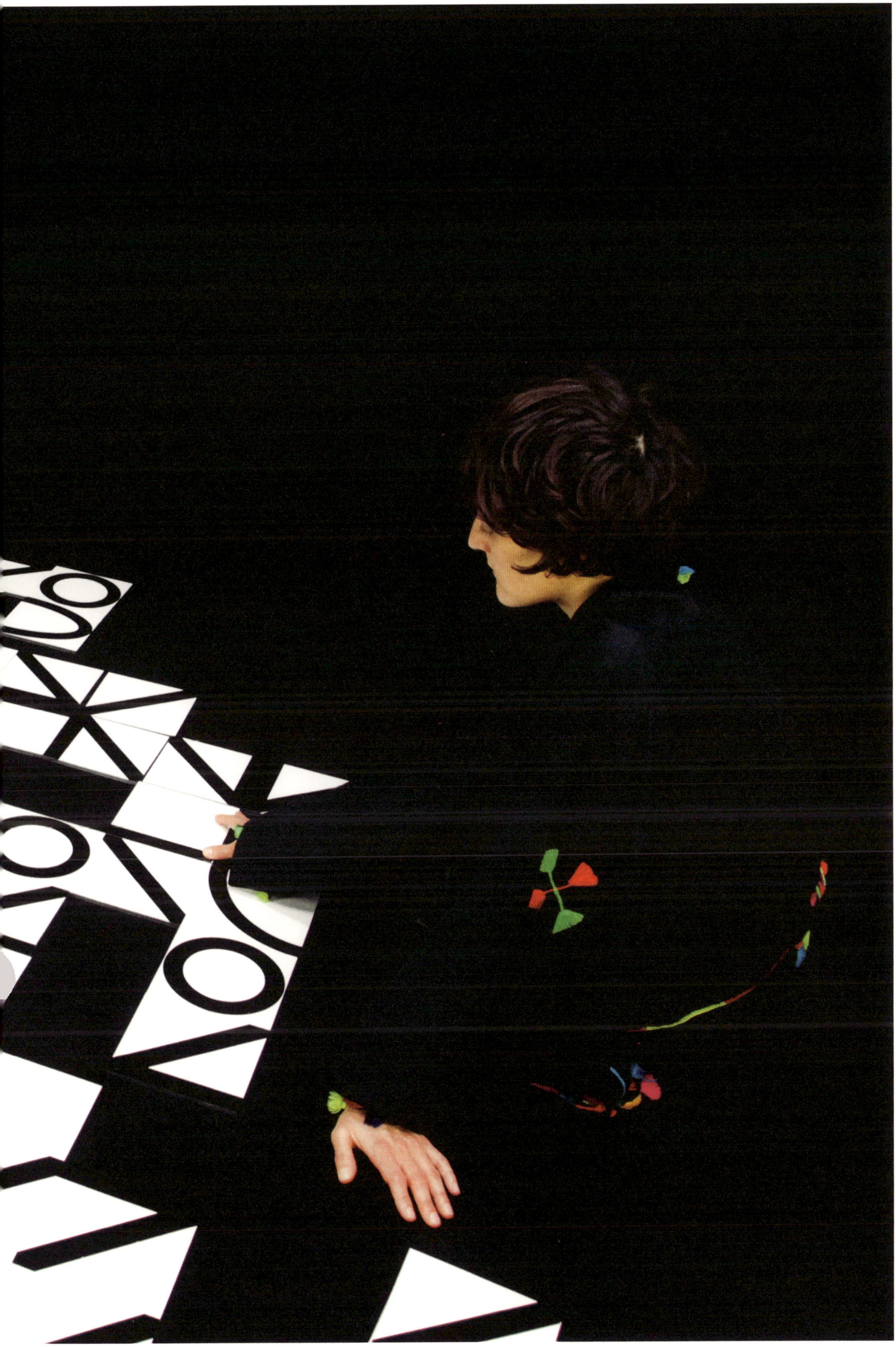

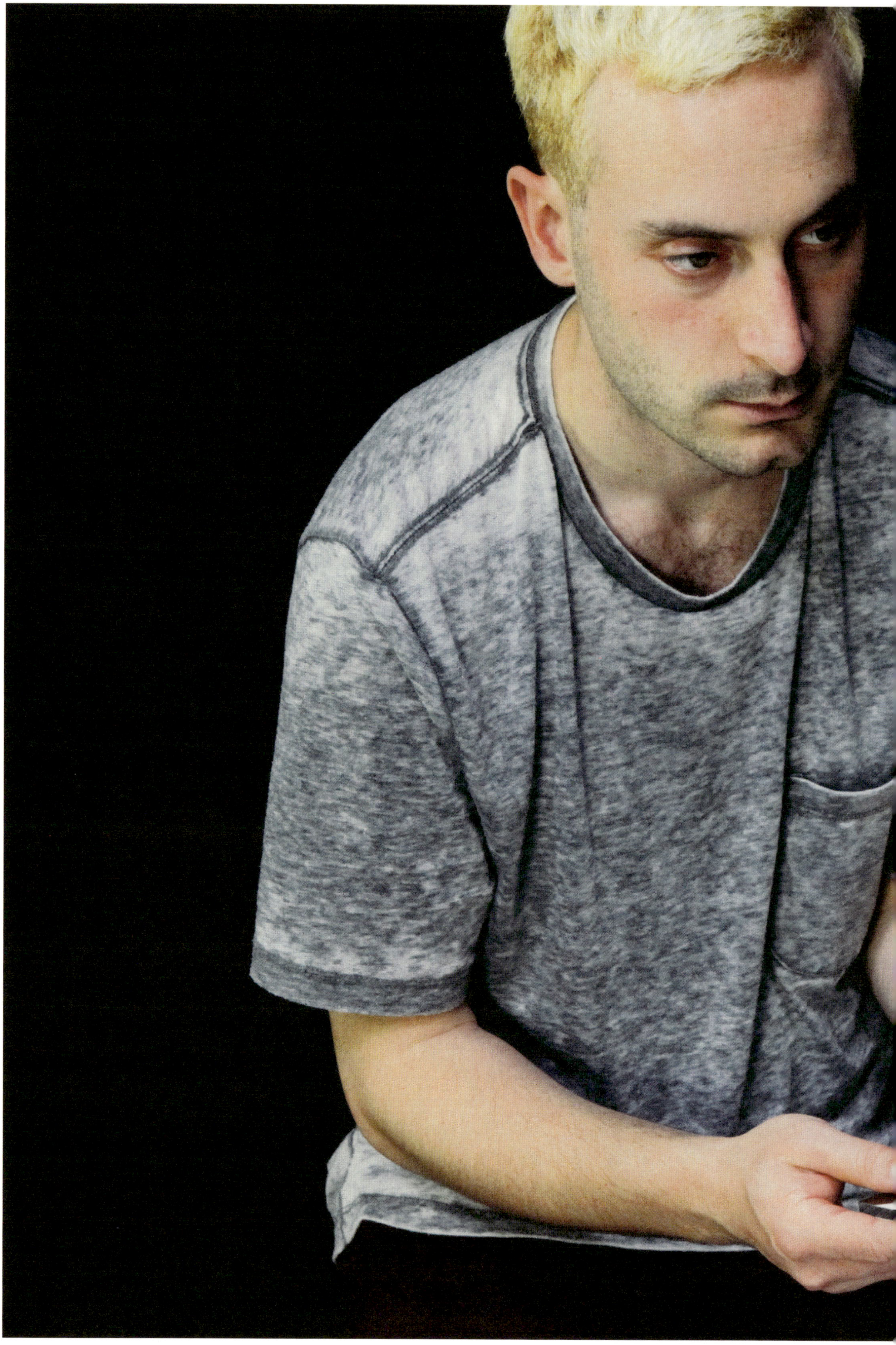

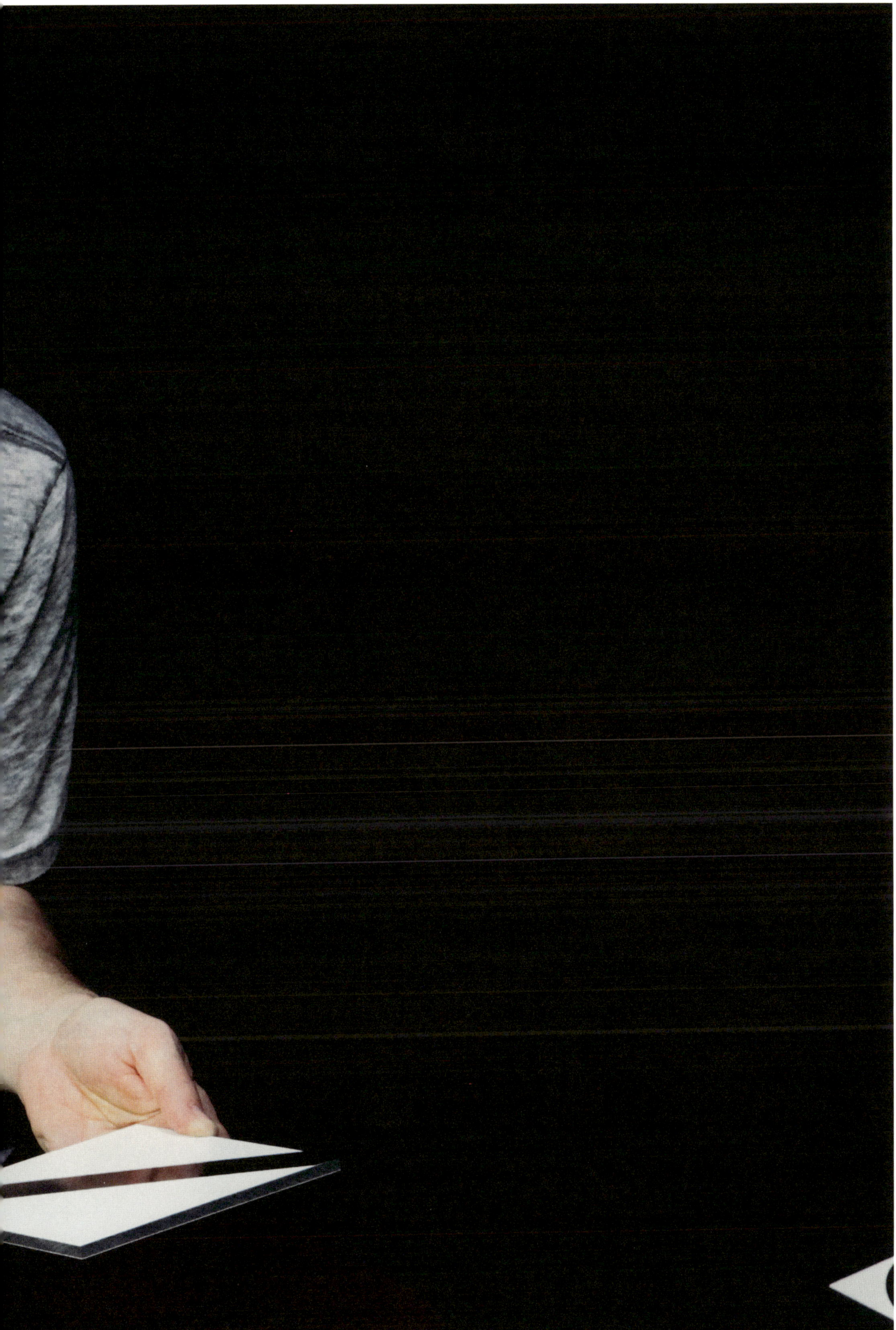

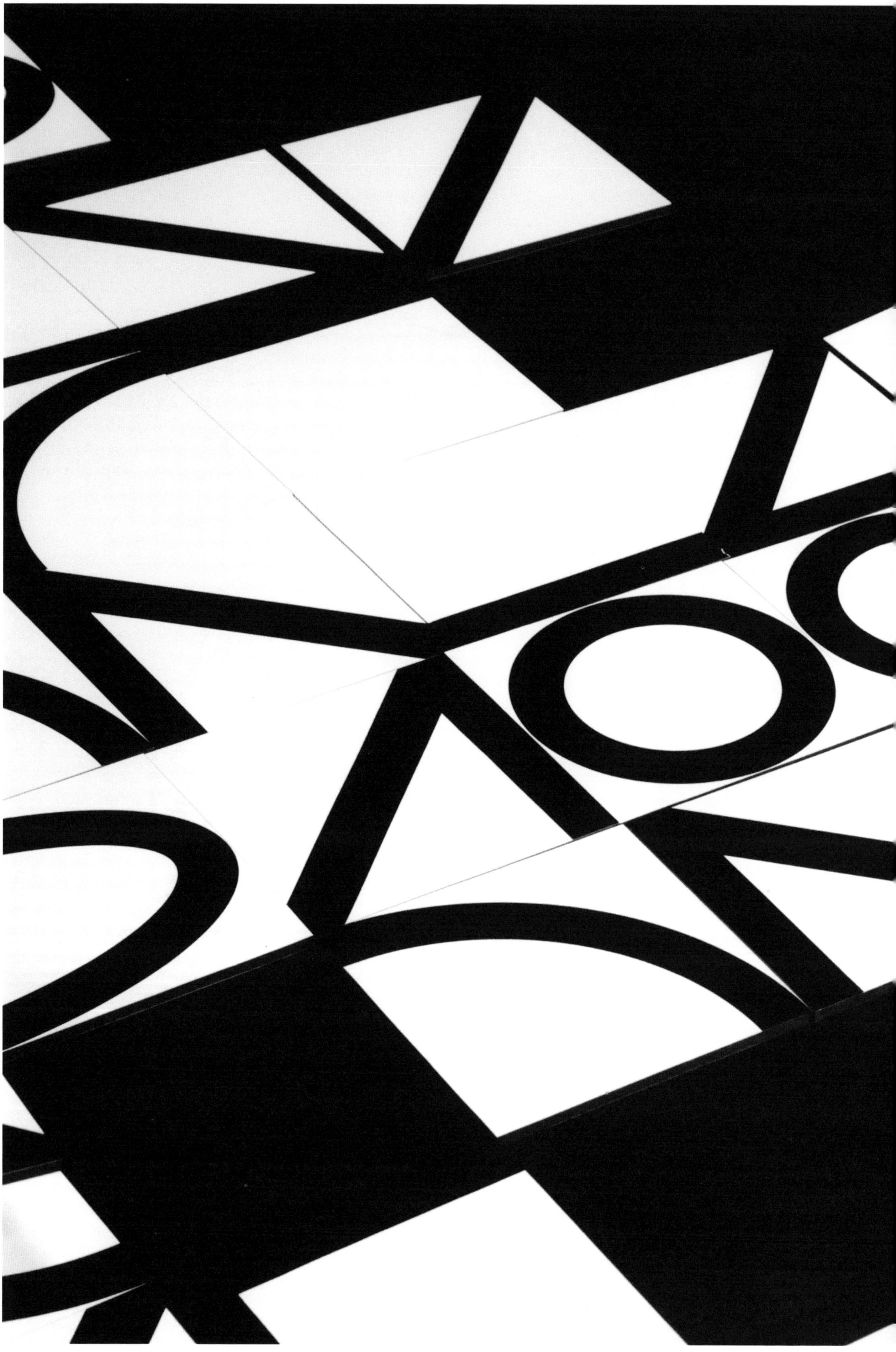

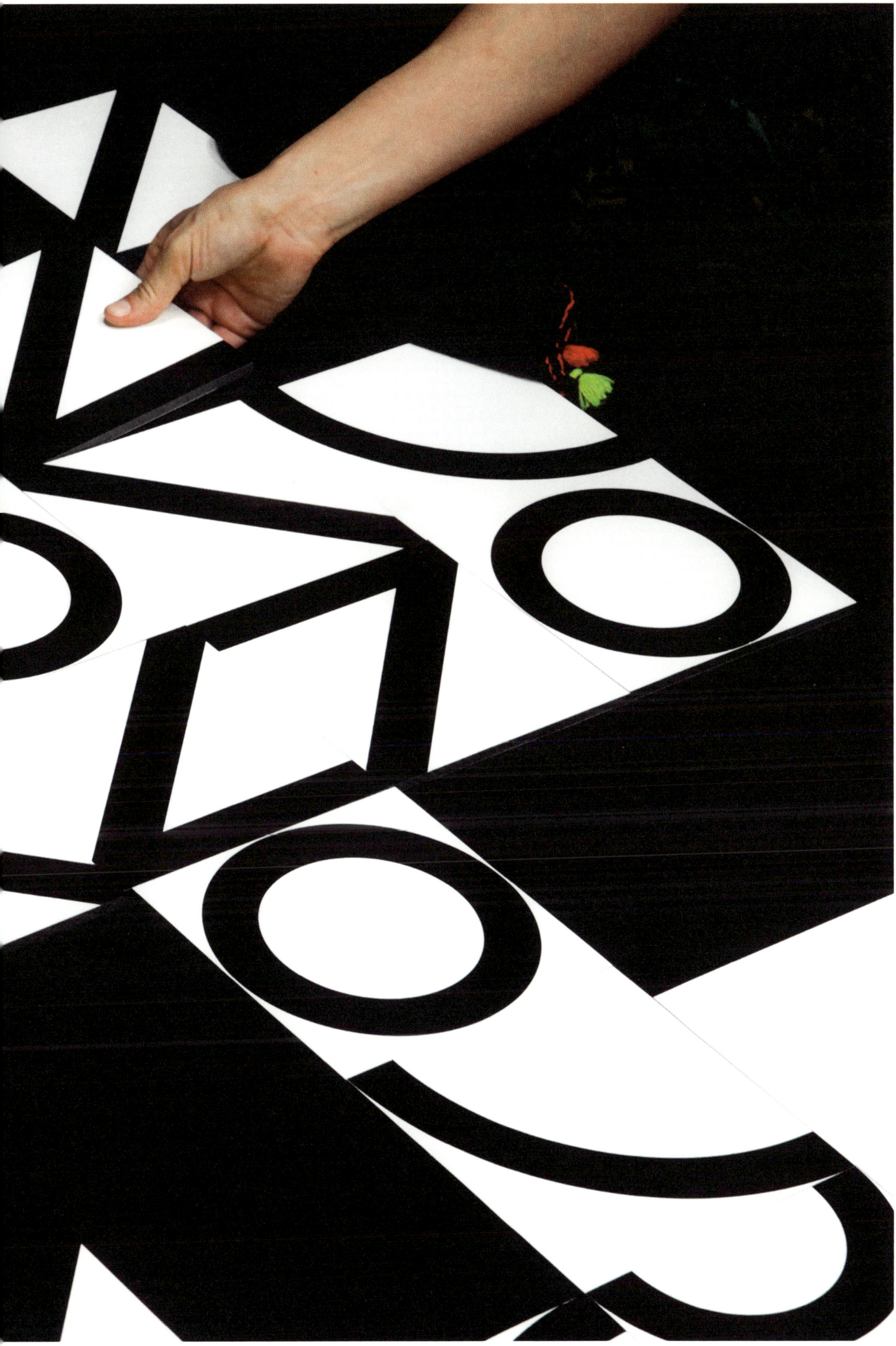

Tara:

The E-X-I-T, where do you think that is? I really have no idea what we're looking for. Ohio?

Ohio:

Tara, we have to think differently, re-consider everything and start from scratch. We need to take entirely new paths. That's what the Oracle says. You understand?

Tara:

Yes, Ohio, I think I'm beginning to understand a little better ...

Tara starts playing the game with black and white shapes on the ground.

... 3, 6, 9. Second row: 5, 10, 12. Third row: 7, 5, ... am not quite sure what the third number is ...

Ohio:

No, Tara. I don't think this is the solution, you see. How about this? A?

Tara:

Alpha.

Ohio

B?

Tara:

Bravo.

Ohio:
C?

Tara:
Charlie.

Ohio:
D?

Tara:
Delta.

Ohio:
E?

Tara:
Echo.

Ohio:
F?

Tara:
Foxtrott.

Ohio:
J?

Tara:
Juliet.

Ohio:
L?

Tara:
Lima.

Ohio:

R?

Tara:

Romeo.

Ohio:

N?

Tara:

November.

Ohio:

U?

Tara:

Uniform.

Ohio:

Y?

Tara:

Yellow.

Ohio:

X?

Tara:

X-Ray!

Flash light. The image dissolves. Tara and Ohio are teleported into another scene.

S-C-E-N-E 13

The Dot turns optical.

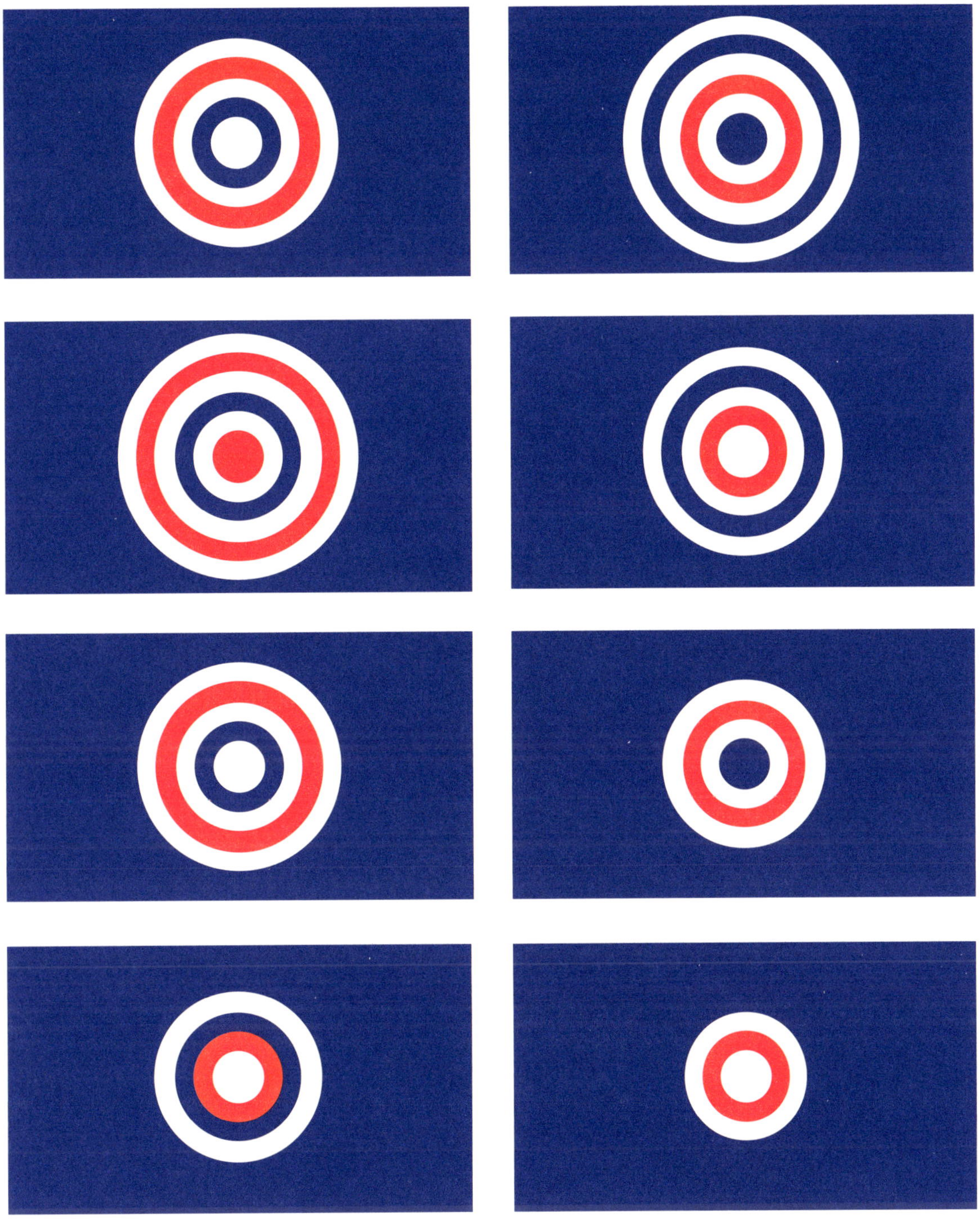

Dot:

Don't be afraid! This is only the beginning. This is only the beginning. This is only the beginning.

S-C-E-N-E 14

Tara und Ohio stand in "The Room of Noise". The room is entirely covered with acoustic foam. A microphone is suspended from the center of the ceiling. At the beginning of the scene there is total silence. Slowly, muffled noises, as if coming out of a closed car, become audible: a female voice in the background, sounds of a telephone keyboard, ringtones, the beep of a clock. Fragments of music tracks fade in and out: The Chromatics. Running Up that Hill. The soft sound of a supermarket checkout product scanning machine becomes increasingly louder and remains as the only sound in the room.

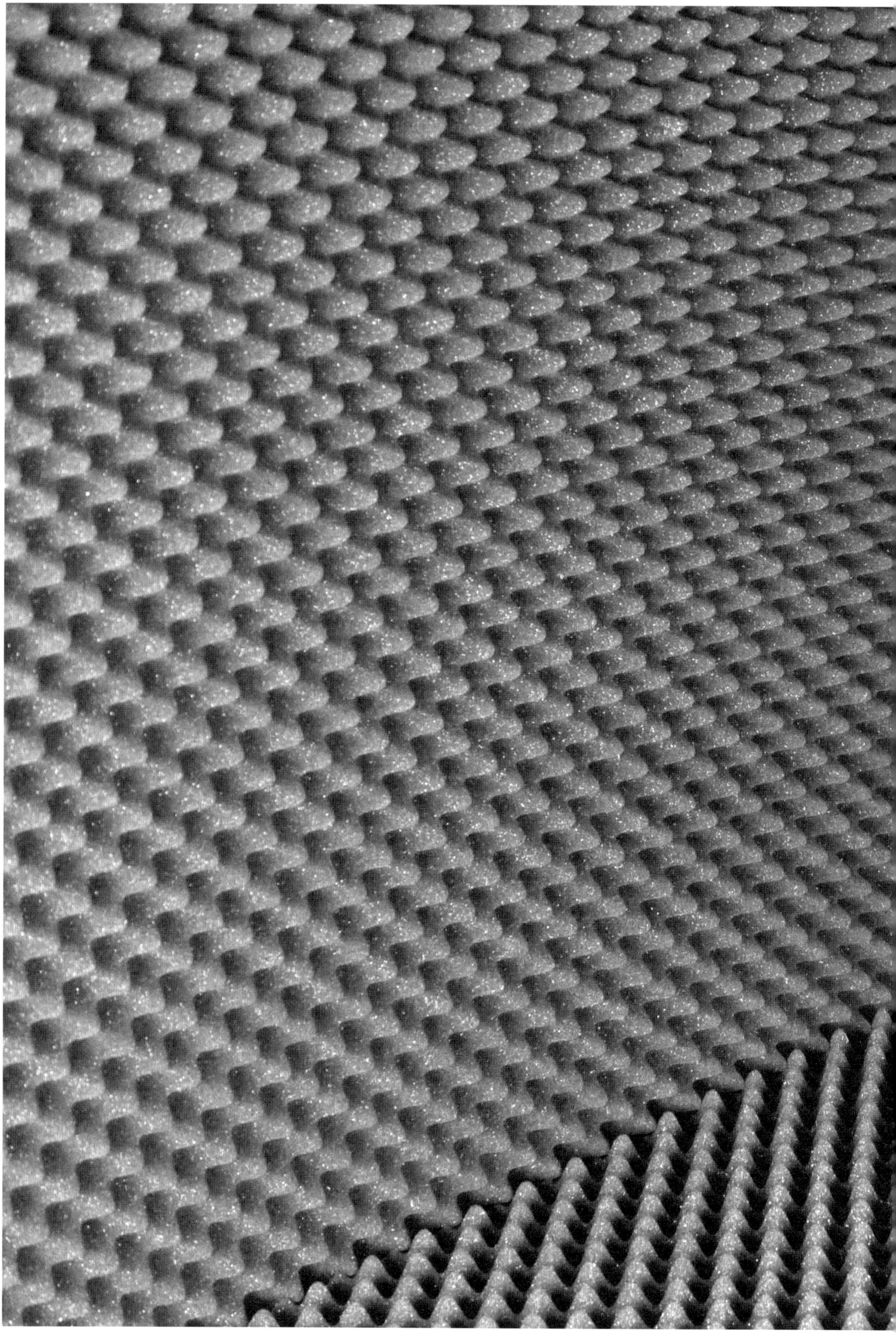

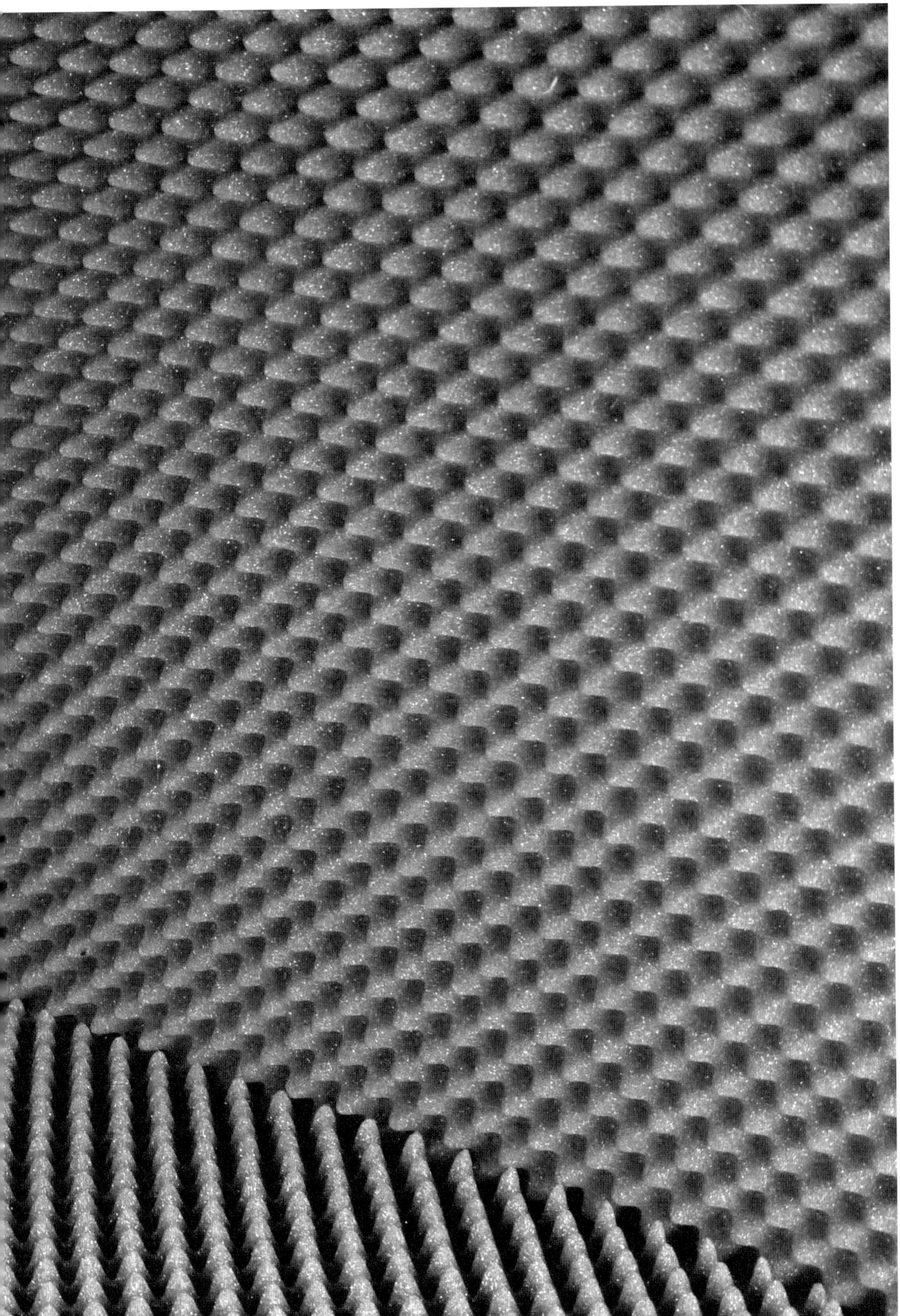

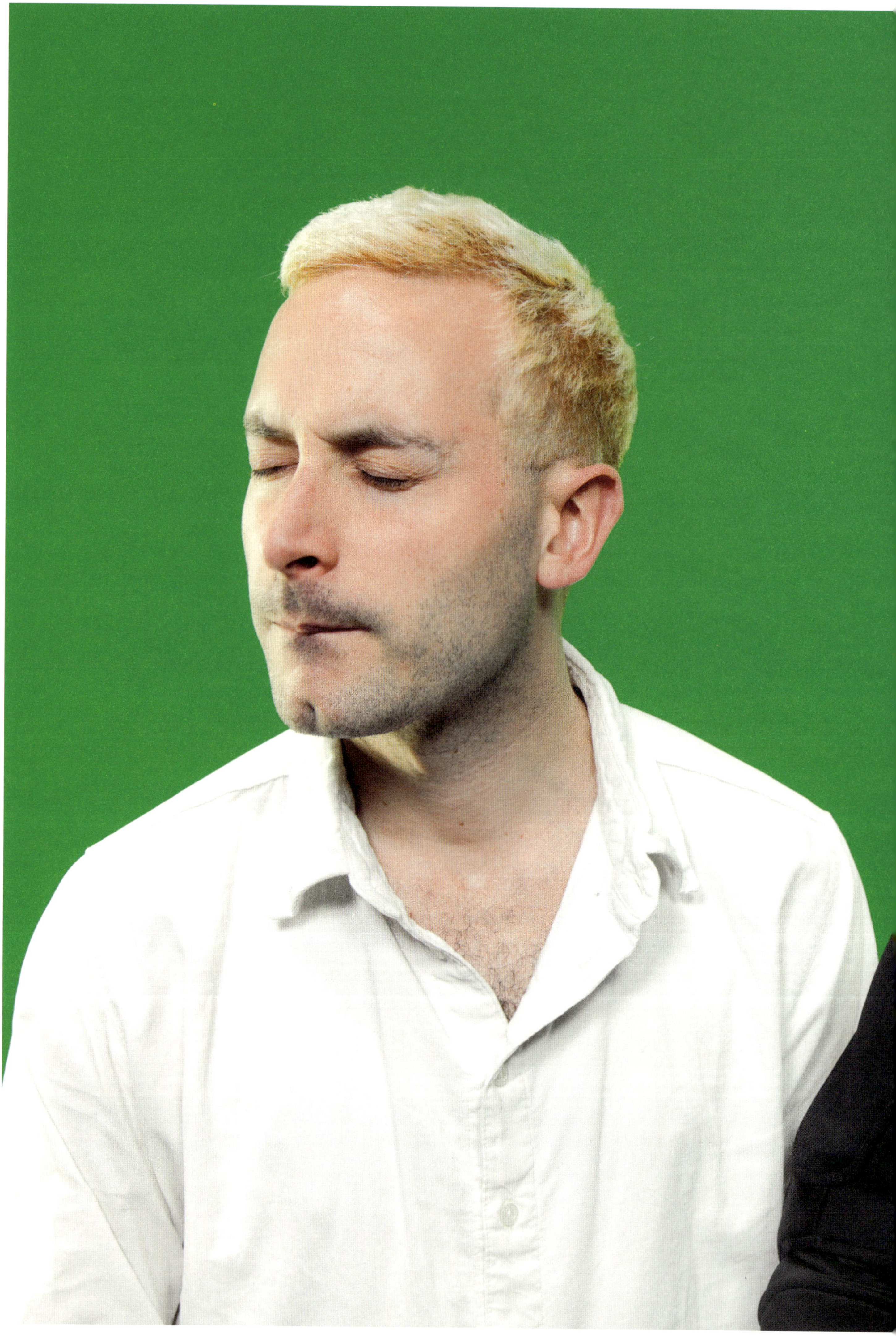

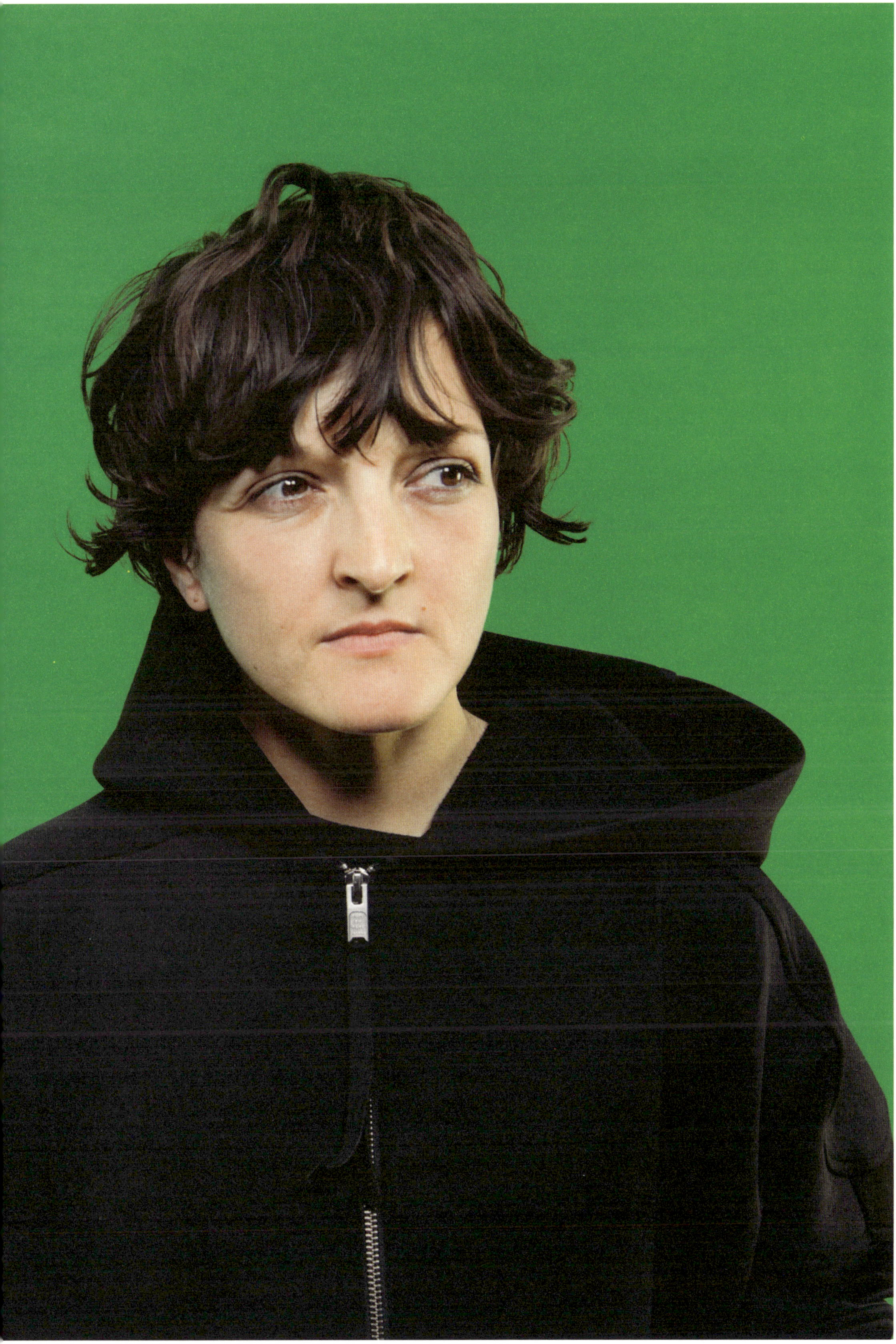

S-C-E-N-E 15

Tara and Ohio are sitting on a bench in a park. Magic Child approaches. He spreads his fingers again and again.

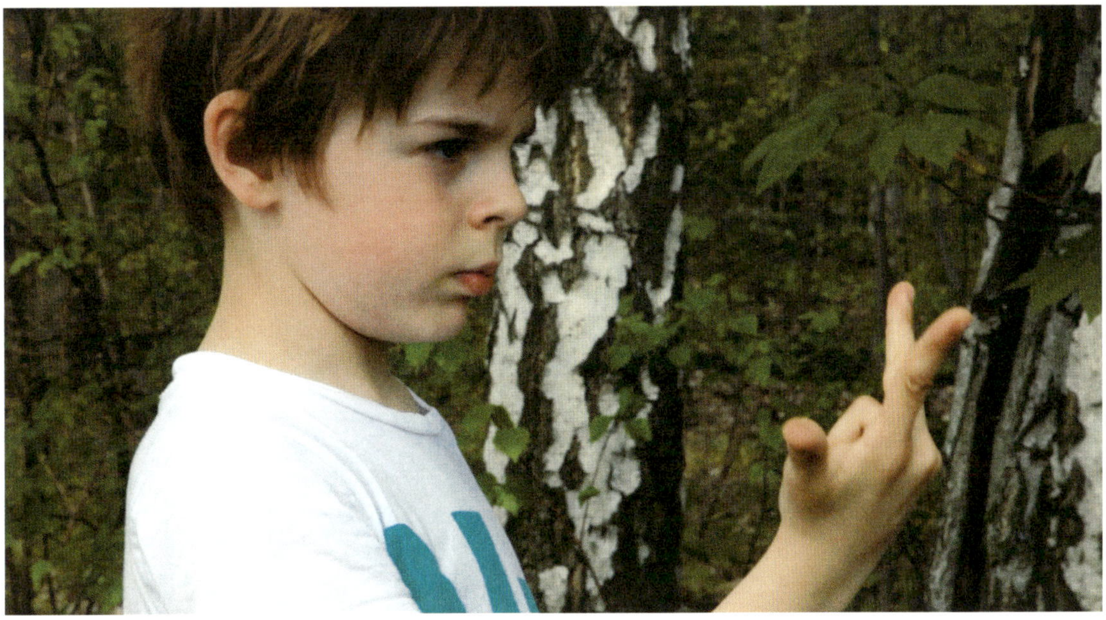

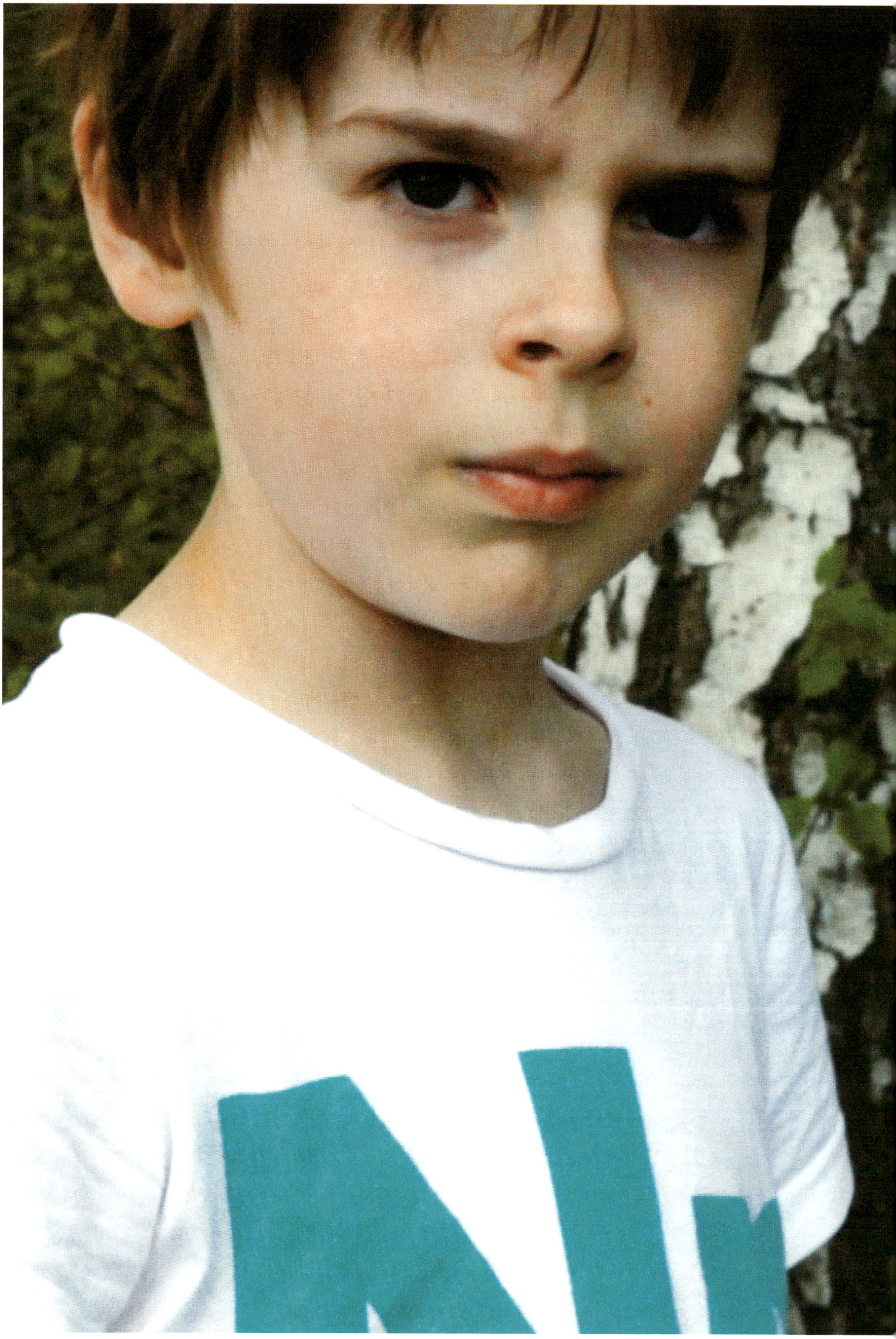

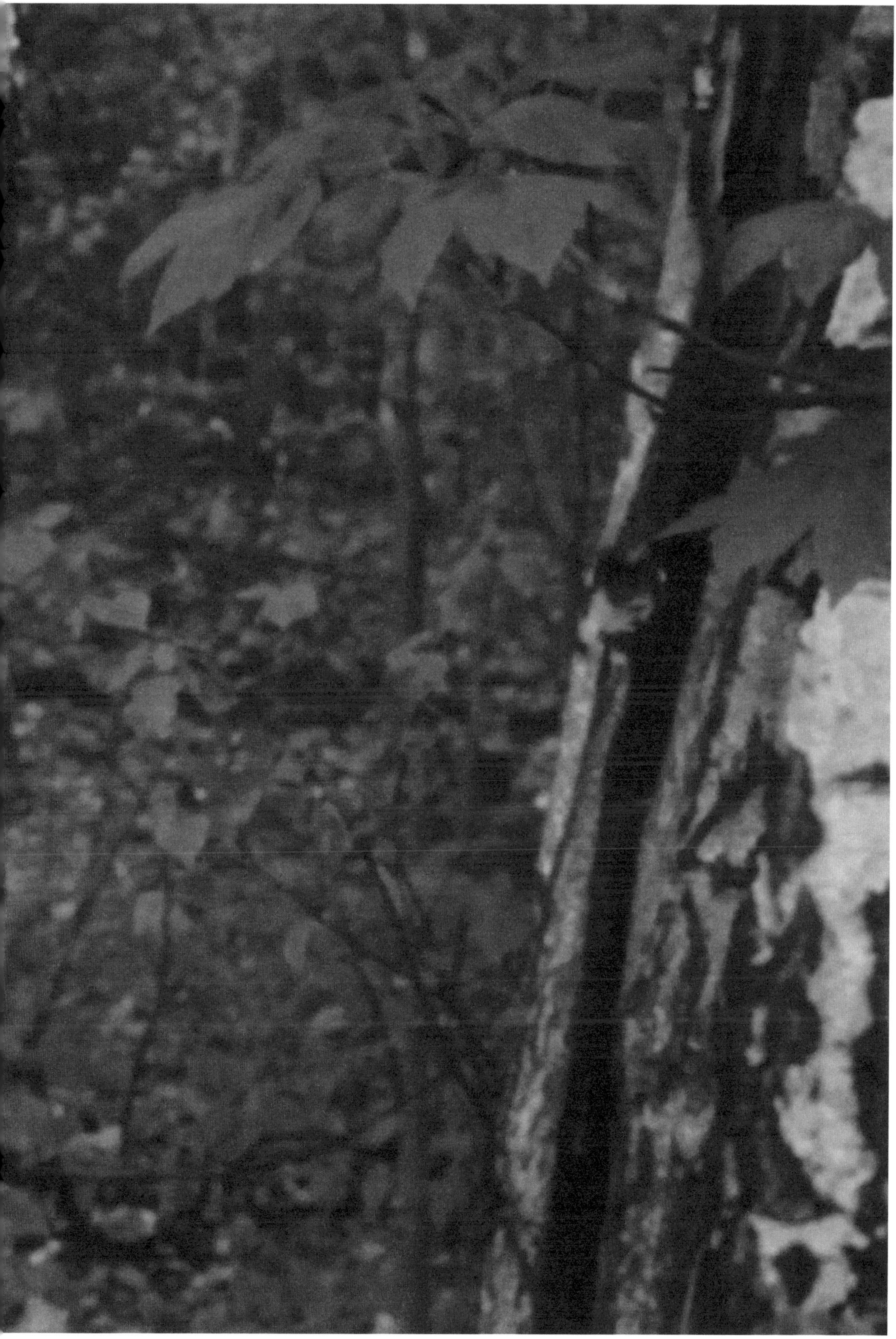

Child:

Do you know what this is?

Magic Child counts until three on his fingers, strangly twisting them.

Tara:

No. I don't know.

Child:

Do you know what this is?

He spreads his fingers in a different way and repeats the same thing a couple of times.

Ohio:

No. We really don't know, we're sorry!

Child:

That's three! Three!

S-C-E-N-E 16

The Oracle is a supermarket cashier. She sits behind a checkout, scanning shopping products.

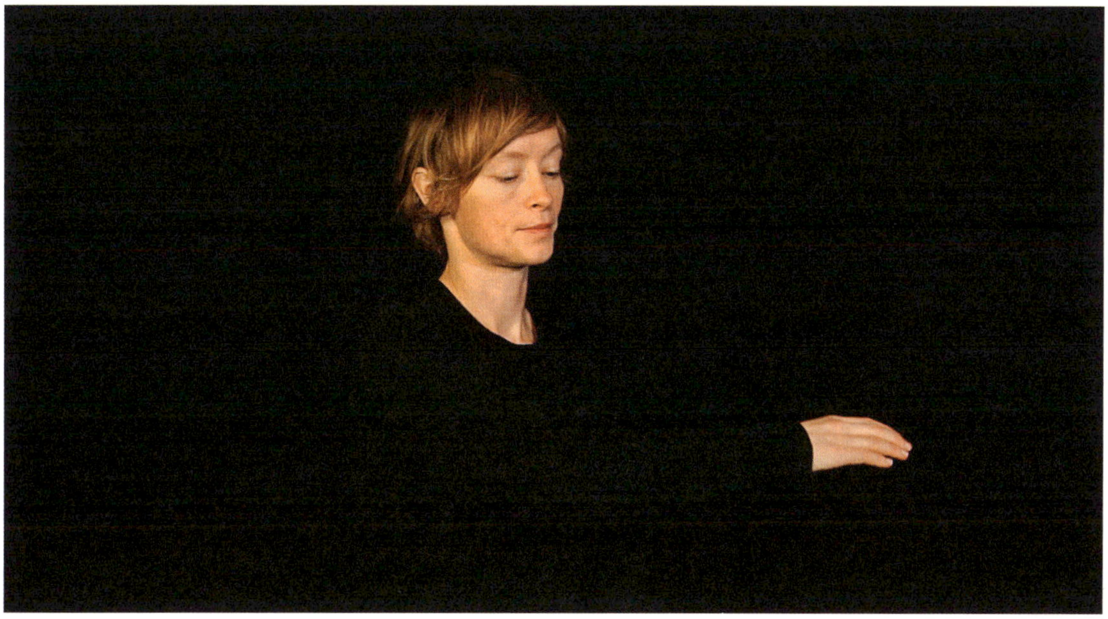

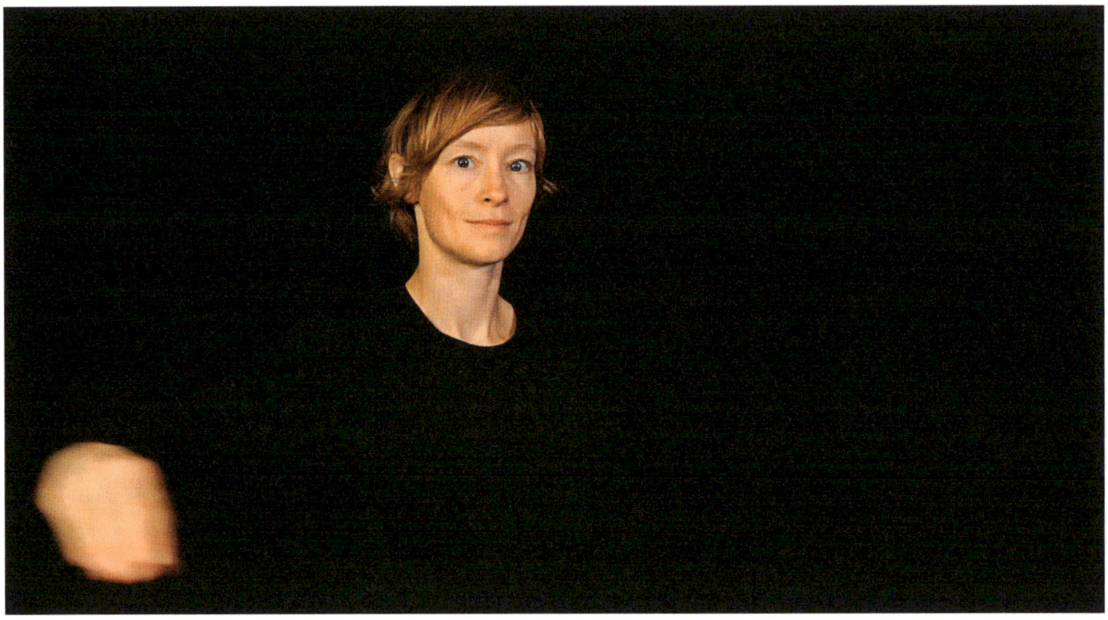

S-C-E-N-E 17

Tara and Ohio are in a monothematic supermarket.

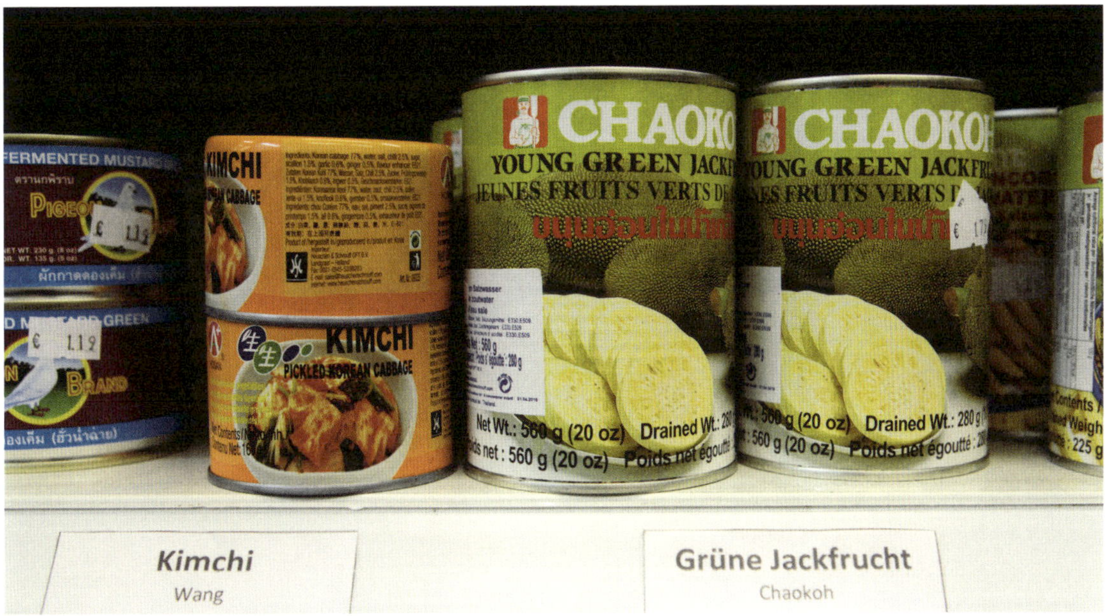

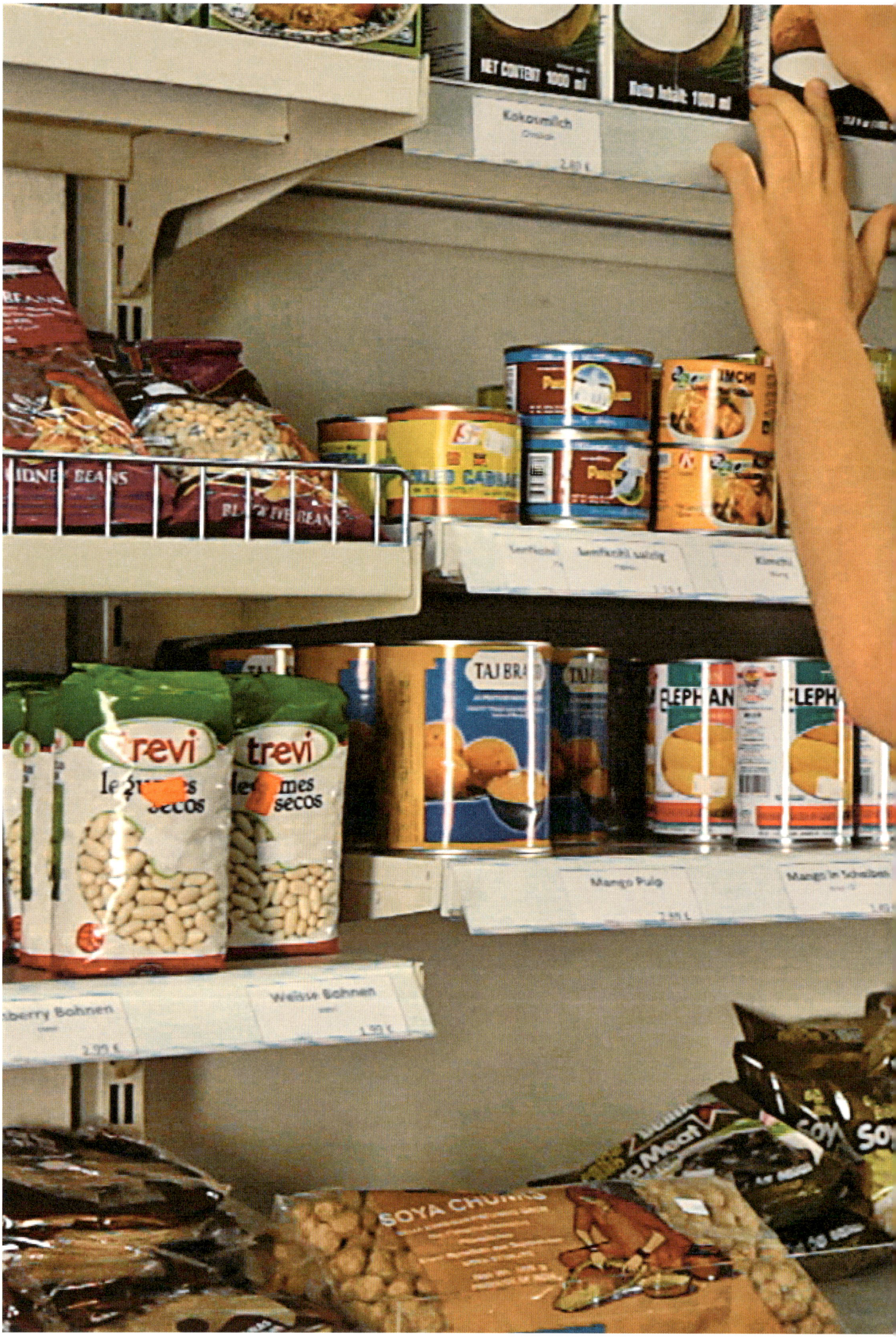
NET CONTENT 1000 ml
Netto Inhalt: 1000 ml
Kokosmilch
trevi
trevi
secos
secos
Weisse Bohnen
Mango Pulp
Mango in Scheiben
SOYA CHUNKS

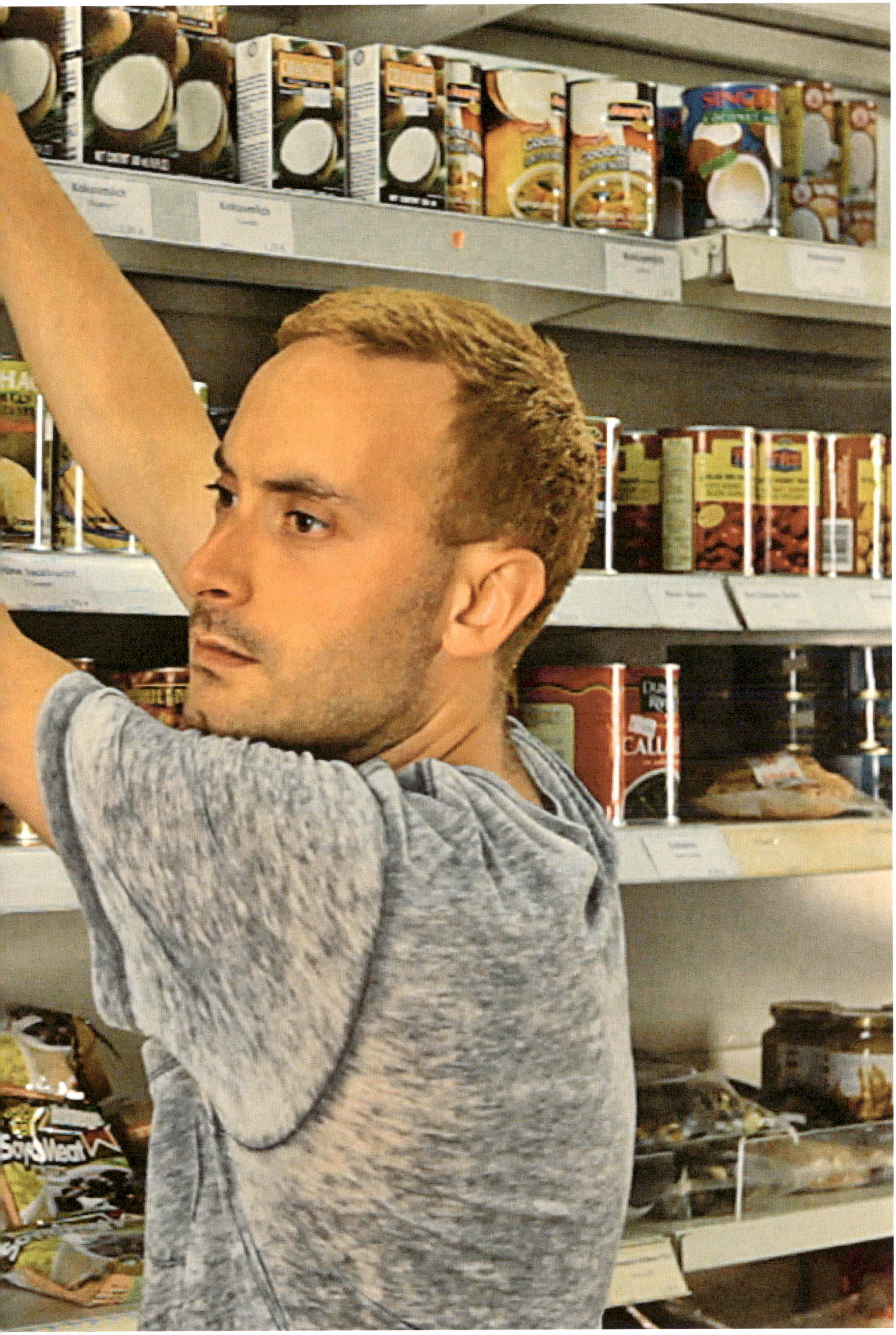
SoyaMeat

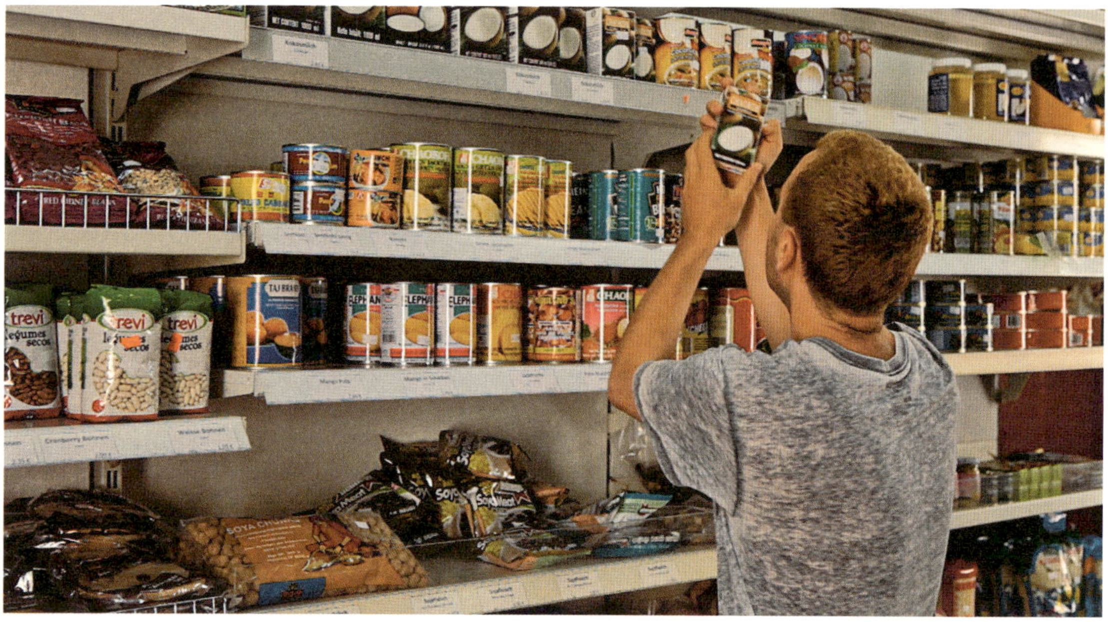

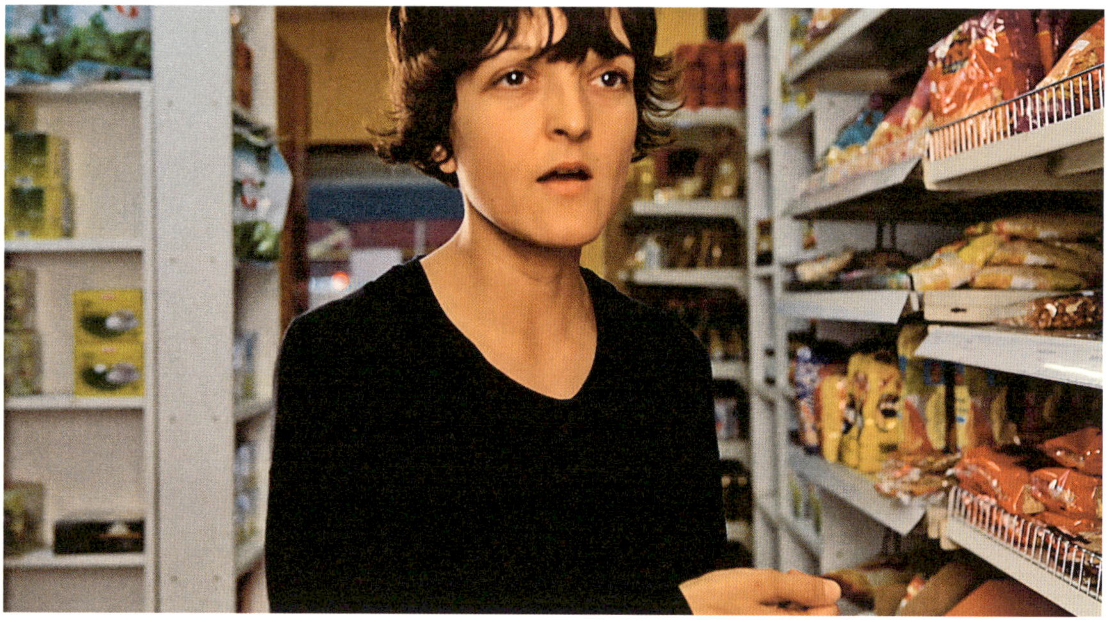

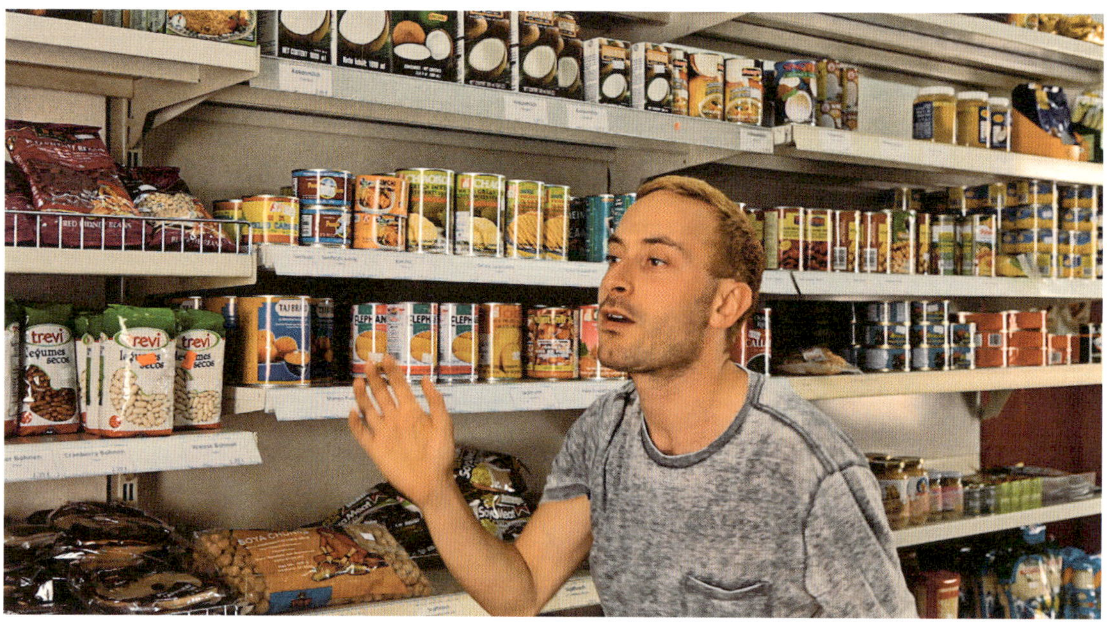

Ohio:

1.69, 1.79, 1.89, 2.49, 2.69, 2.89, 2.99, 3.29, 3.49, 3.79, 3.89, 3.99, ...

Tara:

Oh Ohio, come on! Stop it. Stop all this counting!

Ohio:

3.99, 4.29, 4.69, 4.89, 4.99, I can't stop, Tara, there is a logic in all this, you see. I'm sure there is a reason, a pattern to all of this.

Tara:

Ohio, stop being so paranoid. These are prices that indicate the value of products ...

Ohio:

That is what most people think, Tara. But look, there is a whole conspiracy behind this. High prices are located on the upper shelves whereas lower prices are always on the lowers ones. They are hard to reach, you see. Then there are cameras everywhere. Have you seen them? And have you listened to the music?

Tara:

You have to put them back in their right position, Ohio. Put these products back into their right position. Put them back!

Ohio keeps pulling them out.

Tara:

You are a freak, Ohio! A weird, frustrated, nerdy, paranoid freak! You lost it, Ohio. This is a supermarket, and we were supposed to buy something in here. Instead you are counting again, and come up with ridiculous theories!

Ohio:

But Tara, can't you see. This is our chance: 4.99, 5.29, 5.49, 5,69.

Tara:

Ohio, you are an idiot! I'm not going to stay here anymore!

Tara turns around and leaves the supermarket. Ohio looks surprised, but he starts counting prices again.

Ohio:

0.79, 1.89, 1.99, 2.49, 2.69, 2.89, 2.99, ... I'm sure there is a logic to this ... 3.29, 3.49, 3.79, 3.89, 3.99, ...

S-C-E-N-E 18

The Dot rotating in from far away.

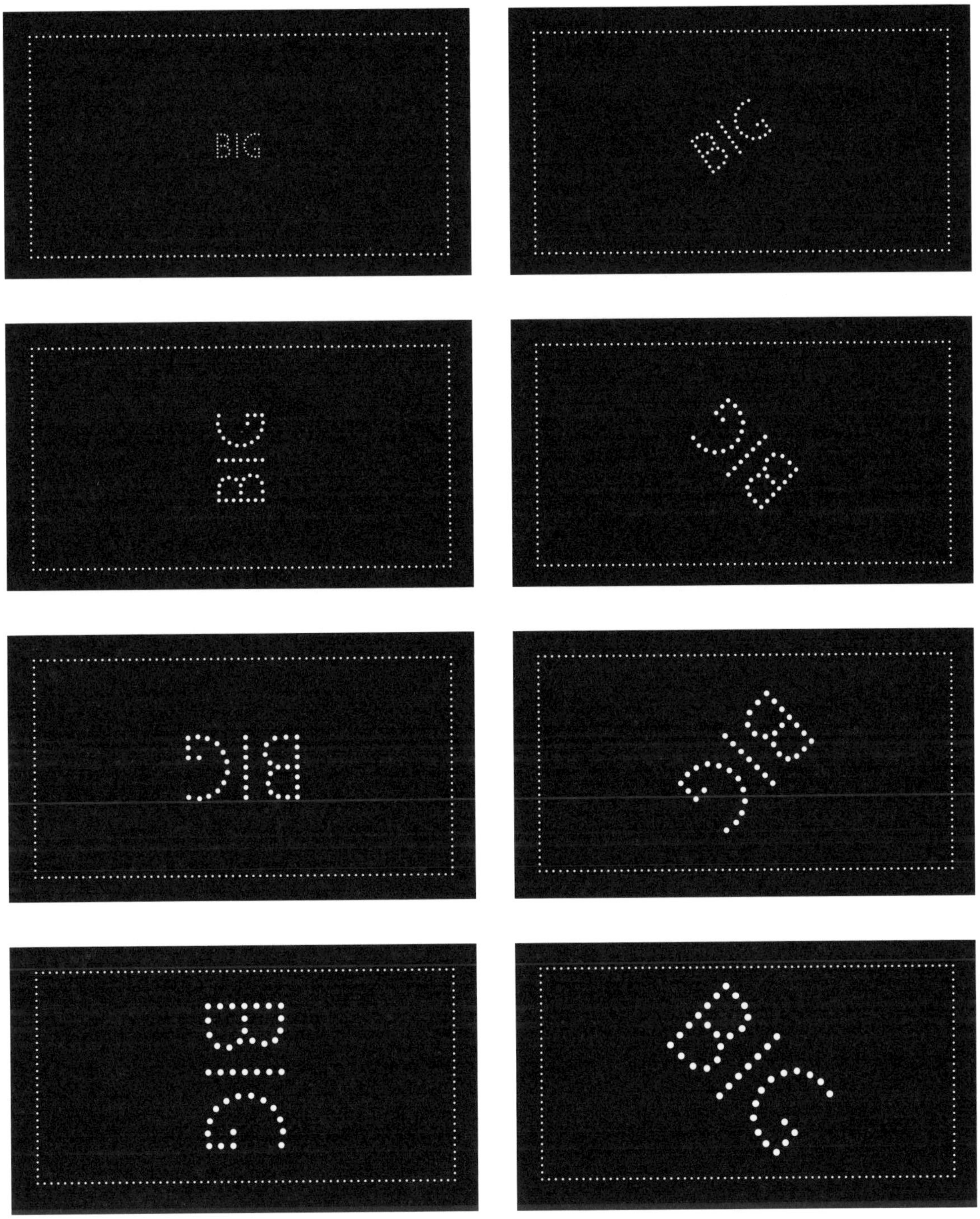

TUR

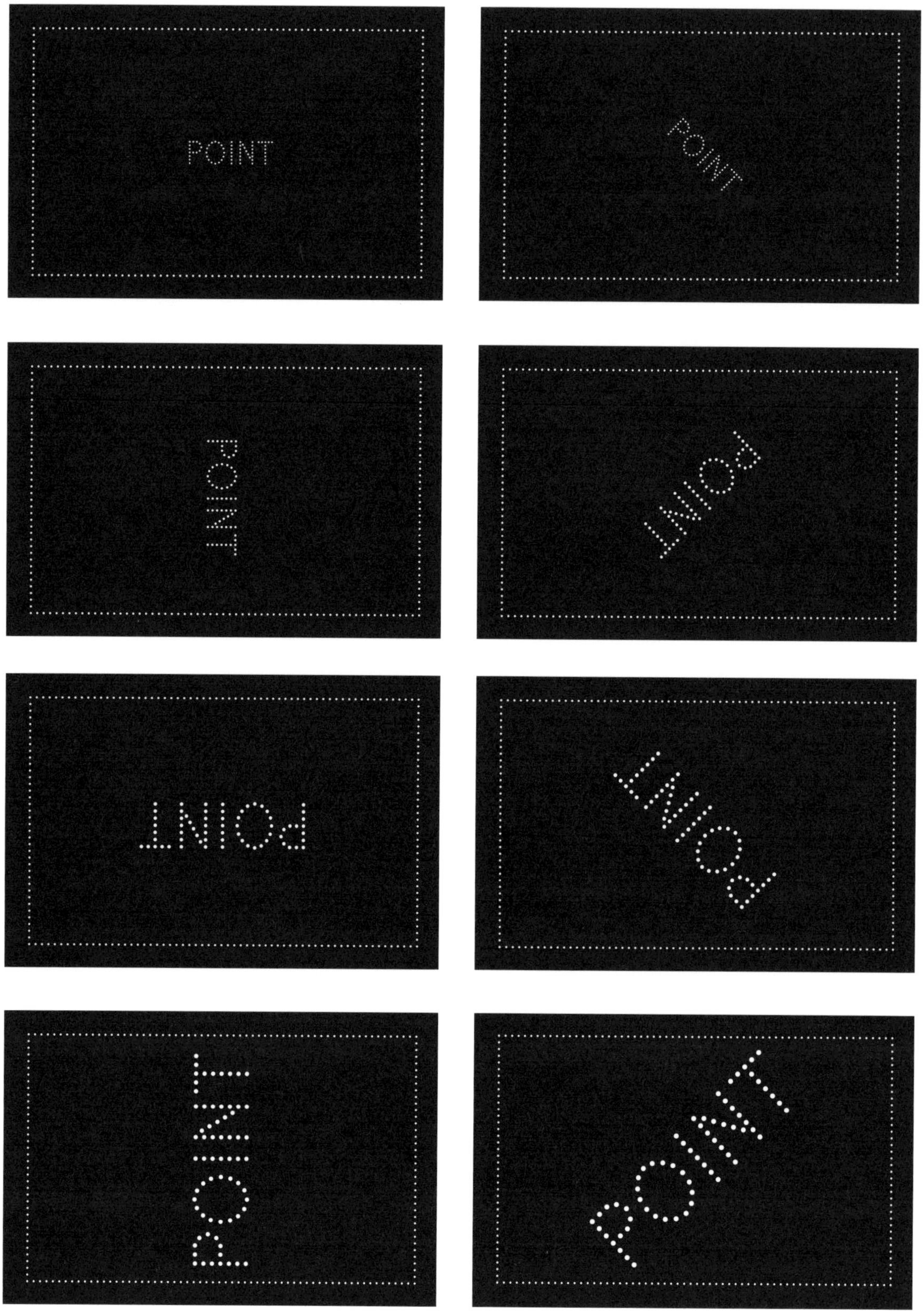
POINT
POINT
POINT
POINT
POINT
POINT
POINT
POINT

S-C-E-N-E 19

Ohio at the parking lot of a supermarket. He is exhausted and sunk in a state of desperation.

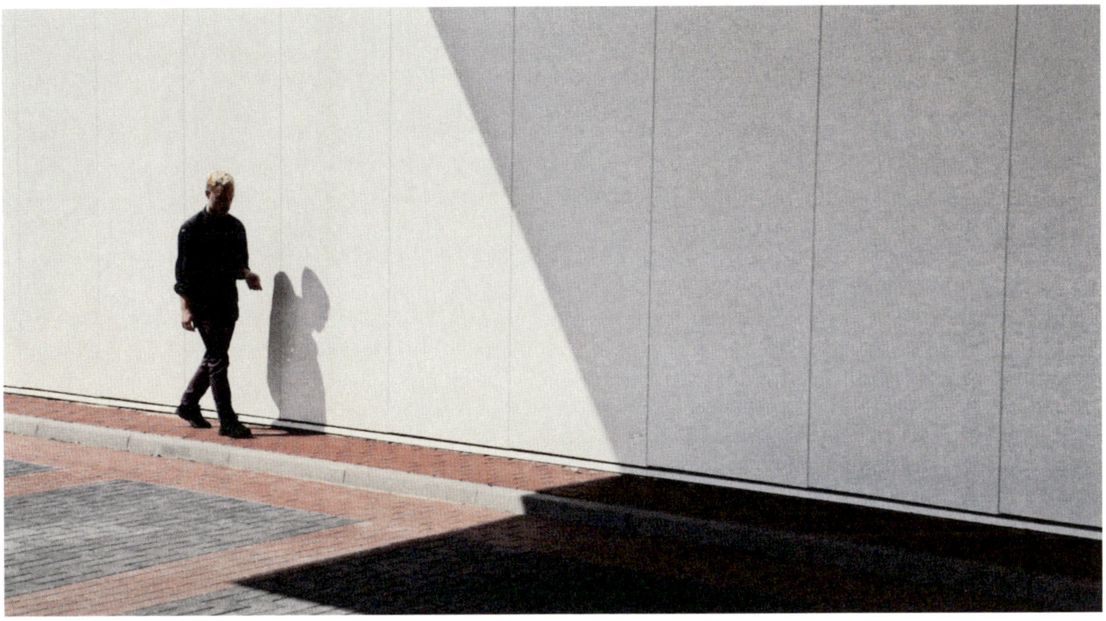

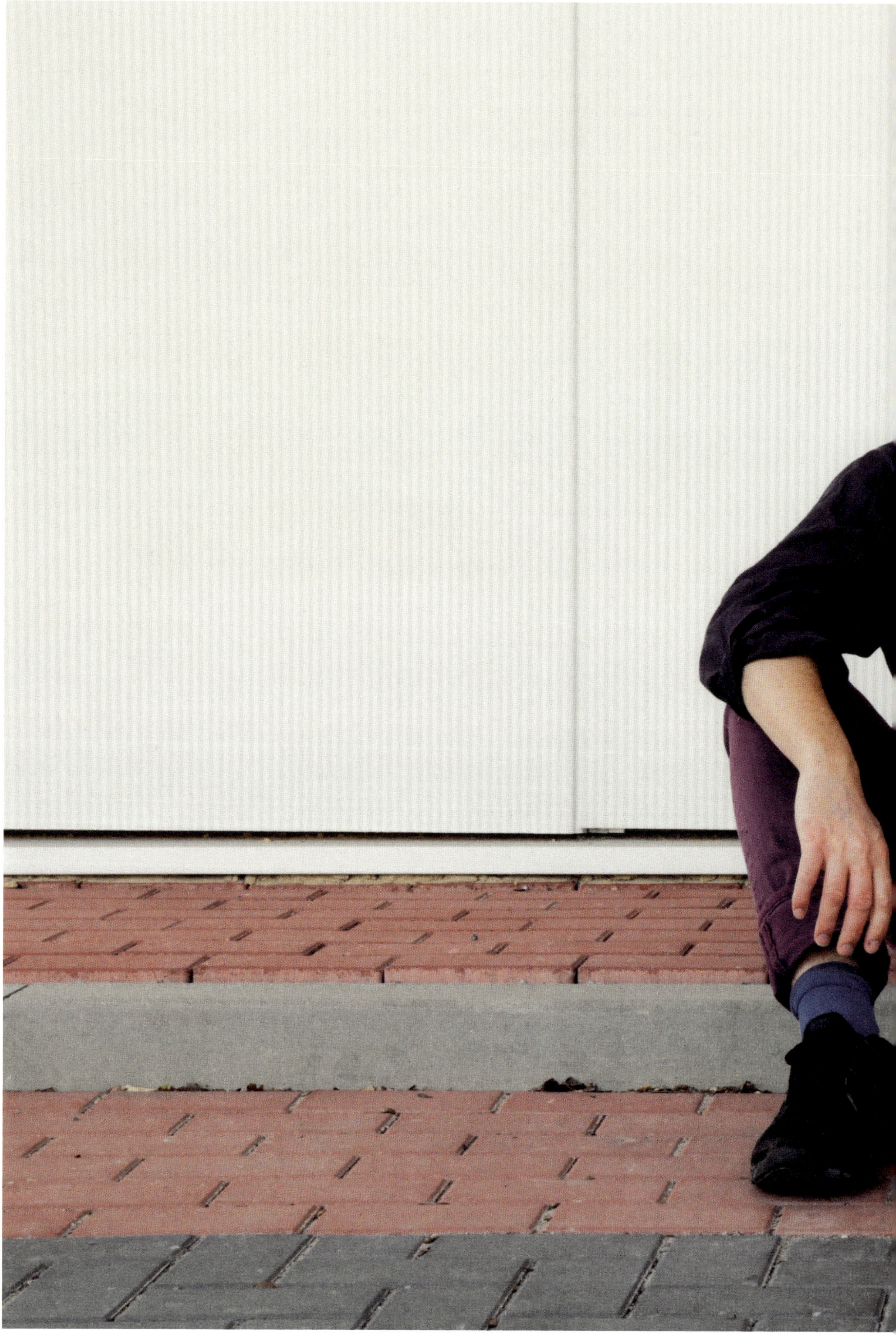

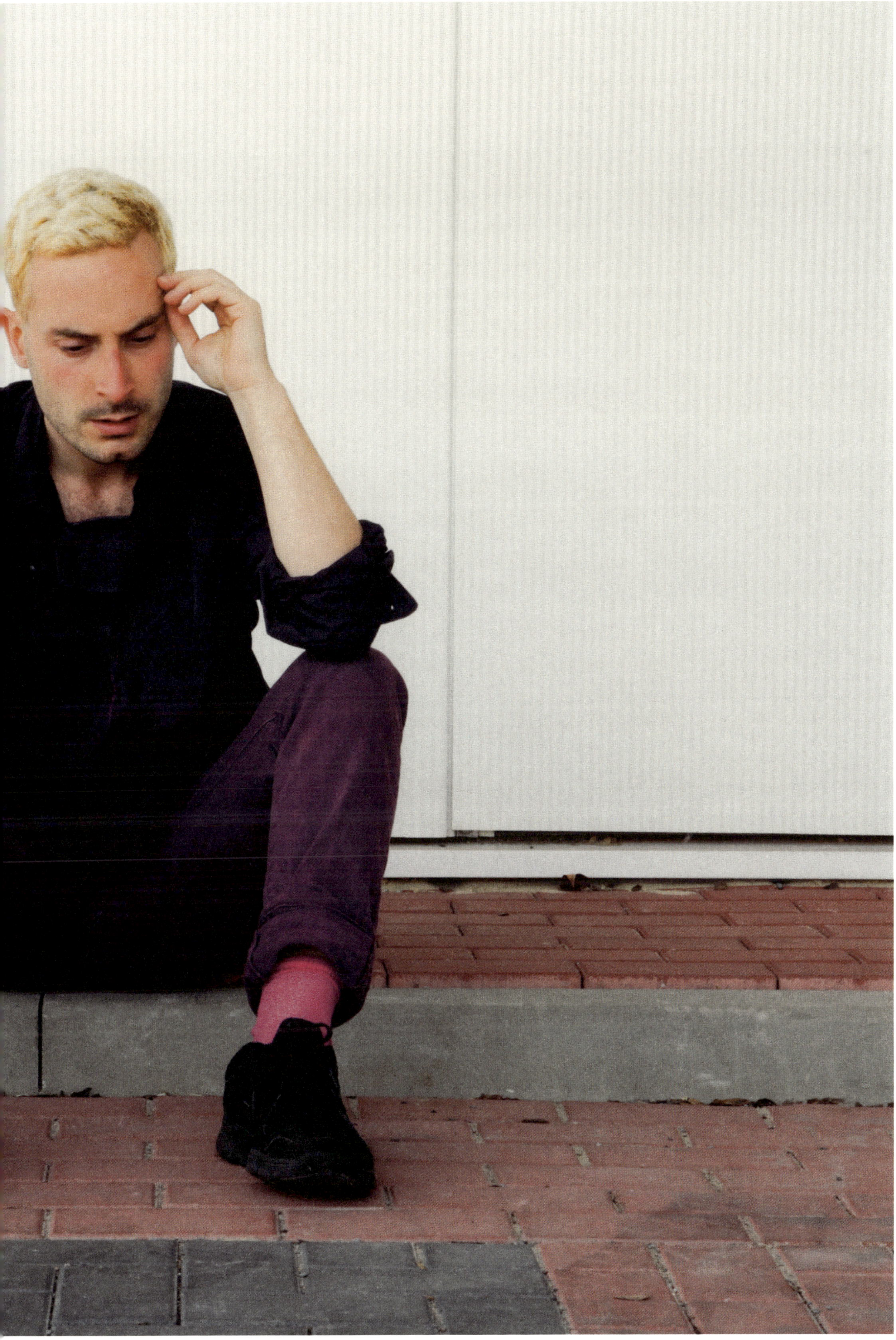

Ohio:

987, 1597, 2584. Why does no one say: I'm sick of searching. I'm sick of not knowing where to look. I'm sick of the unknown, the ambivalence, the unclear. I'm sick of Voodoo, the esoteric, the extraterrestial, the spirtual, the horoscope. I'm sick of supermarkets, waiting lines, administrative letters, pin-numbers and login codes. I'm sick of the telephone bill.

S-C-E-N-E 20

The Dot transforms into different graphs.

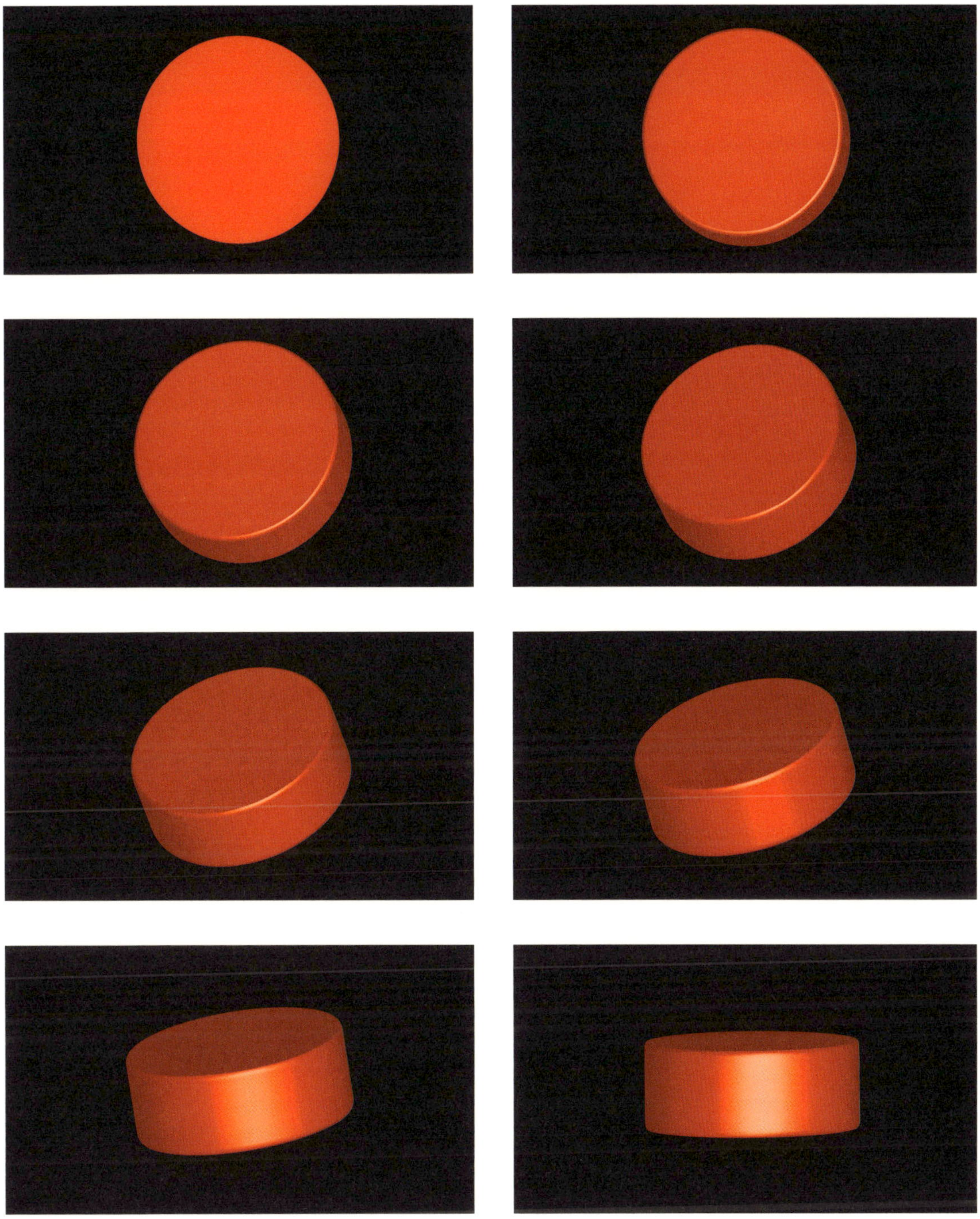

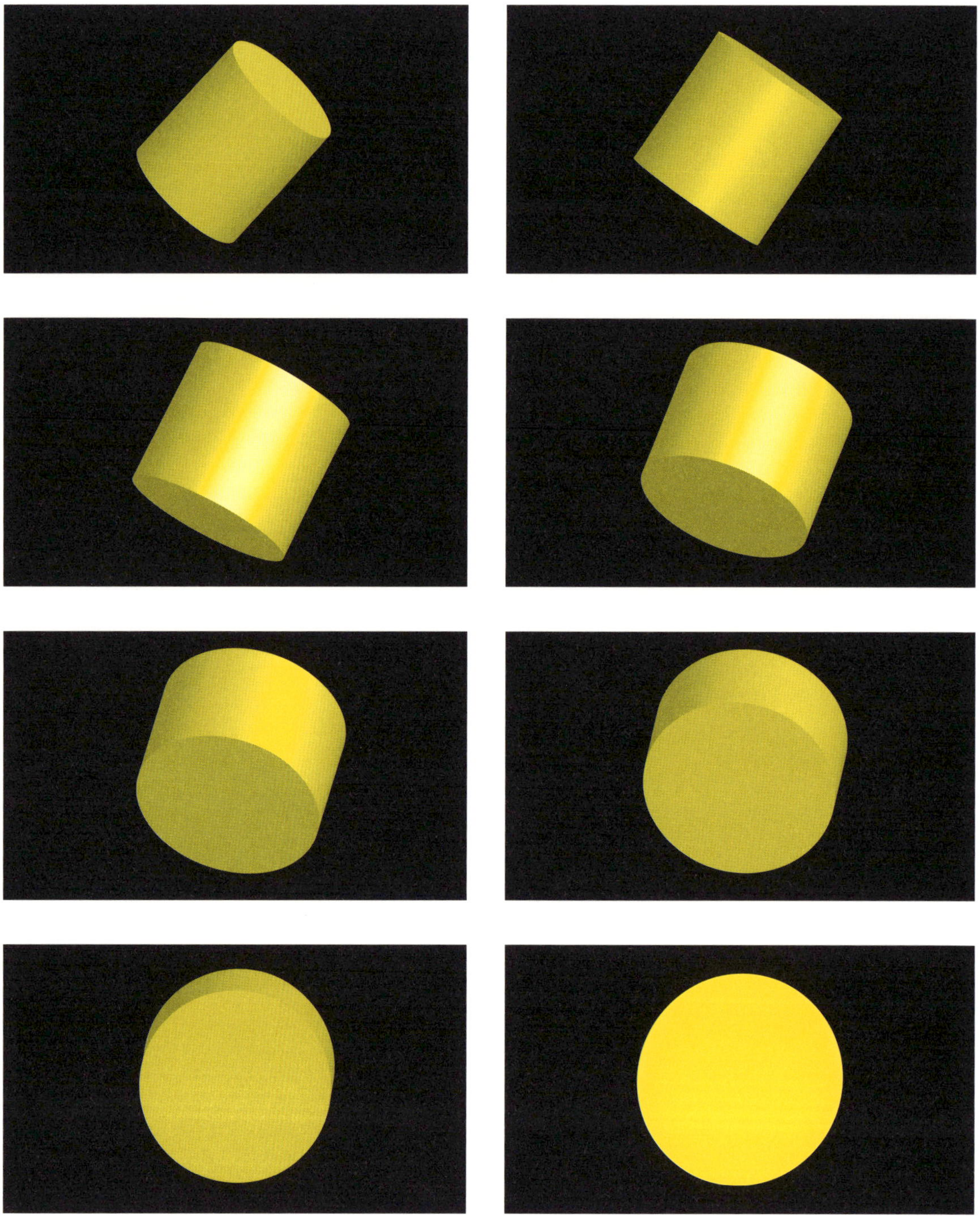

S-C-E-N-E 21

The Oracle performs a magic trick.

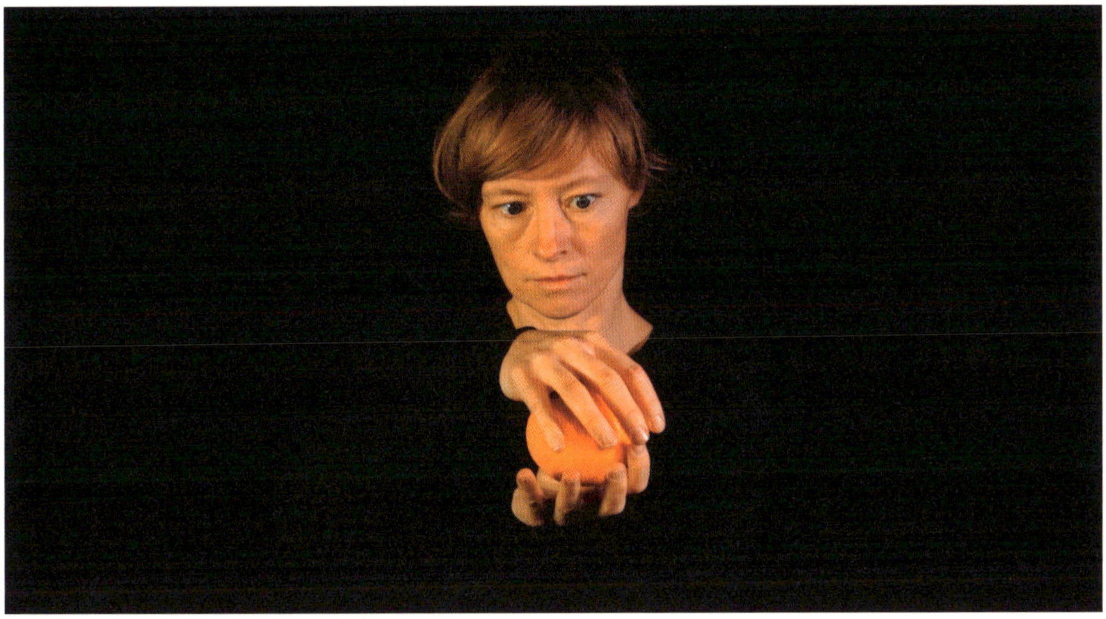

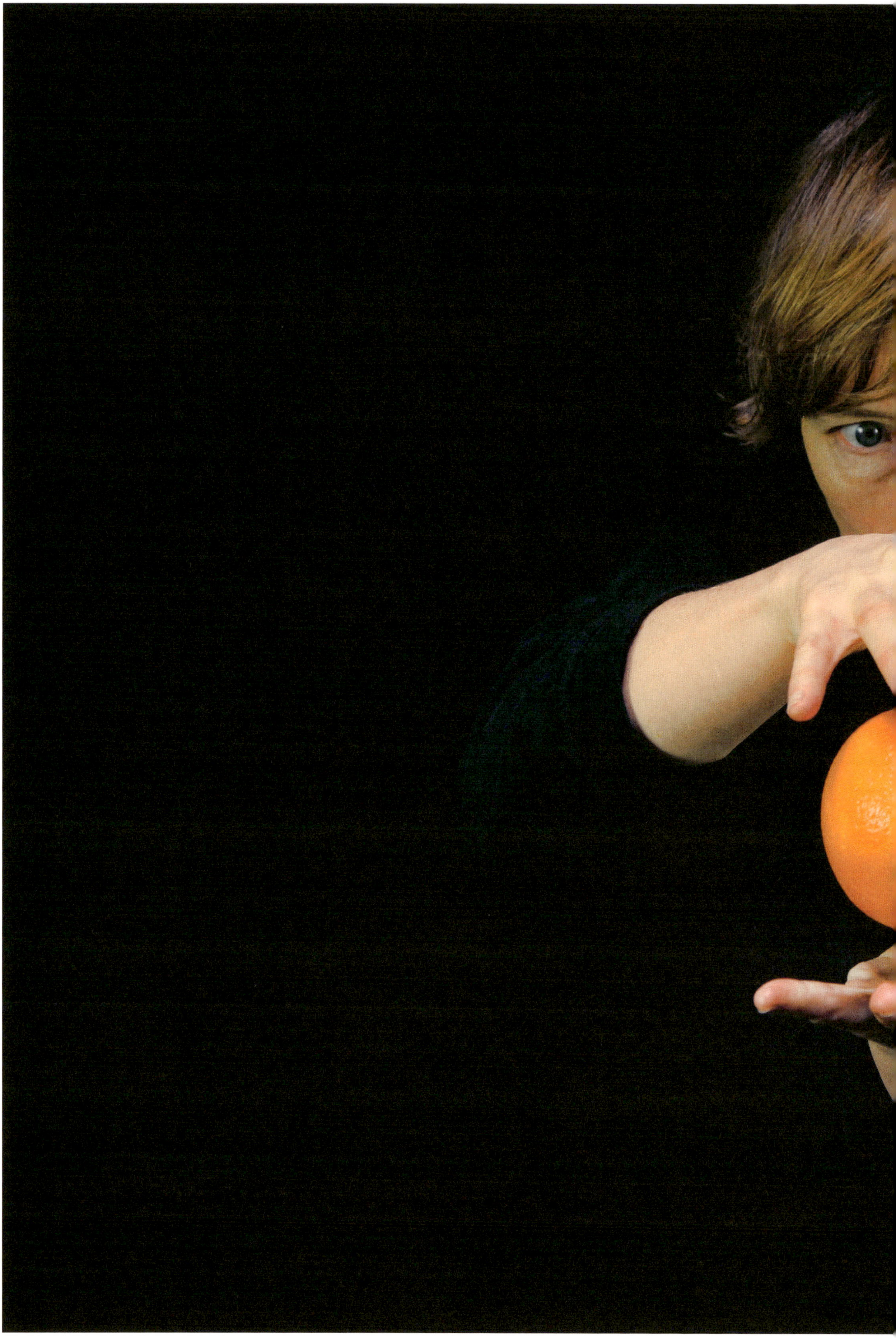

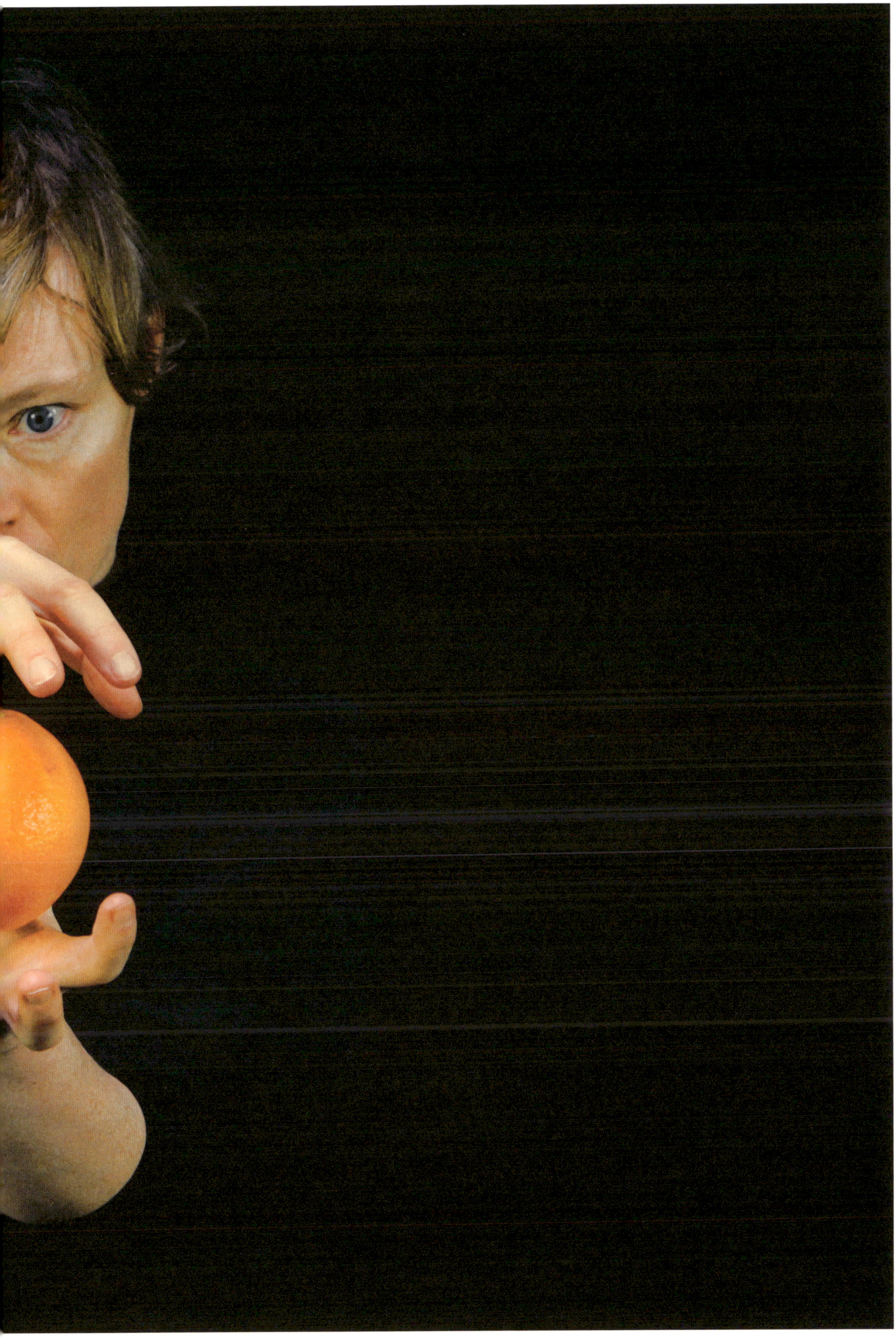

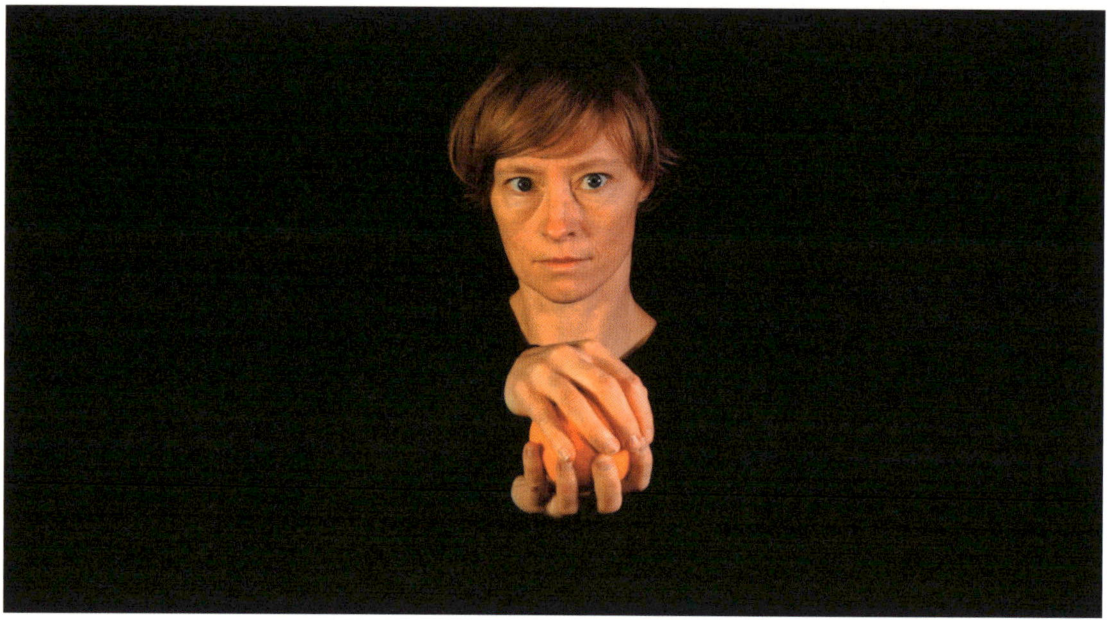

S-C-E-N-E 22

Ohio walks along a river. He sees Magic Child standing on top of a tree trunk, staring at the sky. Ohio stops walking.

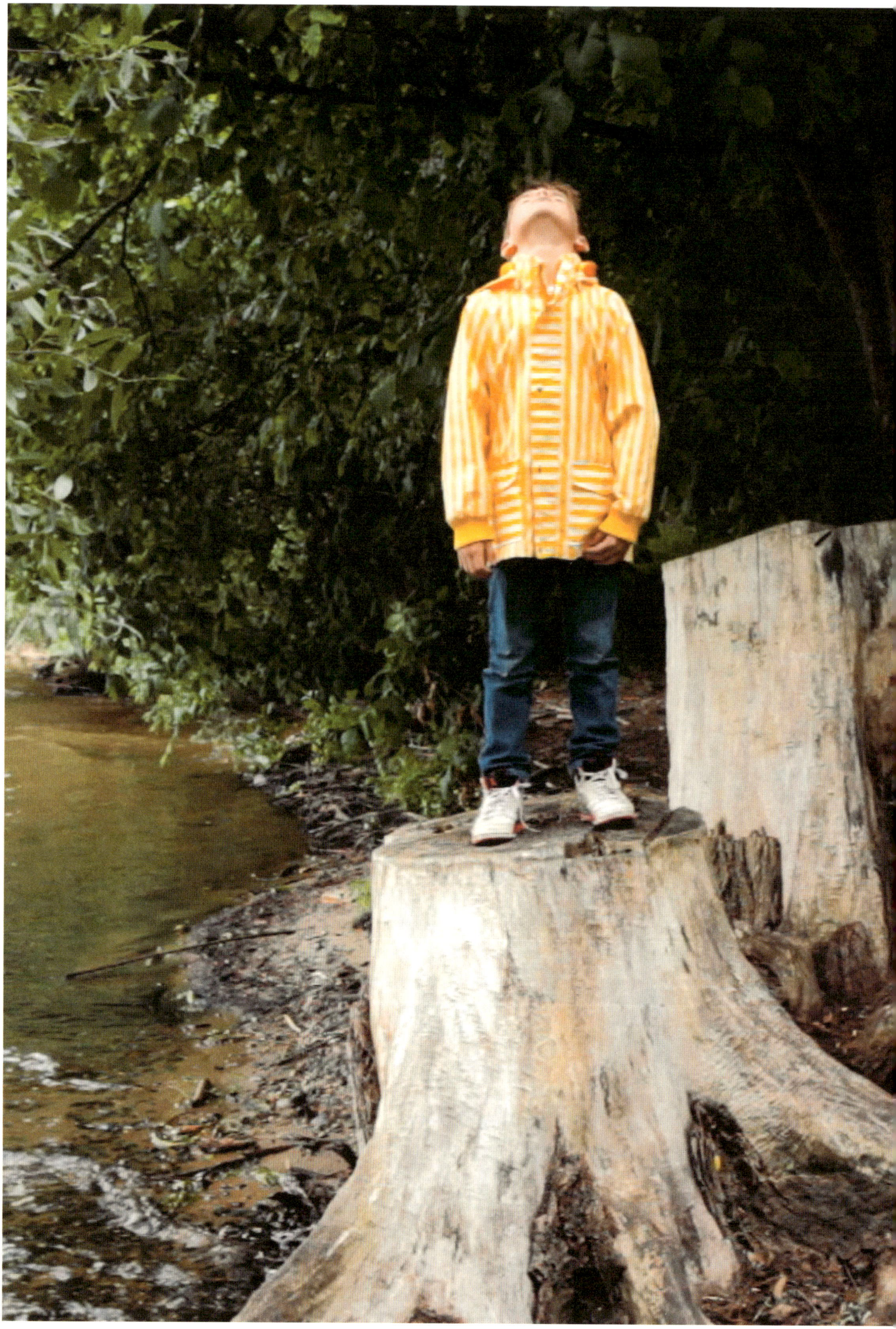

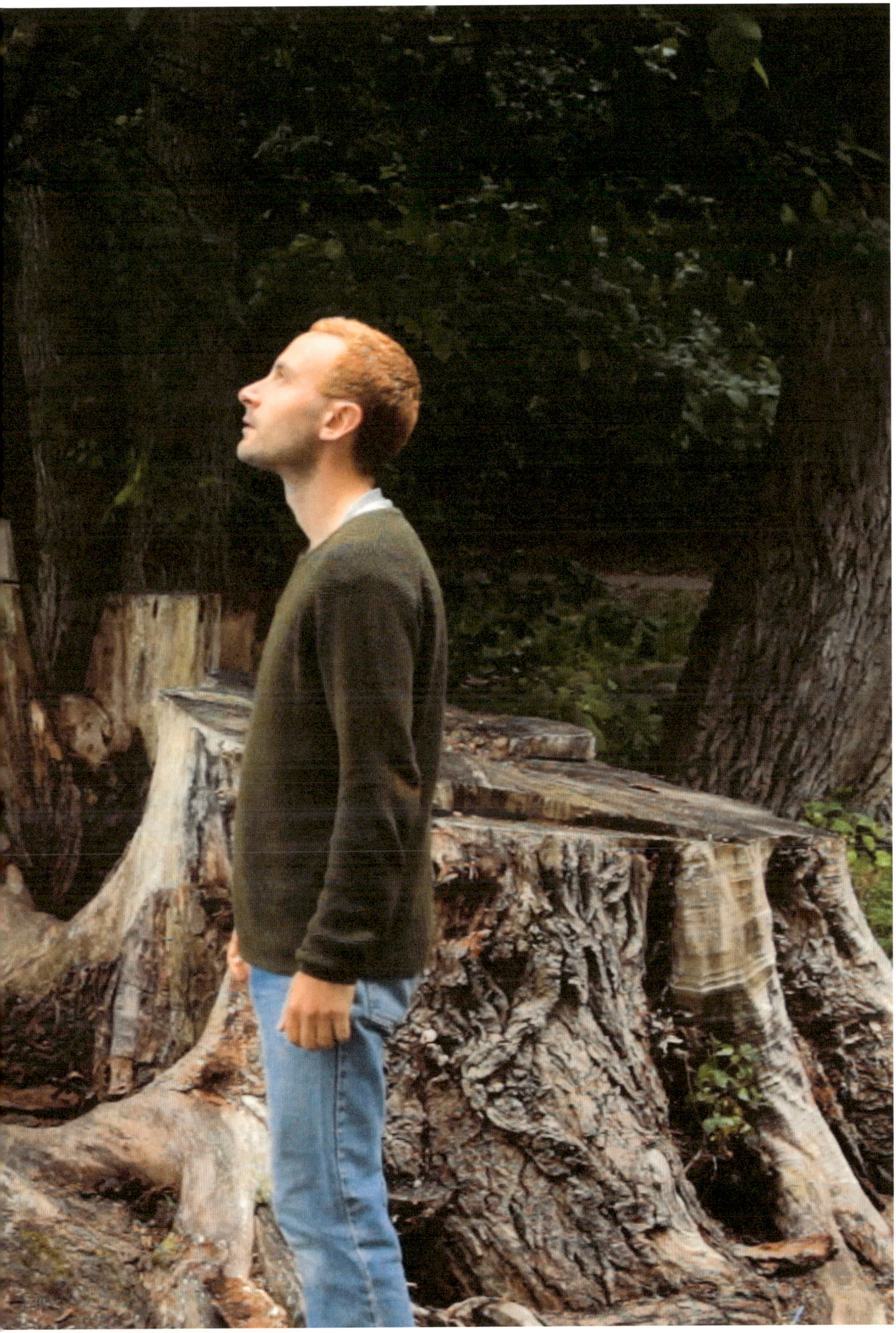

Ohio:

What are you looking at?

Child:

There was an airplane before.

Ohio:

Have you been here all day?

Child:

Yes, since this morning.

Ohio:

But you don't have to stand in the same spot. You can see airplanes from every direction.

Child:

Are you really sure?

Ohio:

Absolutely. Let's see if we can find some over here.

Magic Child climbs off his tree trunk and comes with Ohio. They walk away together.

Child:

What's your name?

Ohio:

My name is Ohio.

Child:

That's a funny name.

S-C-E-N-E 23

Tara sits in the waiting area of what might be a travel agency. Palm trees decorate the room, magazines are spread out on a low table. On the walls there is a picture of the Carribean Sea.

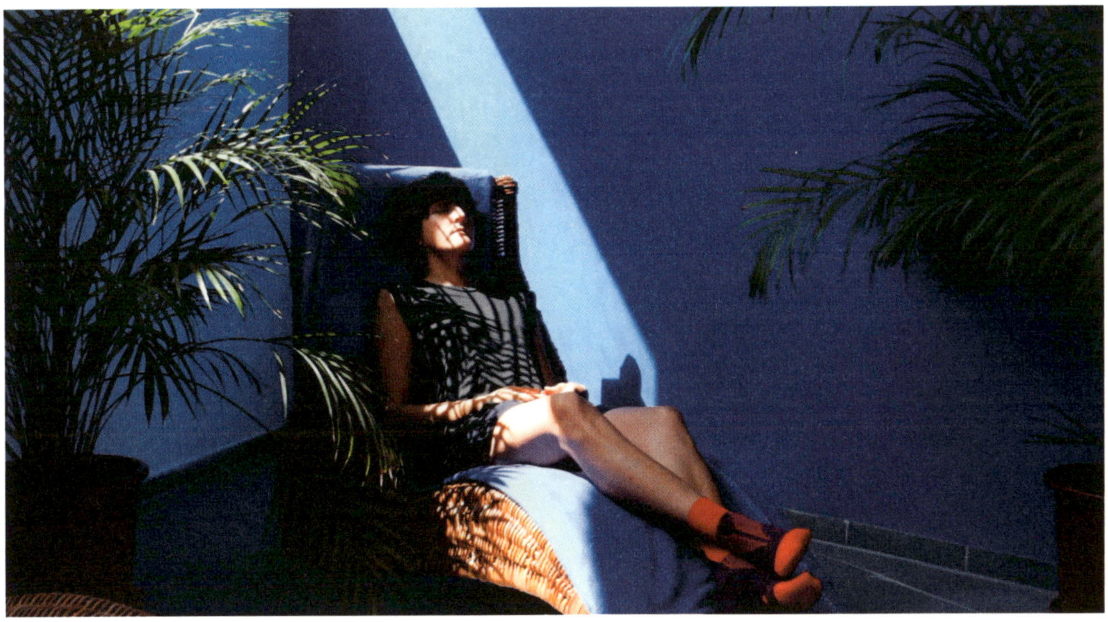

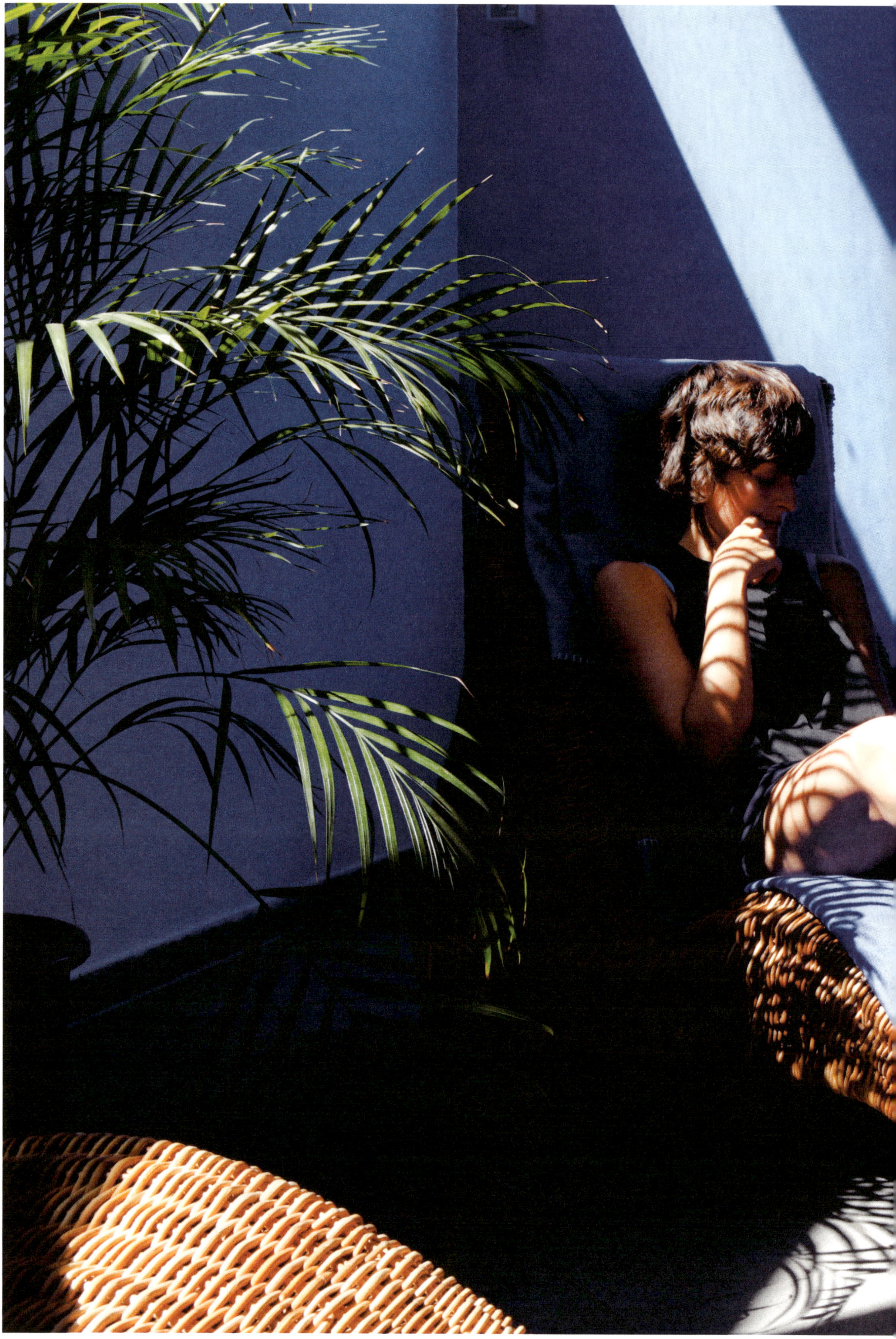

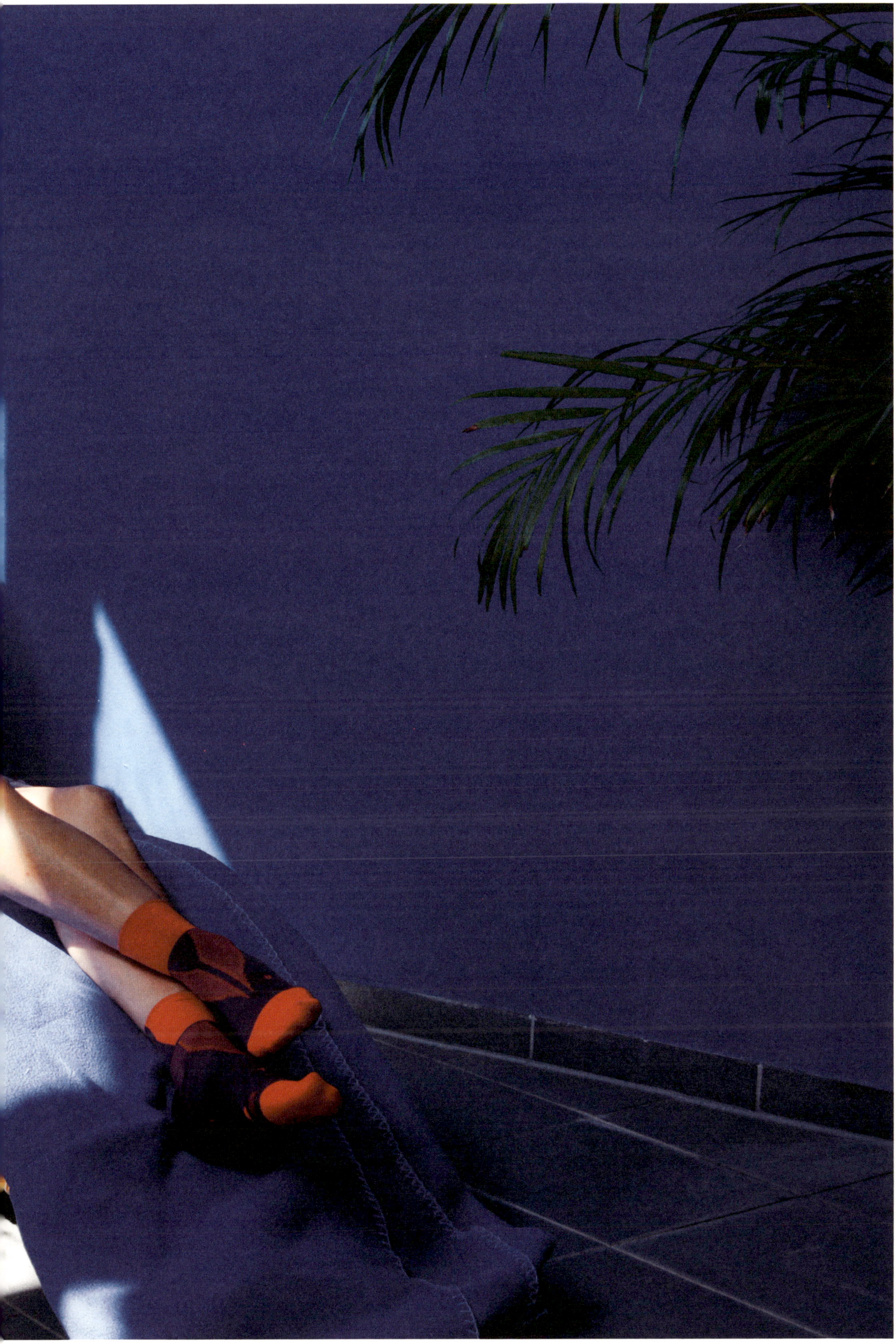

Ohio:

Tara!

Tara:

Ohio!

Ohio runs towards Tara, they fall into each others arms and hug.

Tara:

I'm so glad to see you!

Ohio:

I'm so glad to see you too!

Ohio kisses her softly on the lips. First once, then a second time.

Tara:

I've missed you!

Ohio:

I've missed you too!

Ohio starts kissing her more passionately. Tara tries to avoid his kisses. He ignores her refusal and keeps on kissing her.

Tara:

Ohio, stop it.

Ohio does not stop and tries to kiss her again.

Tara:

Stop it, Ohio. I told you to stop it, Ohio! You are horrible!

Tara takes her stuff and walks away. Ohio sits down and starts counting.

Ohio:

... 75025, 121393, 196418, 317811, 514229, 832040 ...

S-C-E-N-E 24

The Dot is counting down.

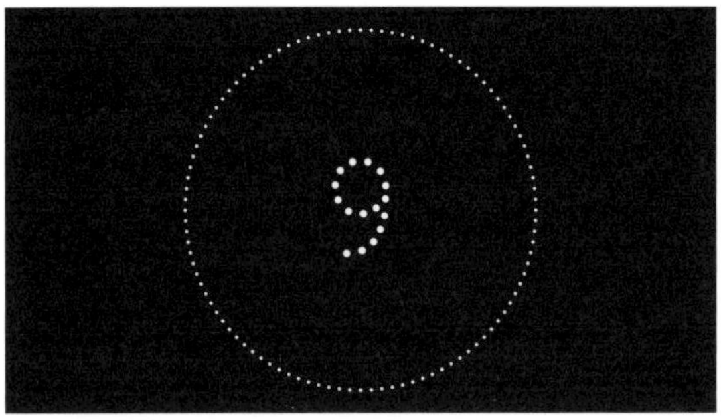

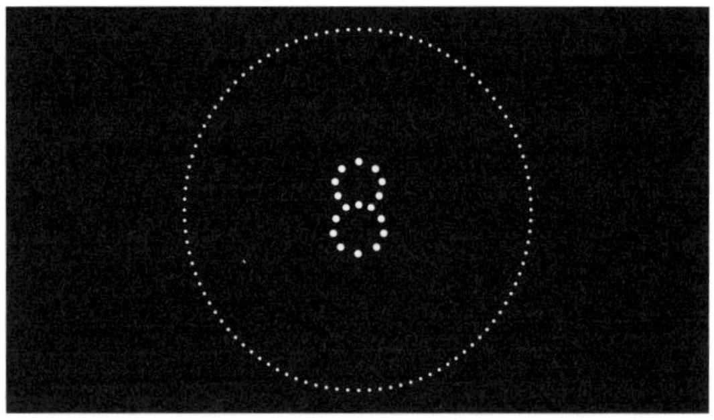

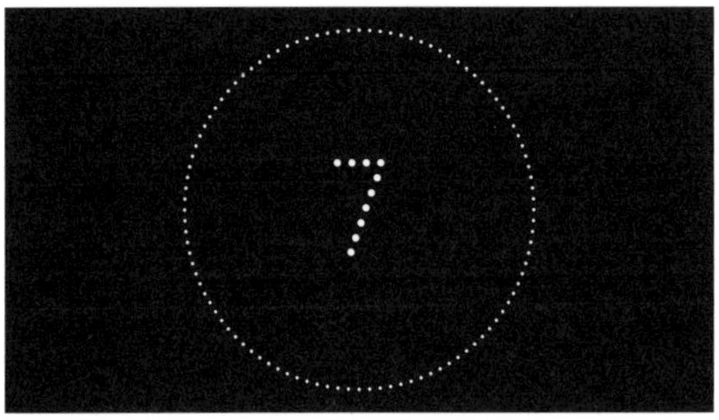

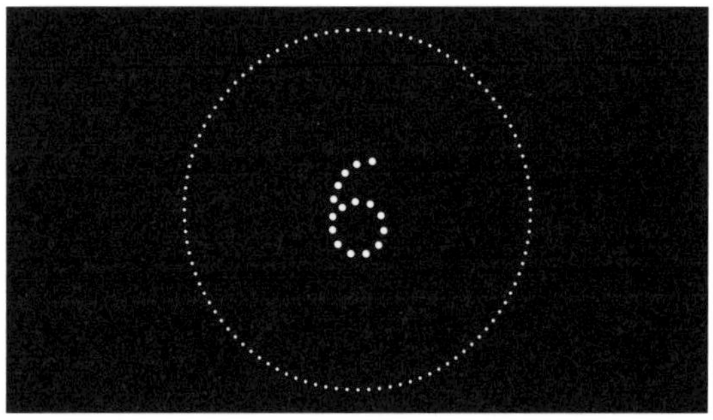

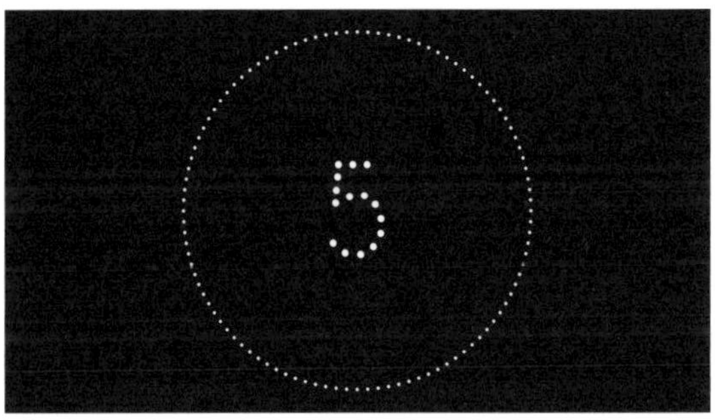

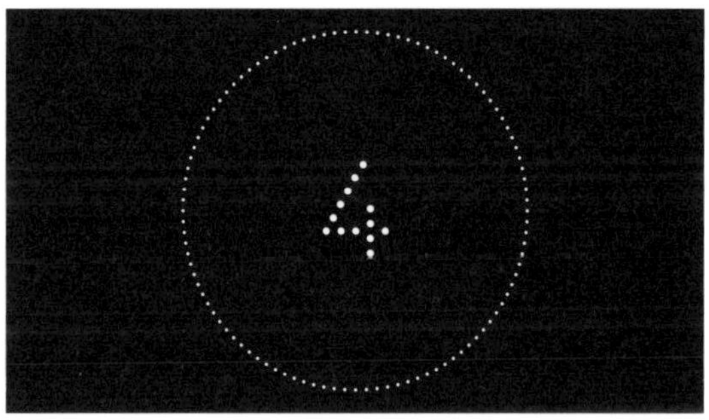

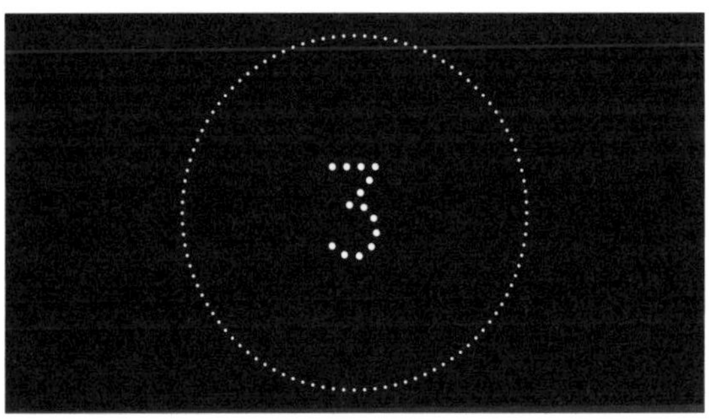

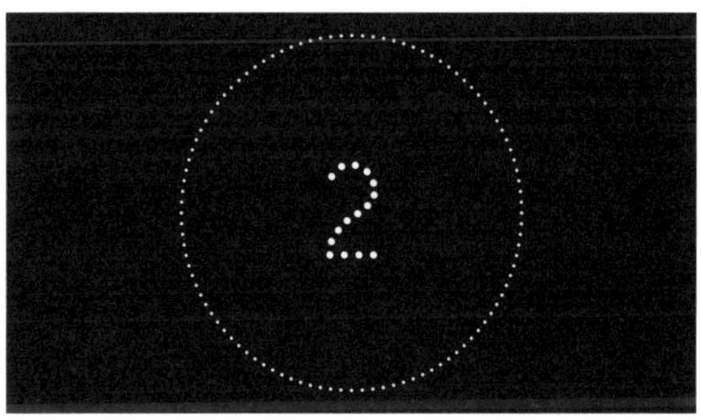

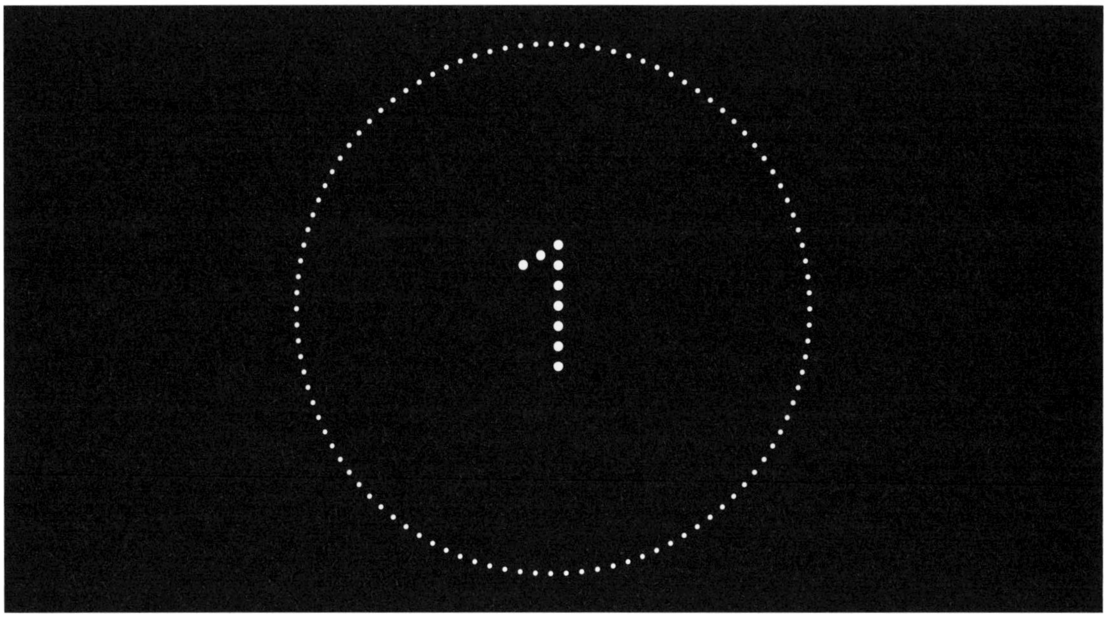
1

S-C-E-N-E 25

The Oracle throws a die.

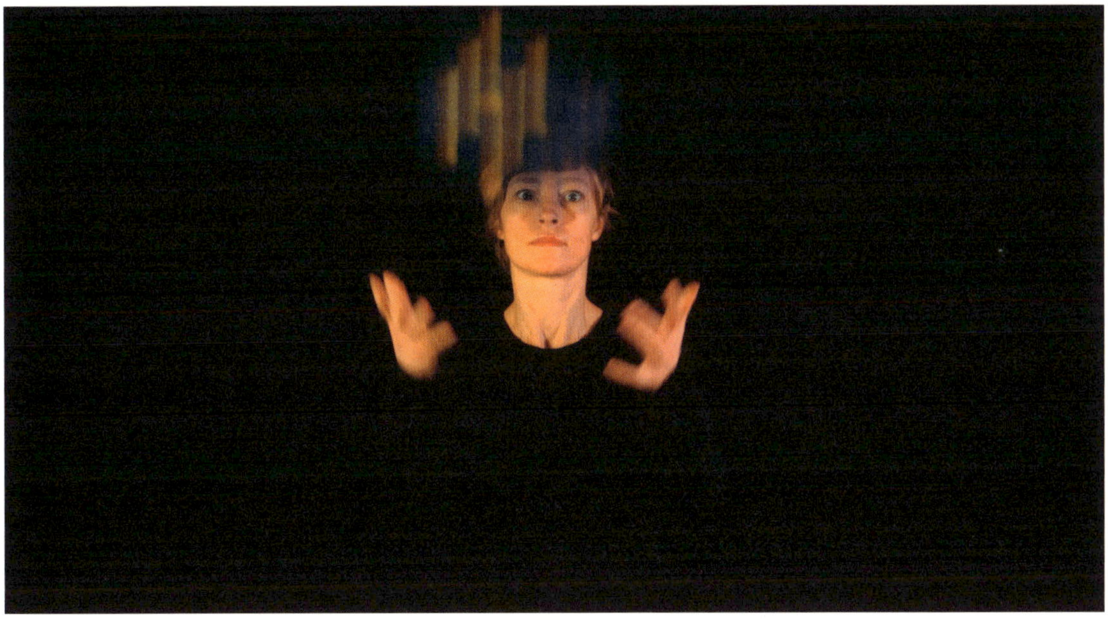

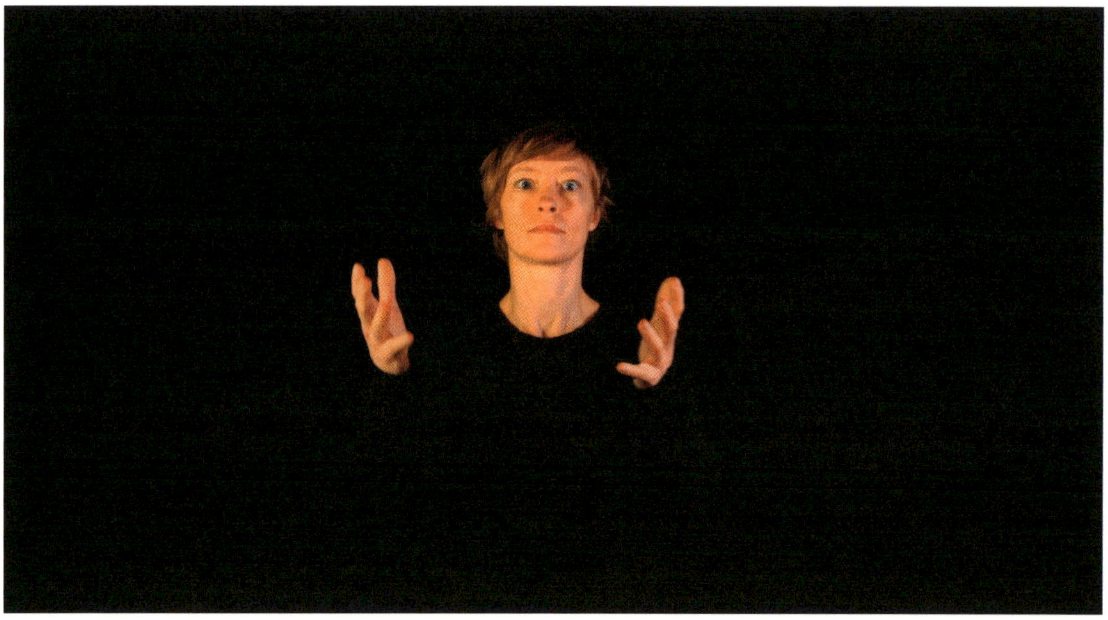

S-C-E-N-E 26

Tara and Ohio are in the “Room of Time”. Light projections form the outlines of a game field. A rumbling noise can be heard. The noise is coming closer. A gigantic ball rolls towards Tara and Ohio threatening to kill them.

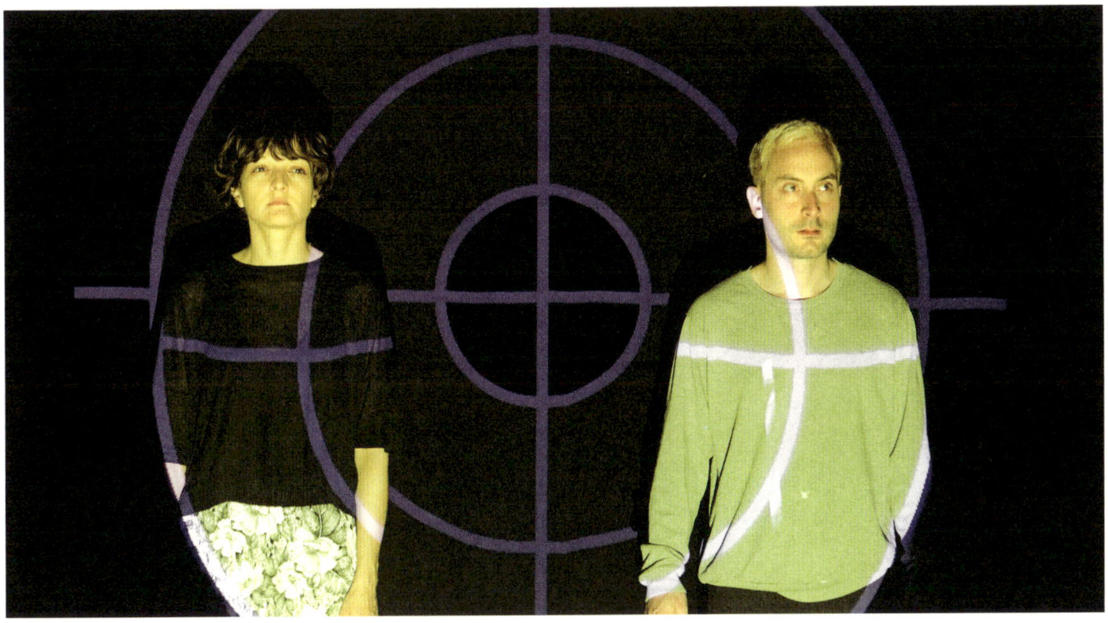

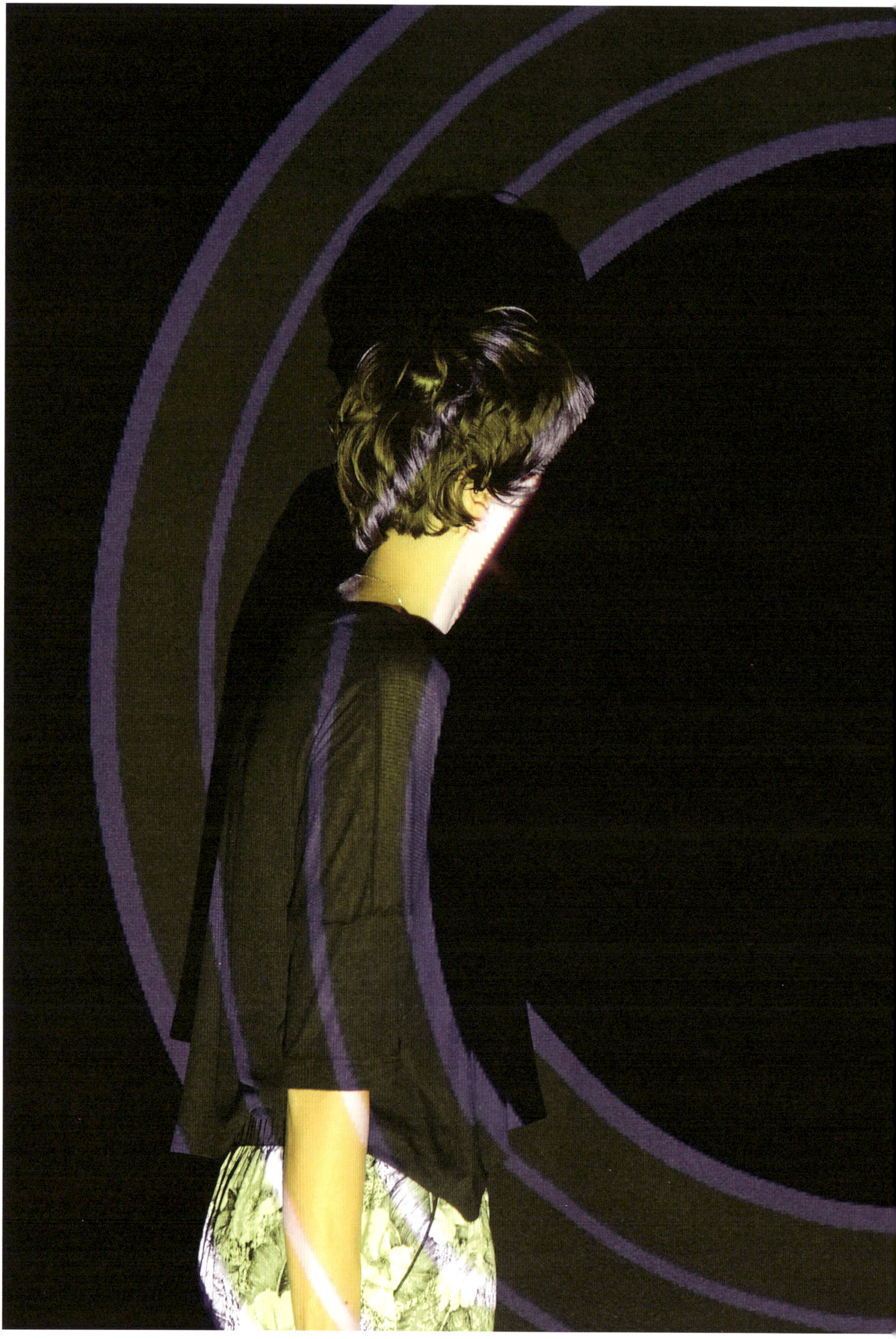

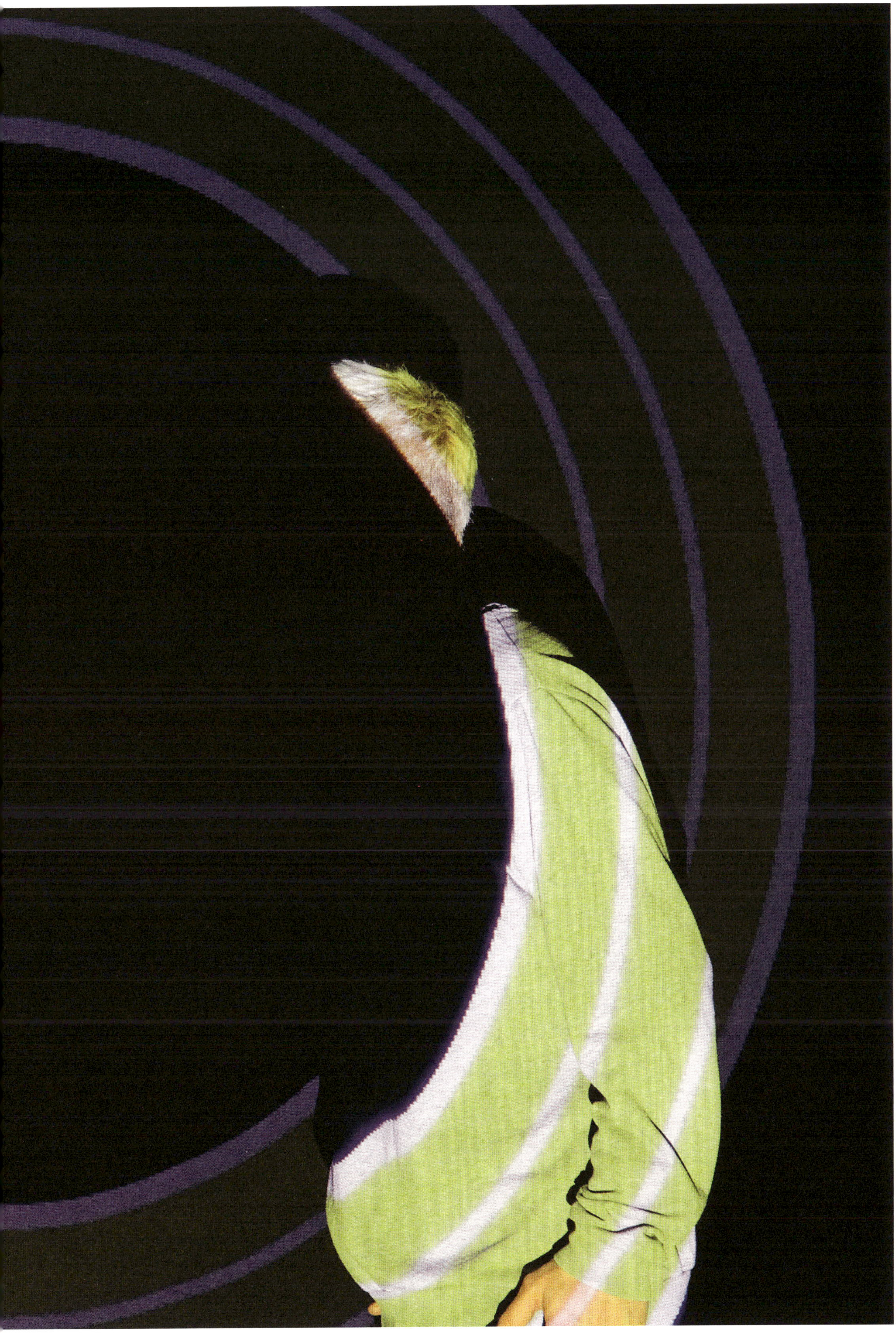

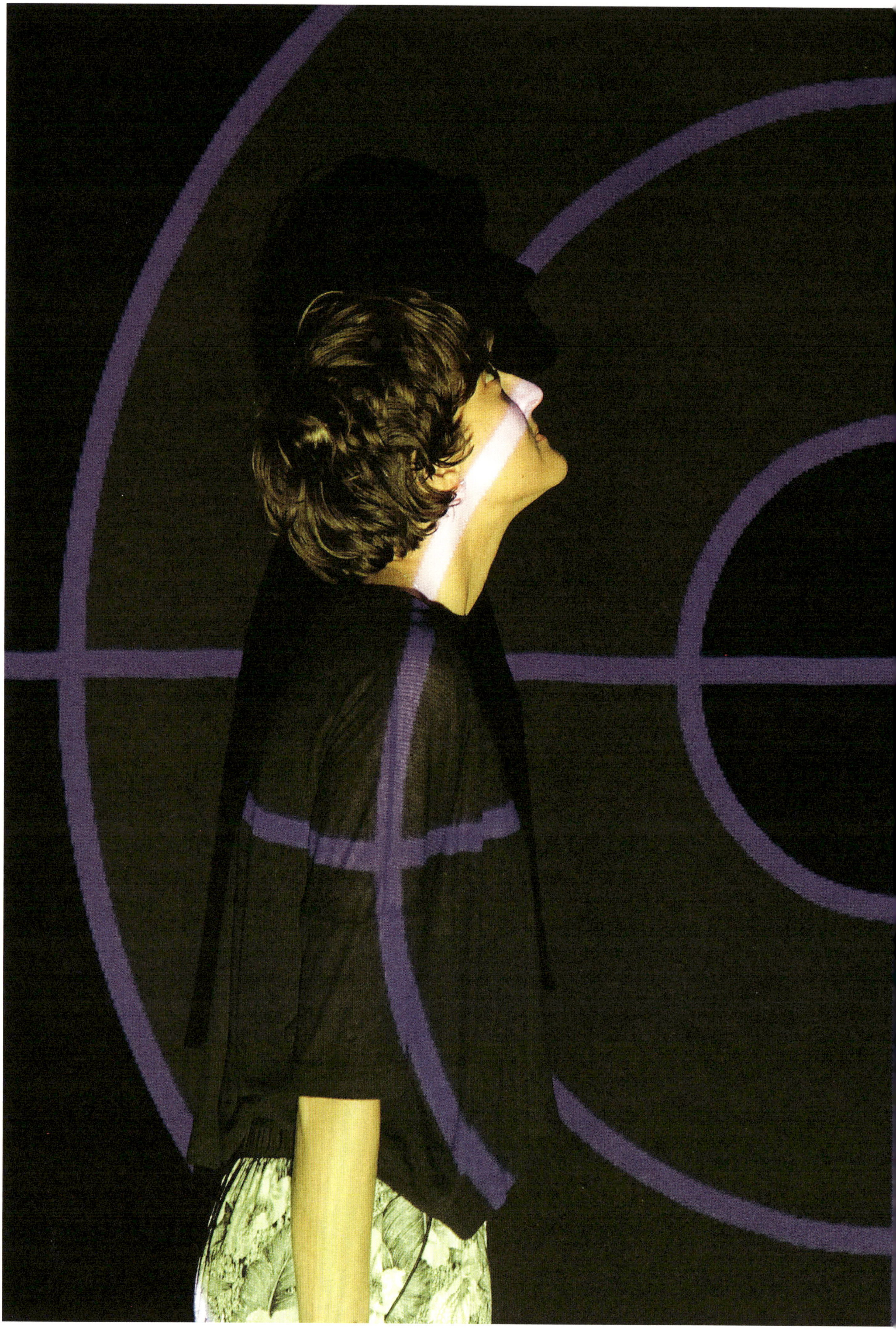

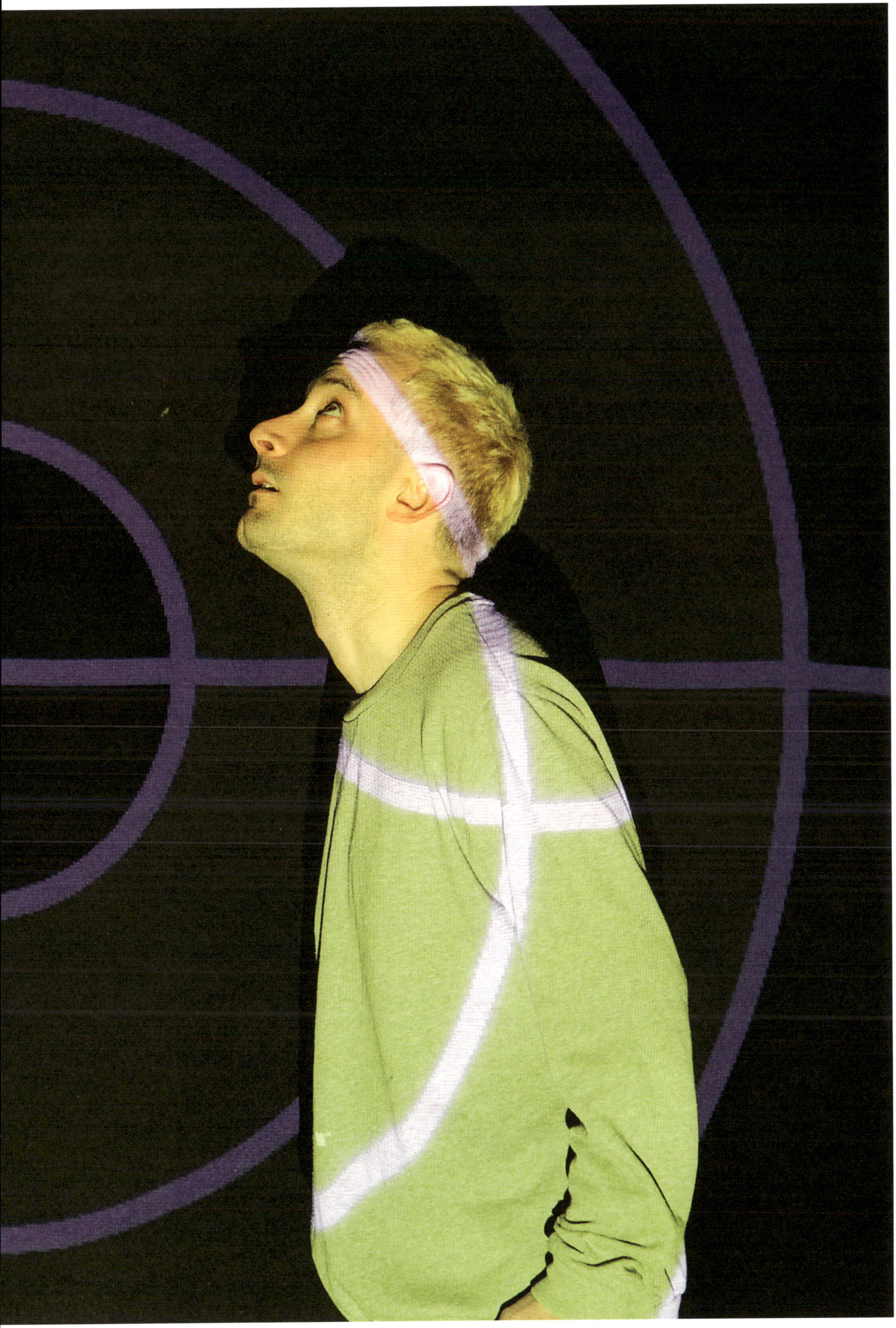

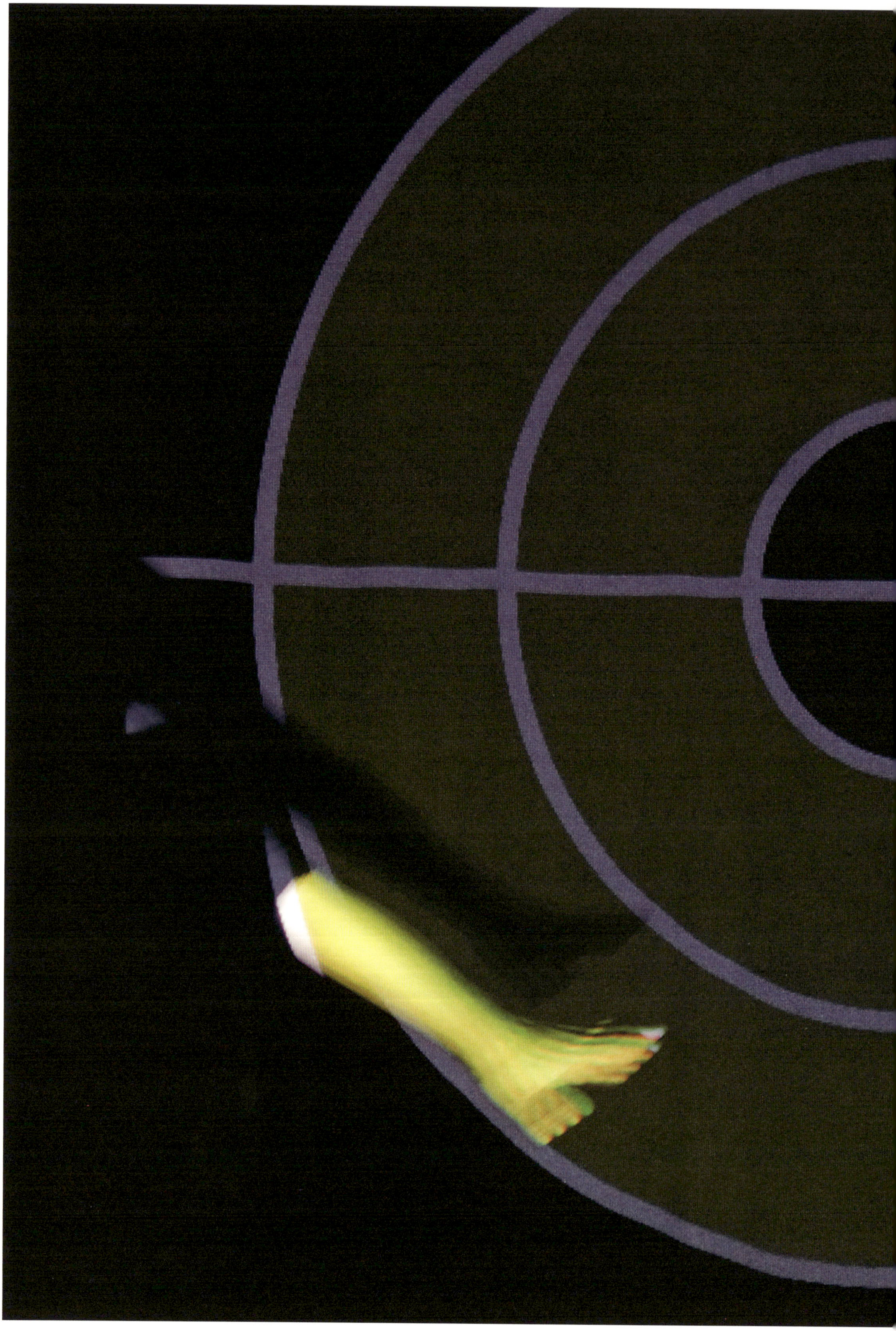

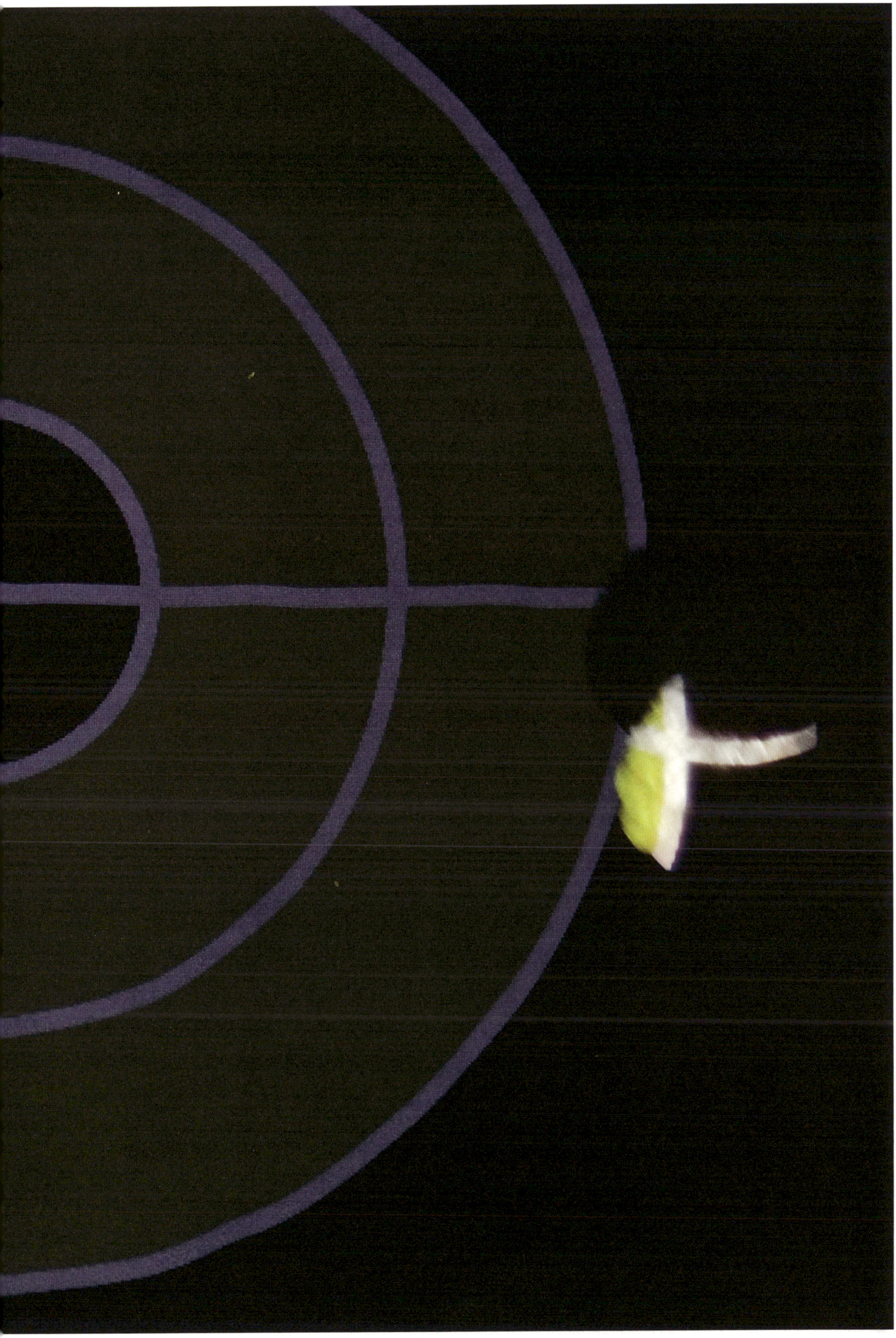

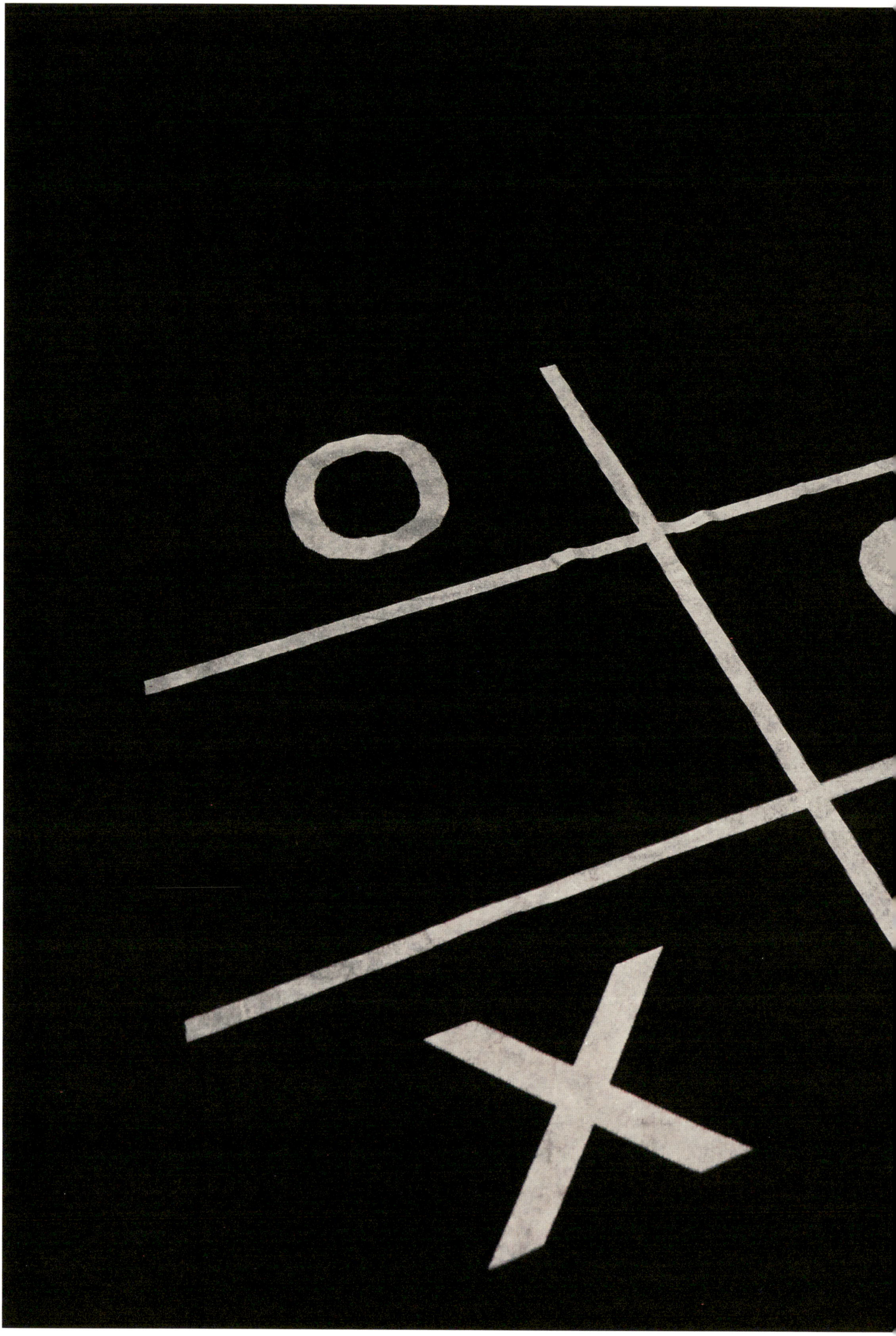

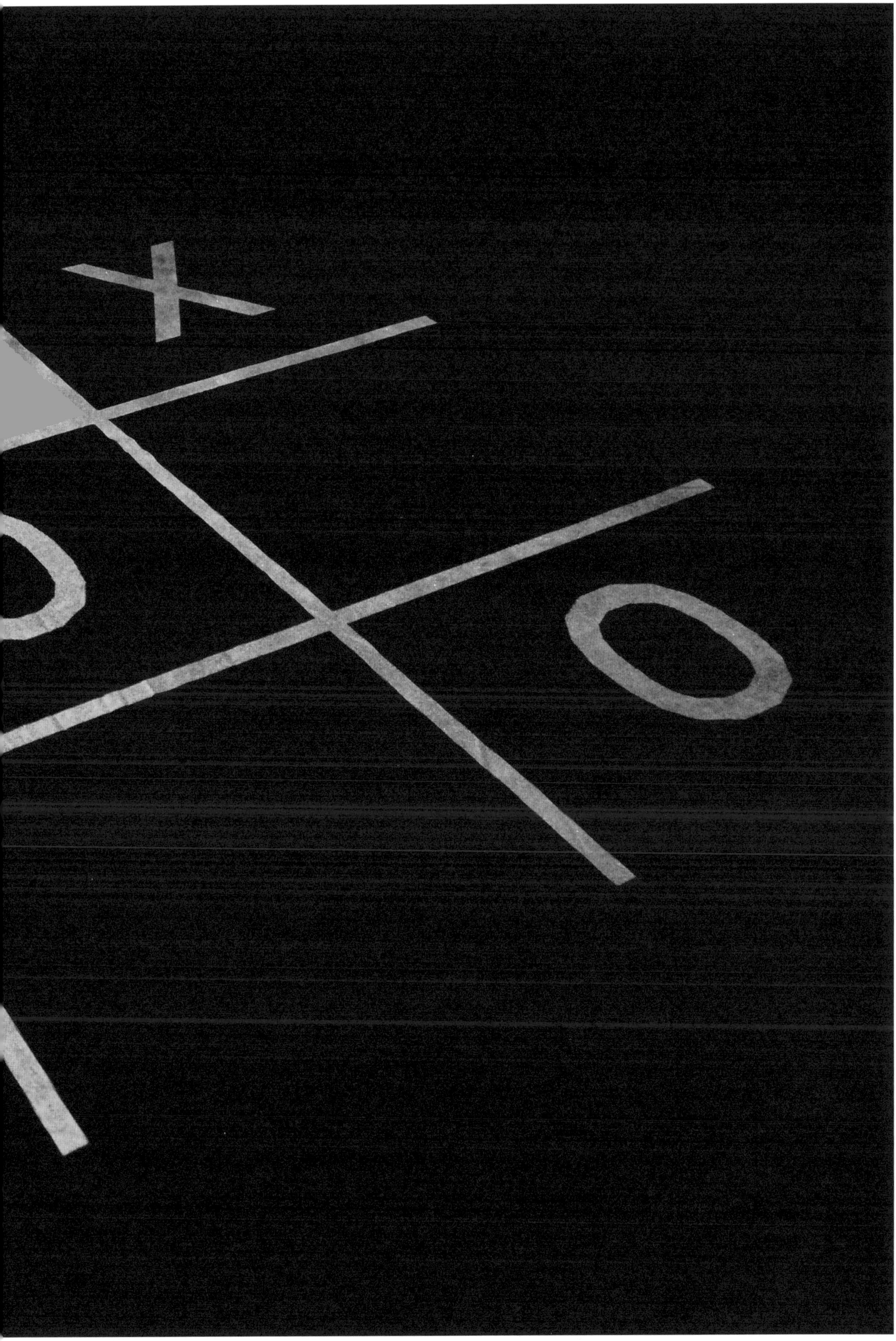

Ohio:

Tara! Tara!

Tara:

Ohio!

The gigantic ball descends rapidly. Only at the very last moment can Tara jump to the side and rescue herself.

Ohio:

Oh, Tara! That was tight! It almost hit you!

Tara:

I'm so afraid! I can hardly move anymore. Ohio, I can't do this any longer!

Ohio:

Tara, remember! The E-X-I-T, the X, the WAY OUT. We can't give up now!

A second game projection materializes in the room. A large Tic-Tac-Toe field is projected on the ground. The Voice appears out of nowhere.

Voice:

Good evening, Tara. Good evening Ohio! I am here to play the G-A-M-E with you!

Tara:

Good evening.

Ohio:

Good evening.

Voice:

Do you know the rules of the G-A-M-E?

Tara:

Yes.

Ohio:

Yes.

Voice:

Excellent. So let's start playing. I am first: "O".

A circle appears on the upper left part of the game field.

Tara:

"X".

A cross appears in the upper right part of the game field.

Voice:

"O".

A second circle appears in the center of the game field.

Ohio:

"X".

A second cross appears in the lower left square of the game field.

Voice:

"O".

A third circle appears in the lower right square and completes a diagonal line of three circles.

Voice:

I WIN! YOU LOSE! HA-HA-HA-HA-HA-HA-HA-HA-HA-HA-HA-HA-HA-HA-HA!

A flash of light. The image dissolves. Cut to the next scene.

S-C-E-N-E 27

Tara and Ohio visit an aquarium. They are standing in front of a fish tank observing fish swarms passing by. The Dot enters as a graphic animation and starts talking to them.

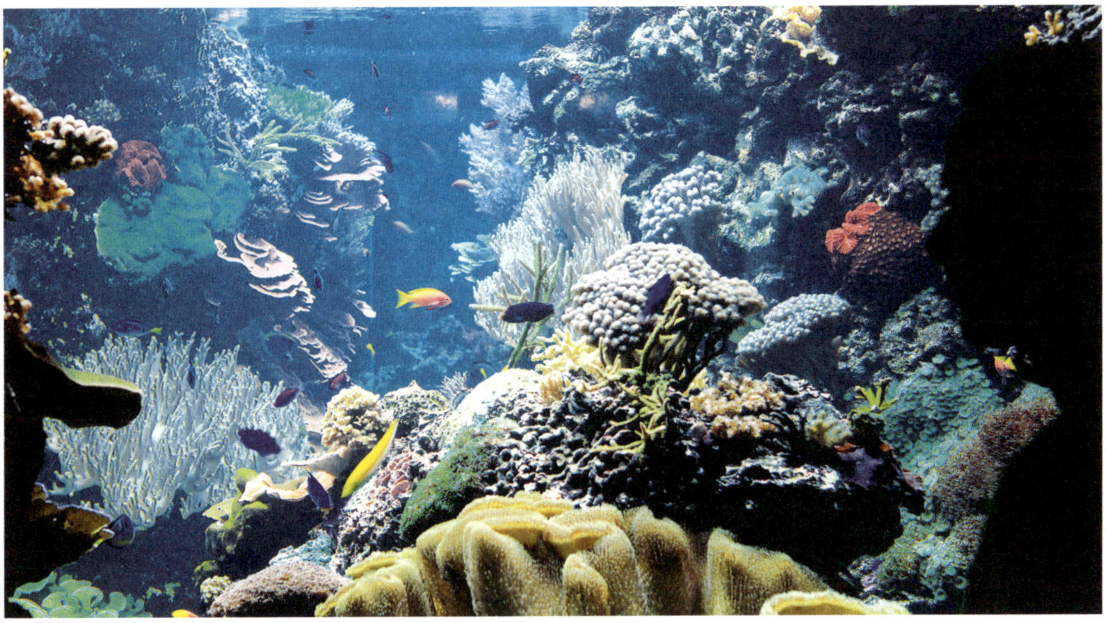

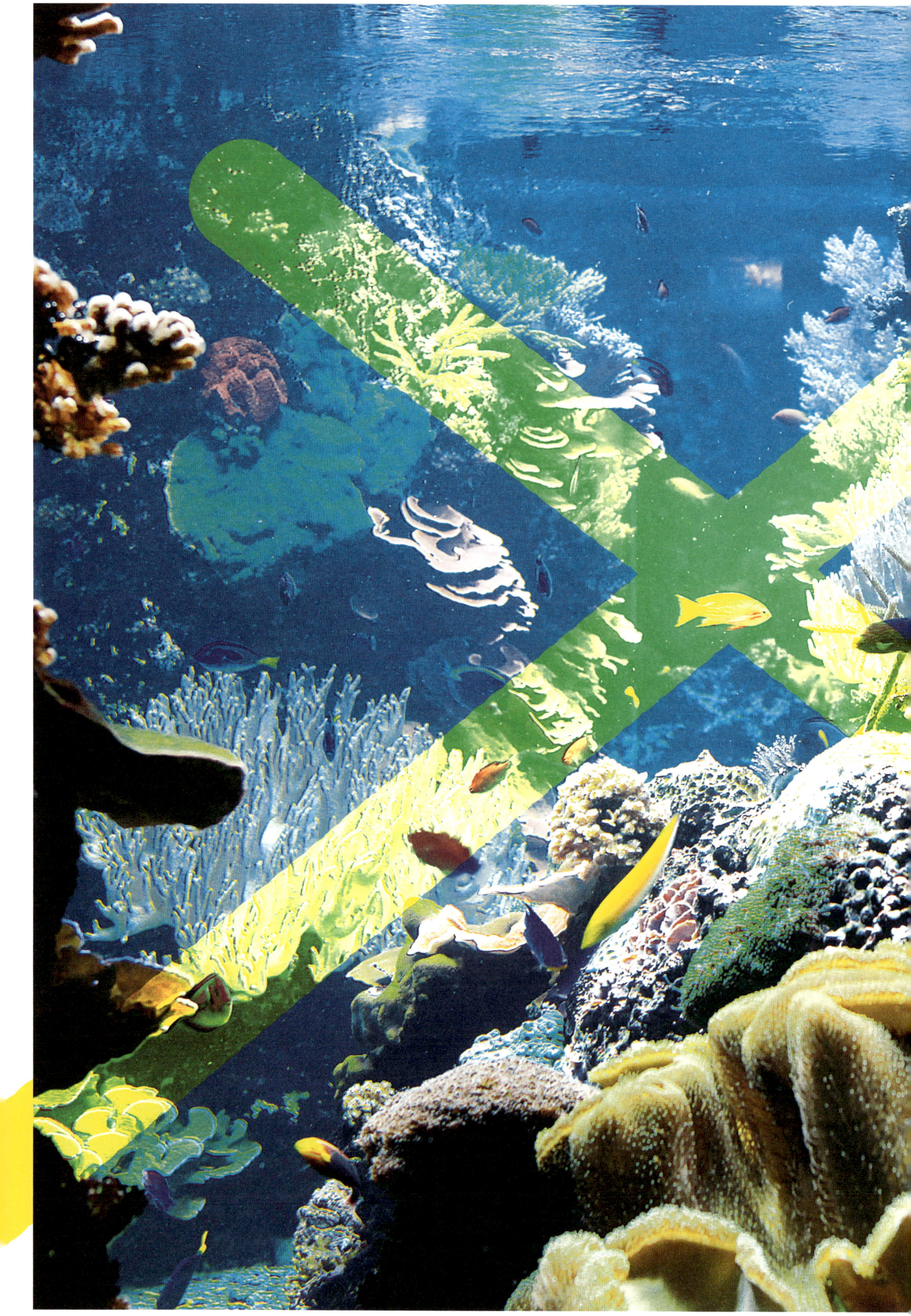

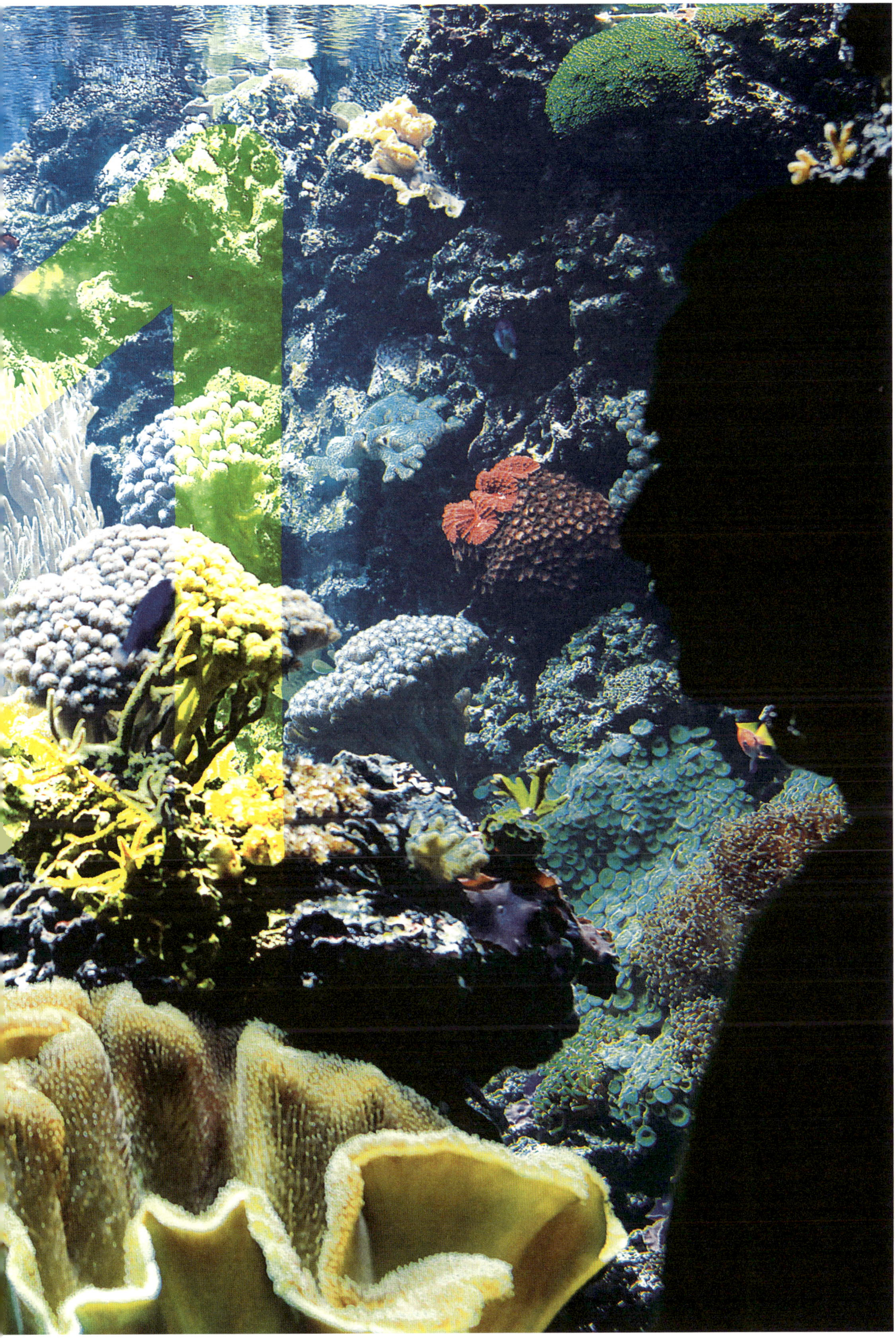

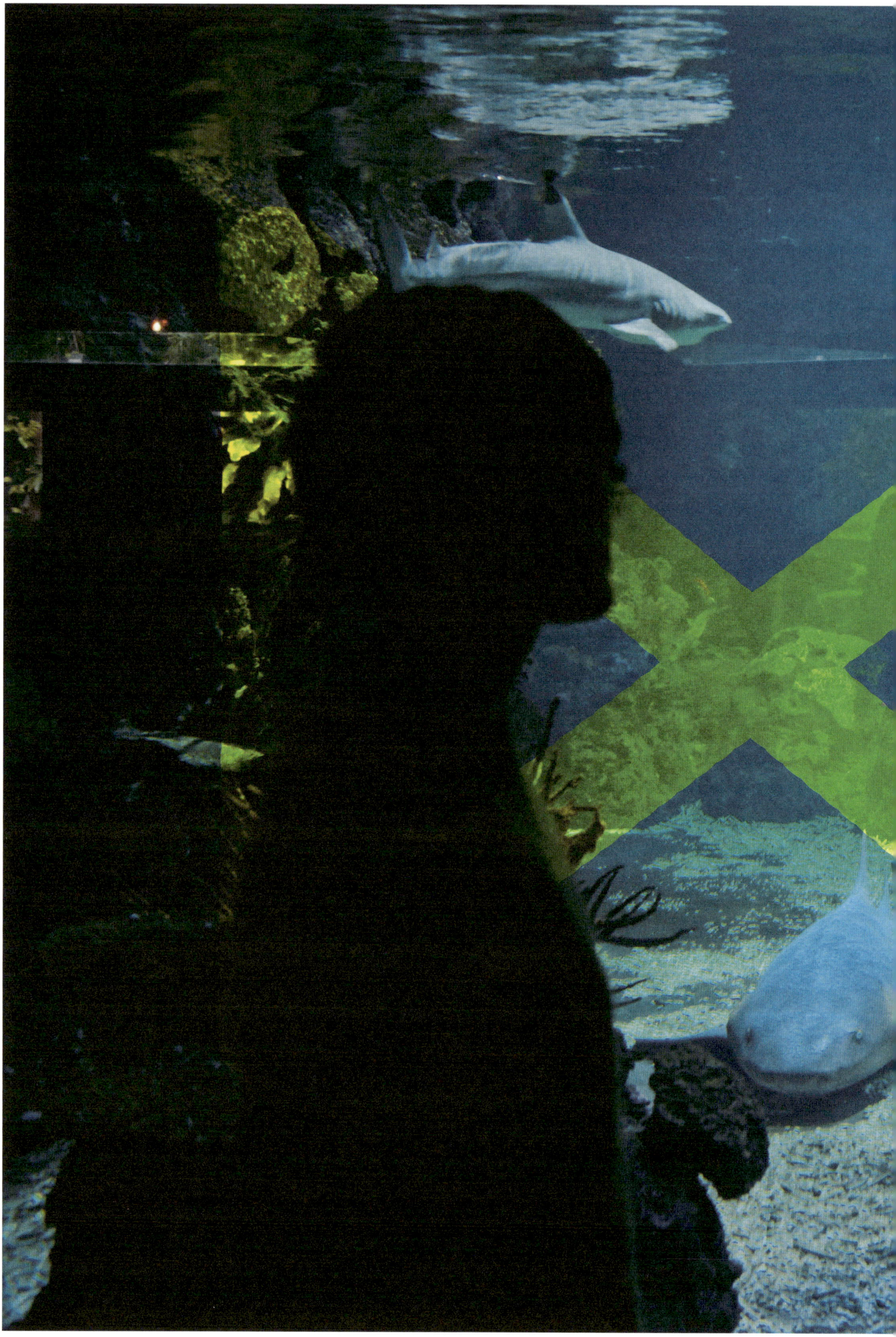

Dot:

Tara, Ohio! Come with me. Look! Look at this! Do you see this here?

Tara:

Yes, I can see it. It’s a goldfish.

Dot:

Now, come with me again.

The dot guides them to a different fish tank. In it, a big shark swims.

Dot:

Do you see this here?

Ohio:

Yes, I can see it. It’s a shark.

Dot:

A shark. In this movie? Ridiculous. Don’t you see that everything in here is illusion? There will never be a WAY OUT!

S-C-E-N-E 29

Tara und Ohio are in a public swimming pool. A sound signal is indicating the start of artifical waves. The waves slowly get bigger until they reach a certain height. They then repeat rhythmically. Tara and Ohio enter the water and start swimming. A conversation starts.

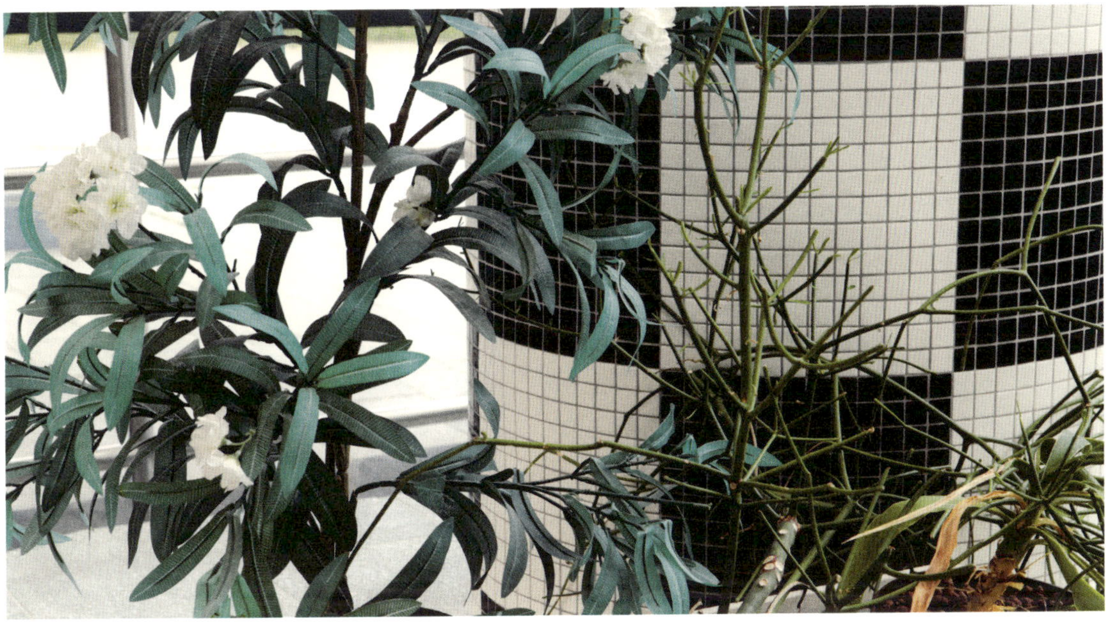

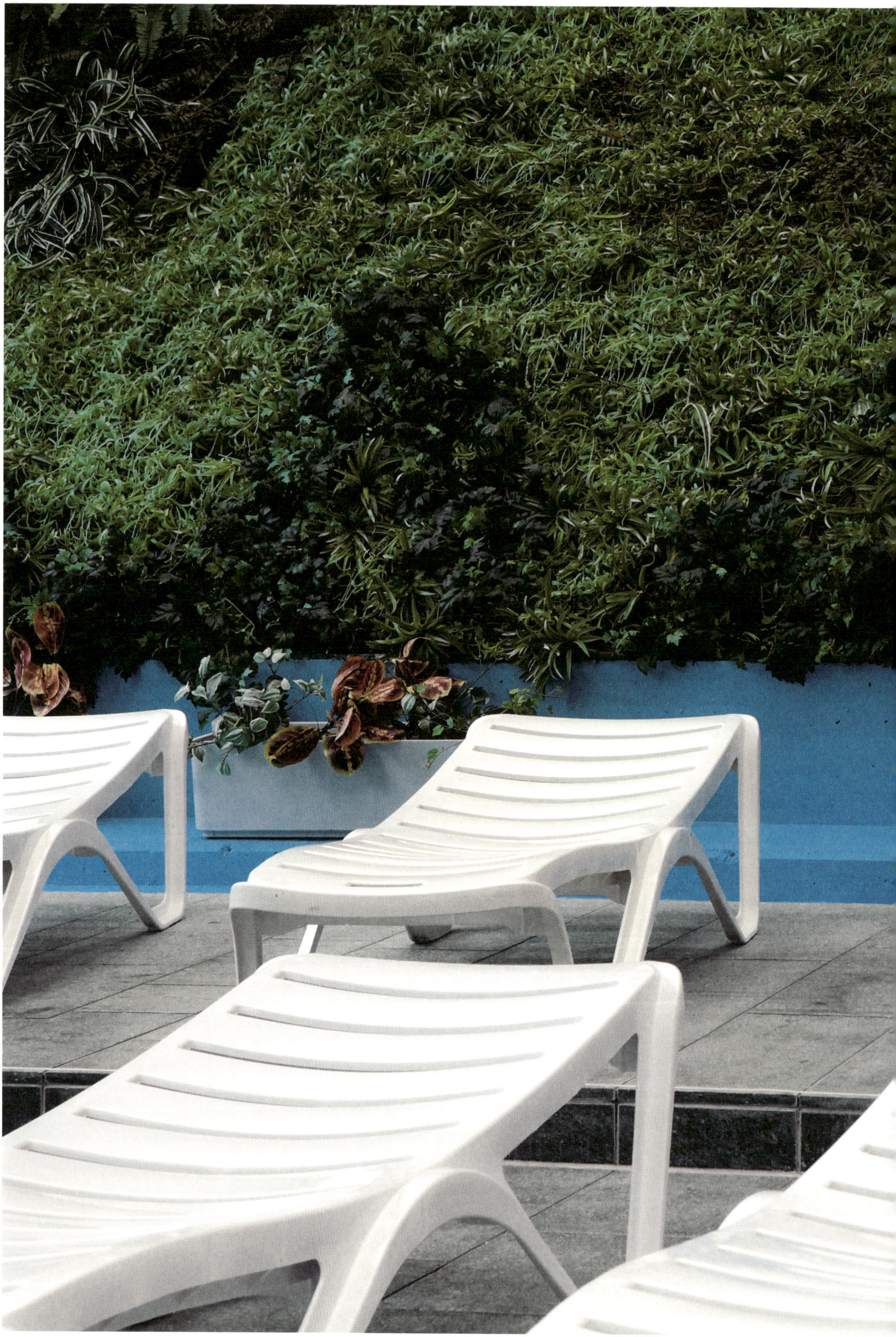

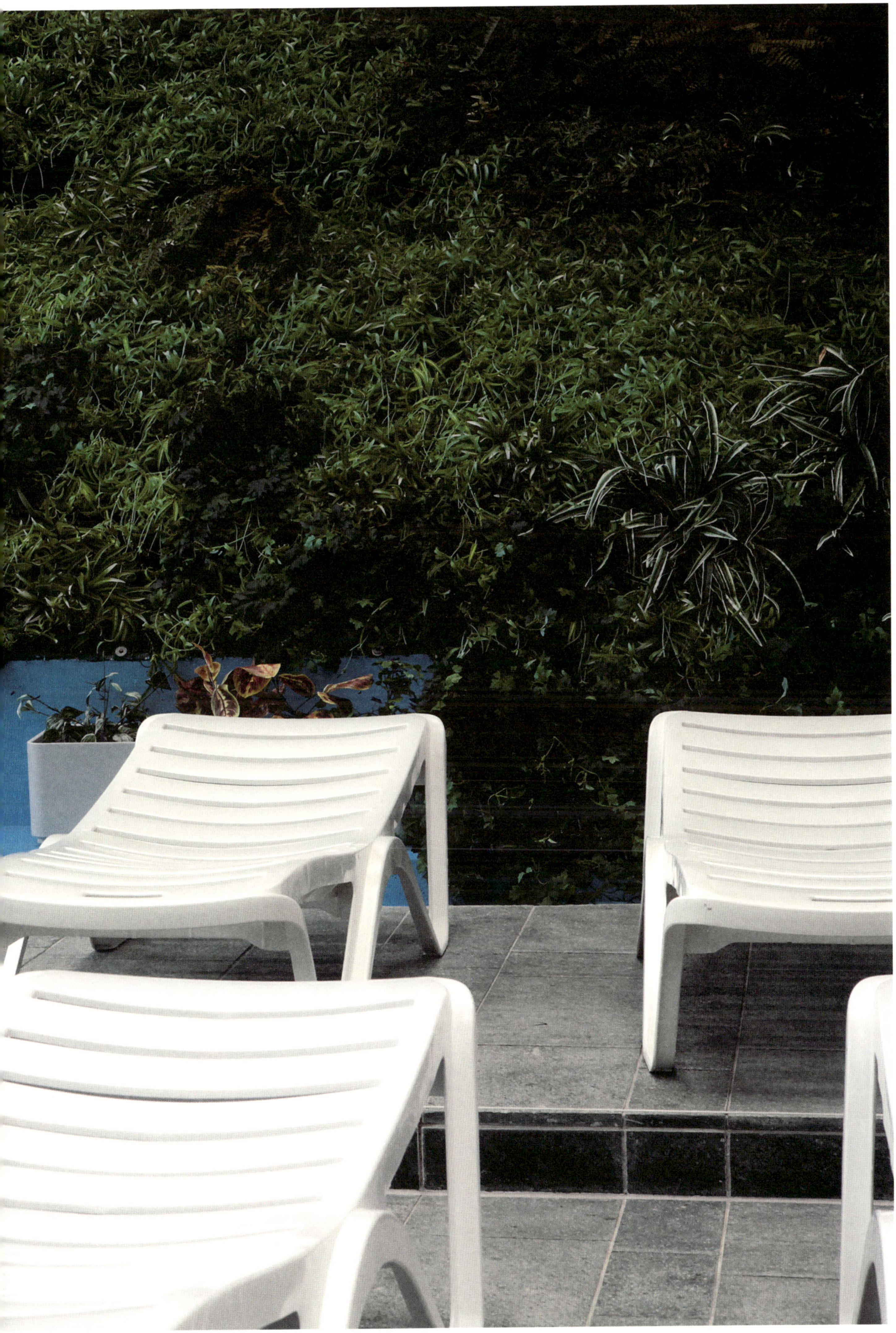

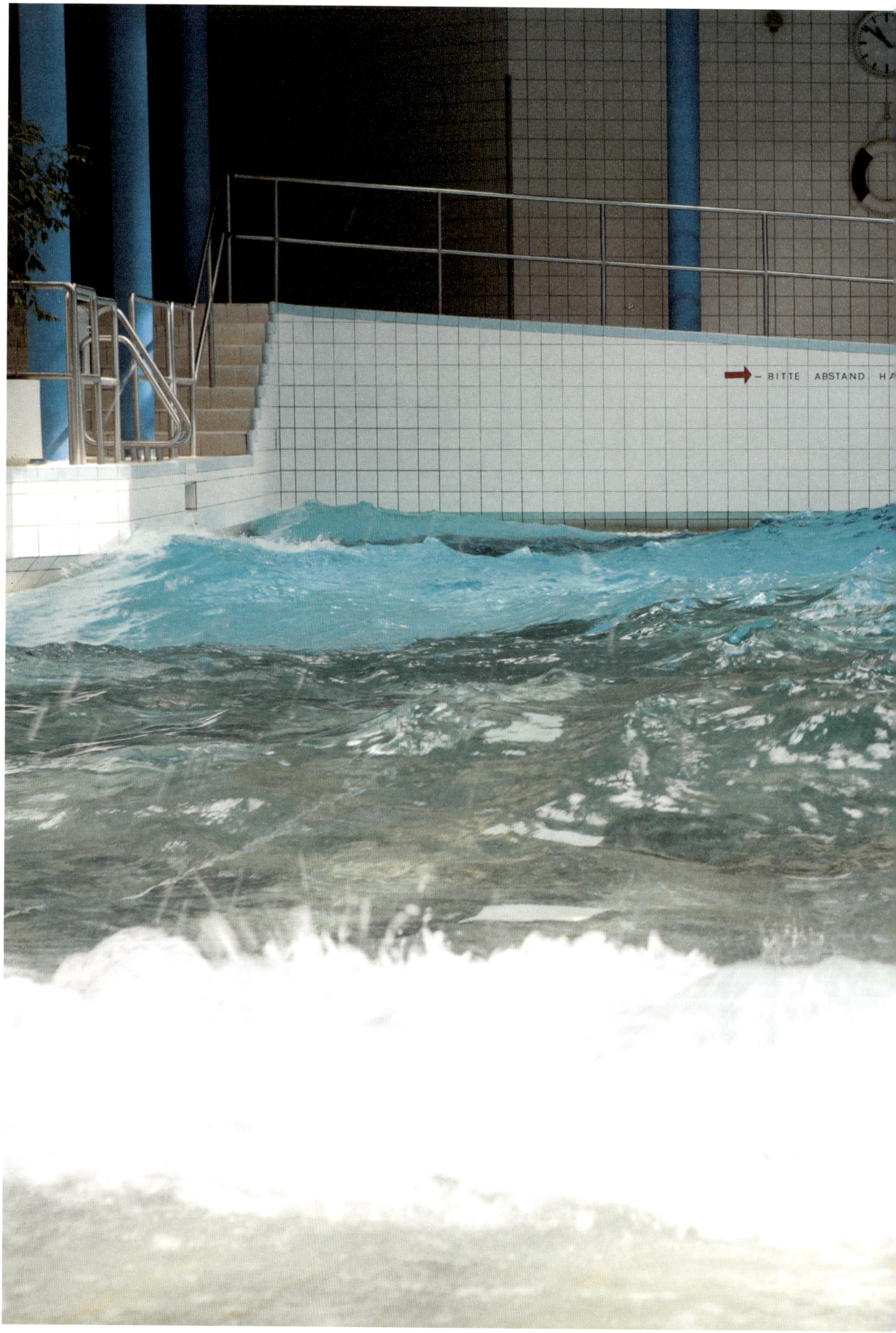
– BITTE ABSTAND

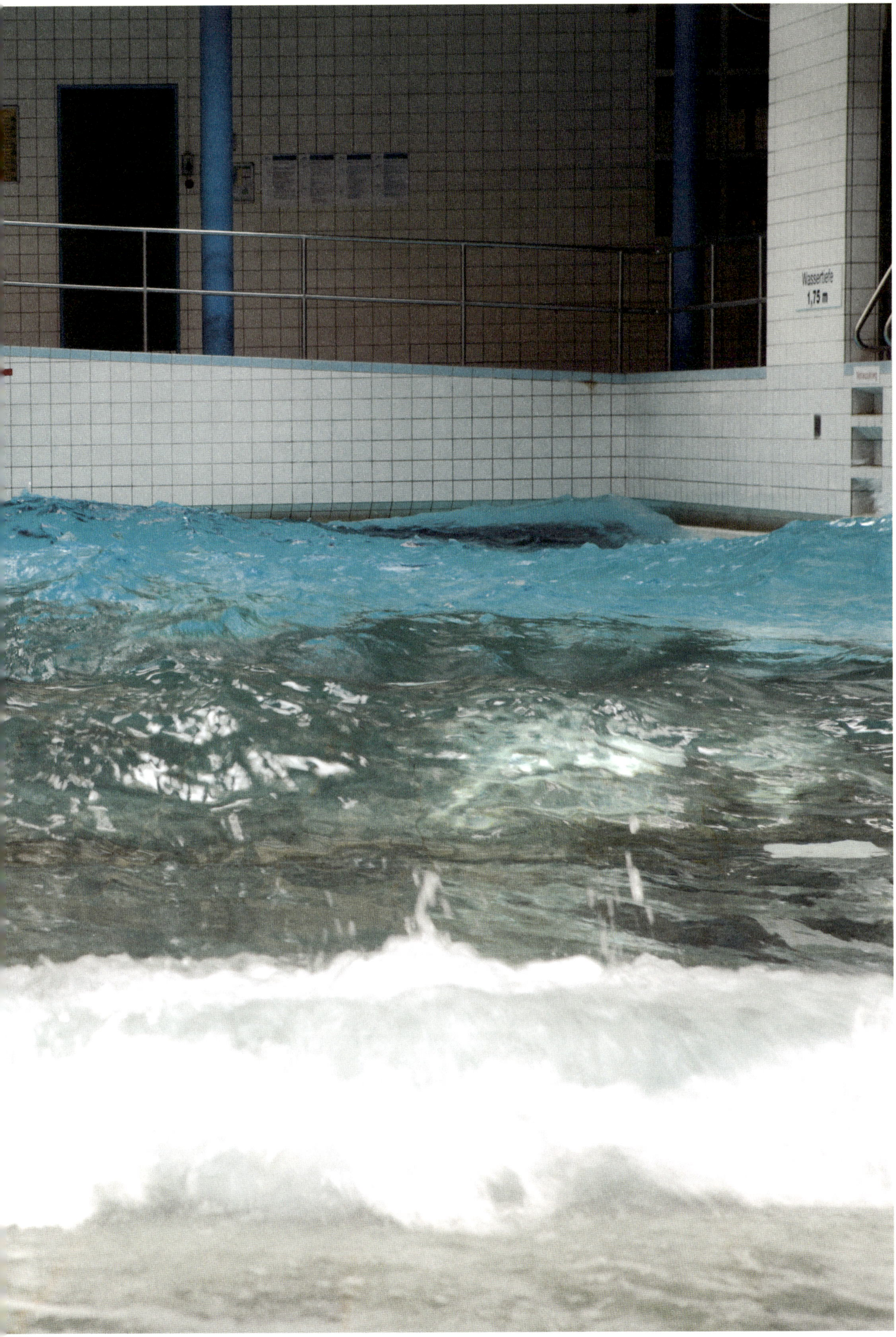
Wassertiefe
1,75 m

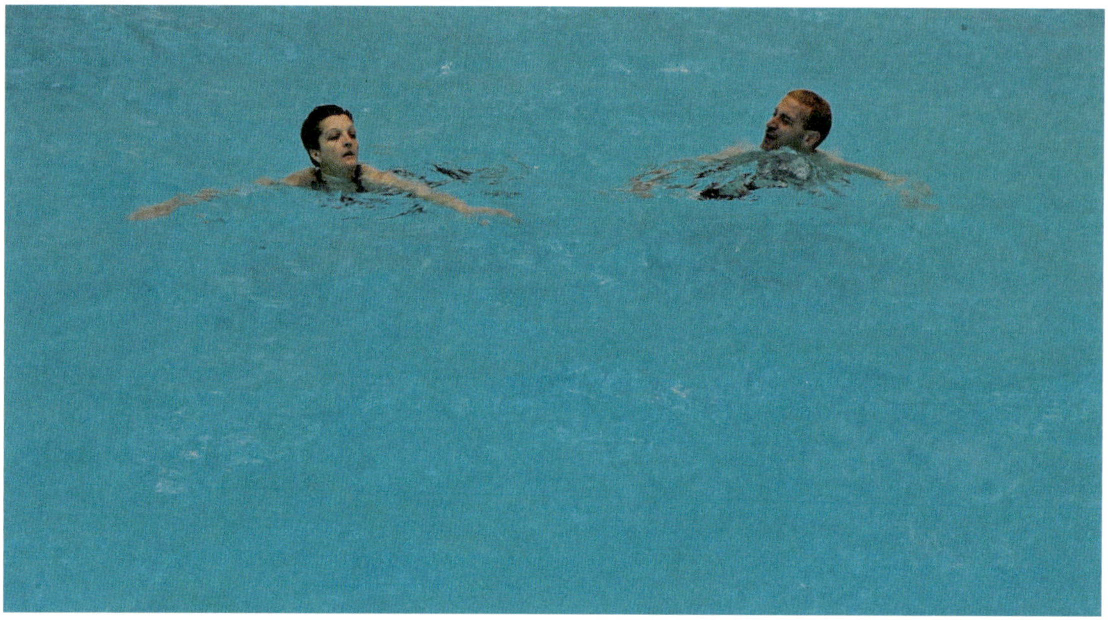
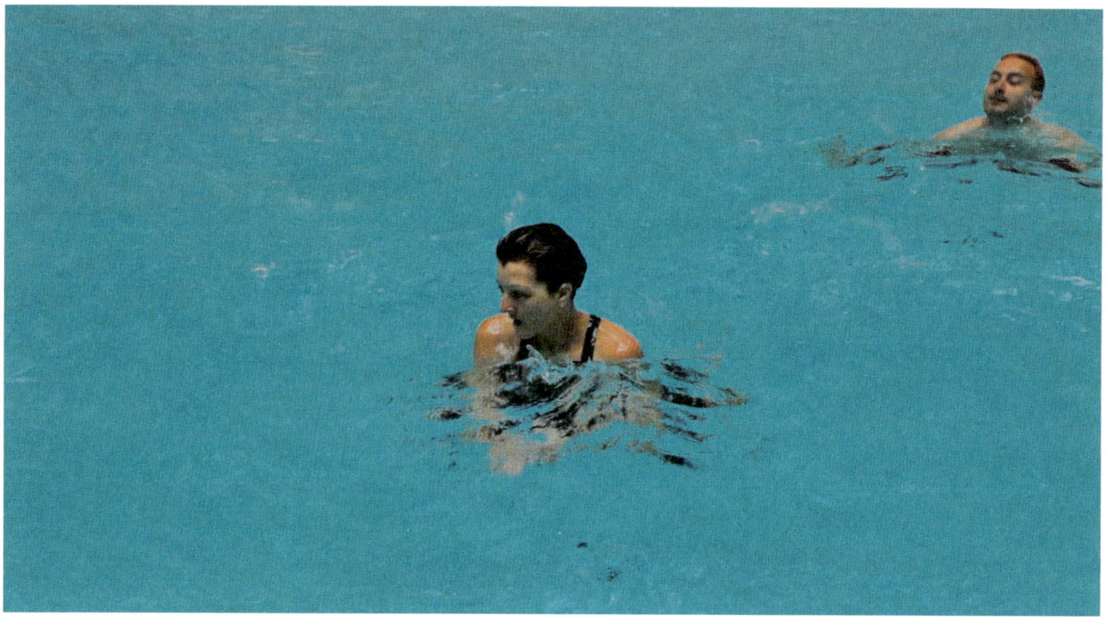
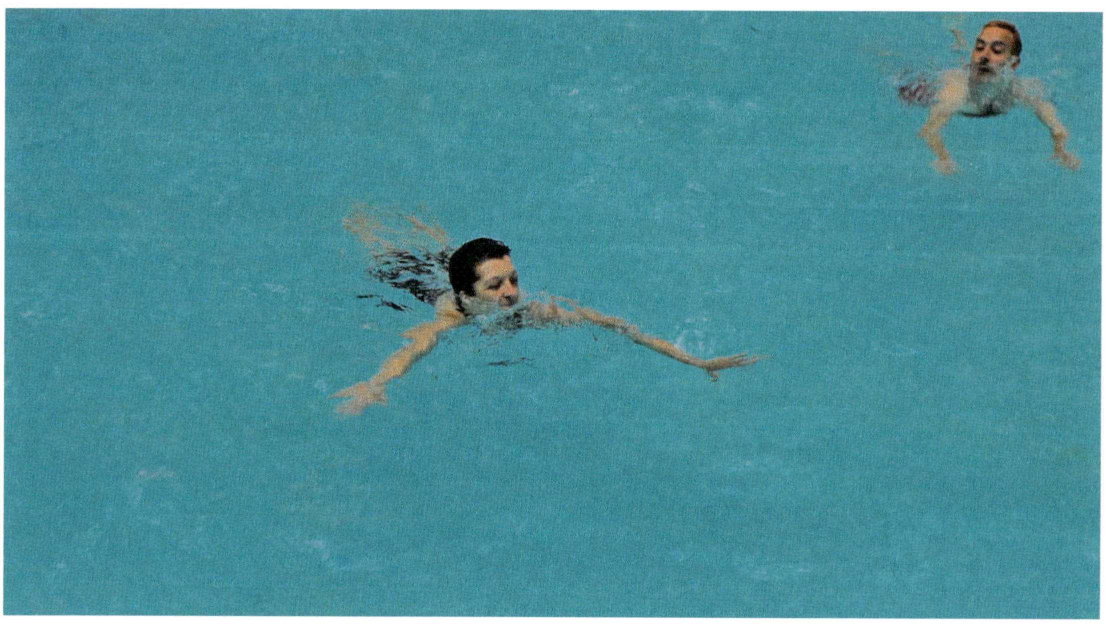

Ohio:

144, 233, 377. It's funny. We grow up listening to the same fairy-tale. We want to hear it again and again. We also want to see the same movie again and again. And we go to the same playground. We want to do things over and over. At one point in our life, we have enough of it, we don't want to listen to it anymore, we are no longer interested.

Tara:

Do you think we loose interest because we've had enough of repetition?

Ohio:

I'm not sure Tara, maybe the repetition is just not exact enough! 377, 610, 987, 1597, 2584.

S-C-E-N-E 28

Tara, Ohio and Magic Child walk in the forest. Magic Child is counting.

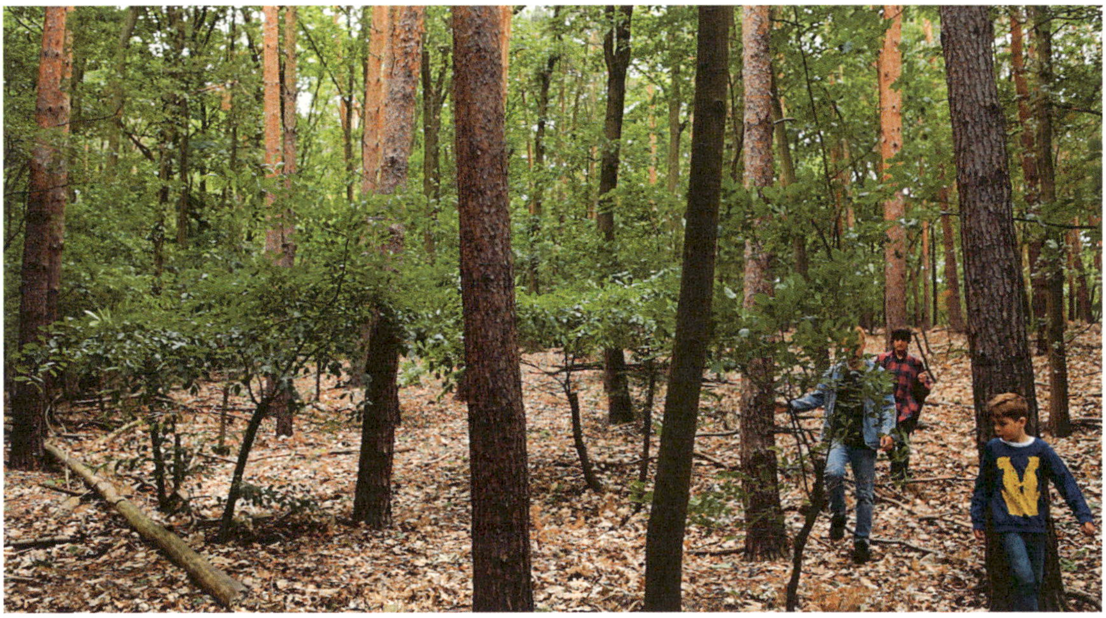

Child:

1, 2, 3, 4, 5, 6, 7, 8, 9, 10. What comes after ten?

Ohio:

11!

Child:

11, 13, 14, 15, 16, 18, 17, 19, 20. And what comes after twenty?

Ohio:

21!

Child:

21, 22, 24, 23, 25, 26, 27, 29, 30. I’m really good at counting.

Tara:

Yes, you certainly are!

S-C-E-N-E 31

Tara and Ohio play tennis.

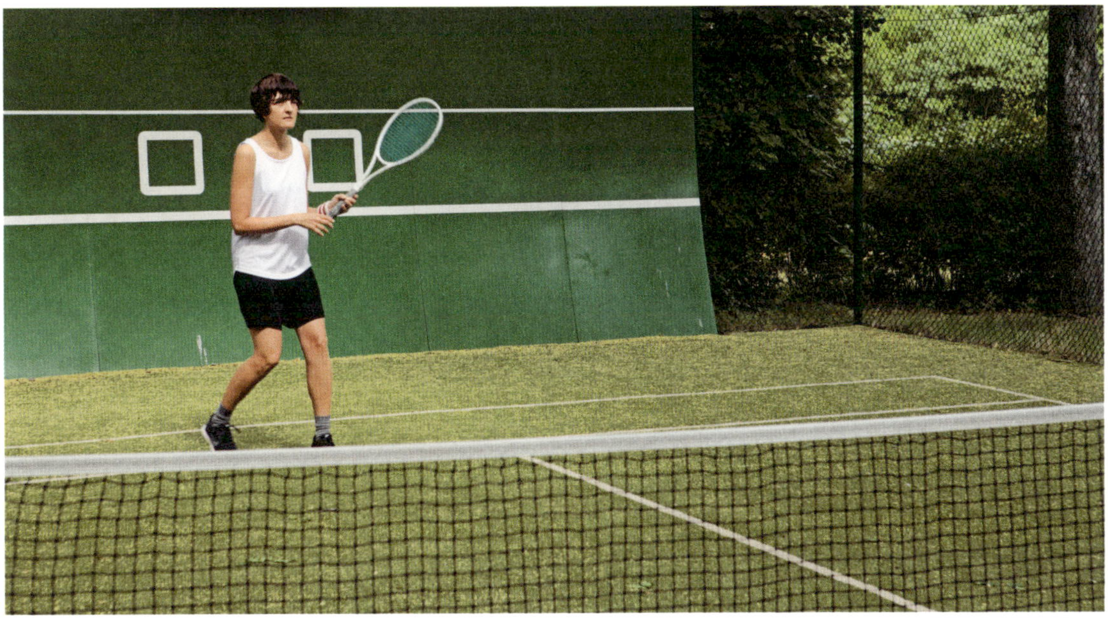

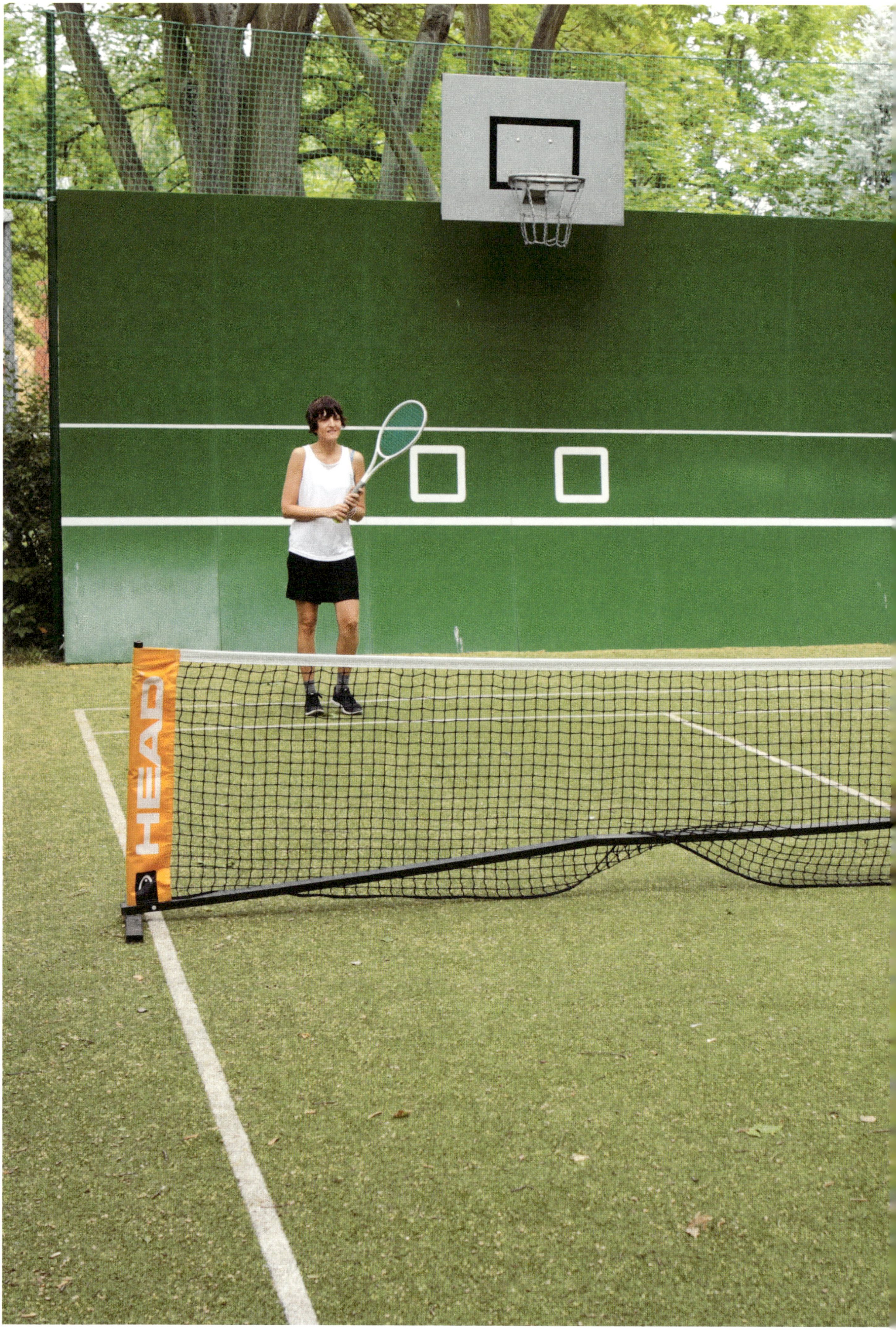
HEAD

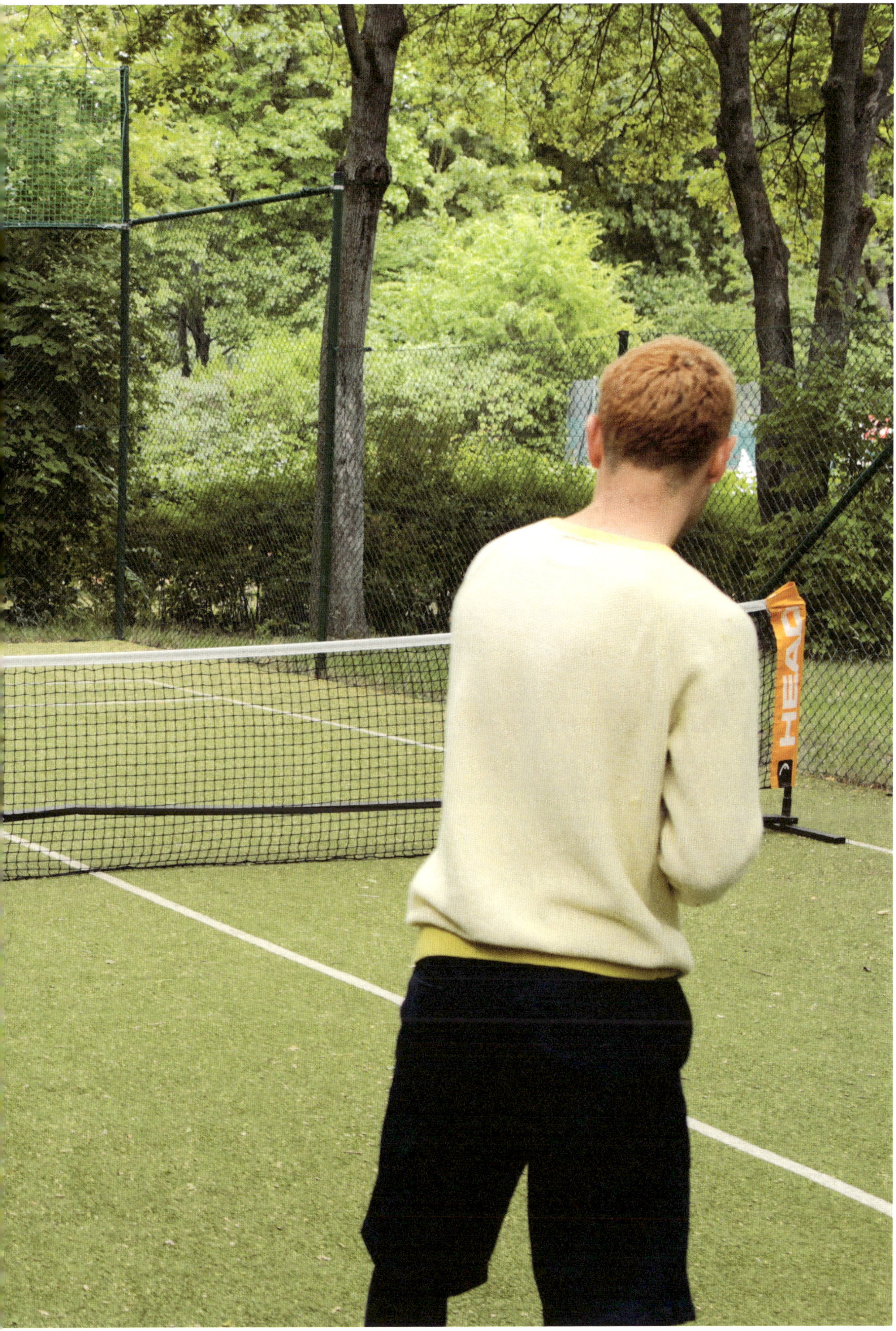

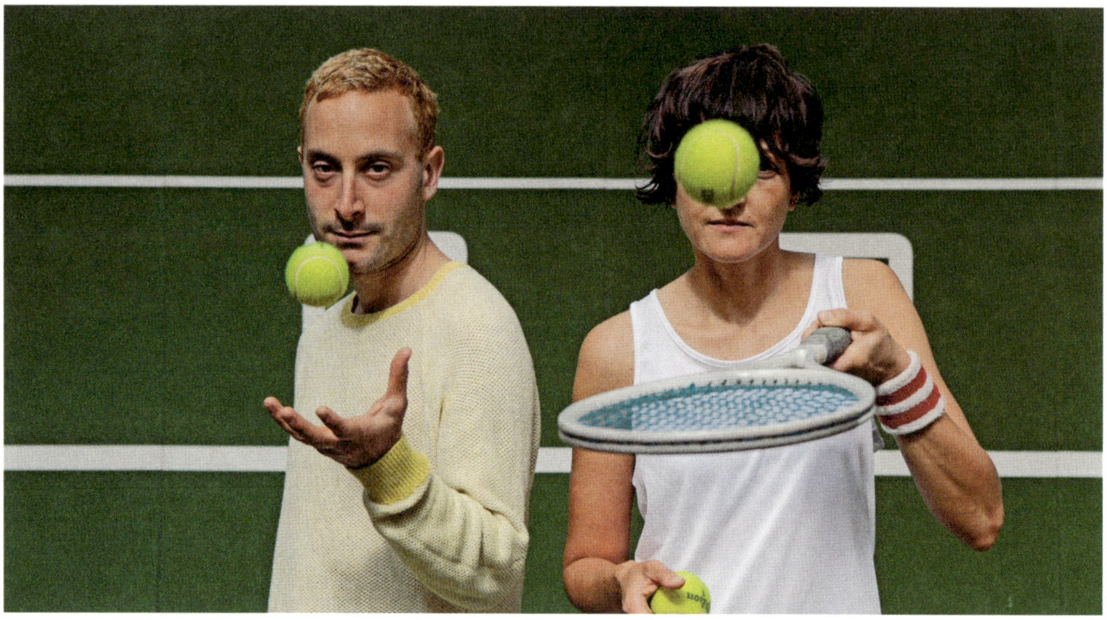

S-C-E-N-E 32

The Dot counting.

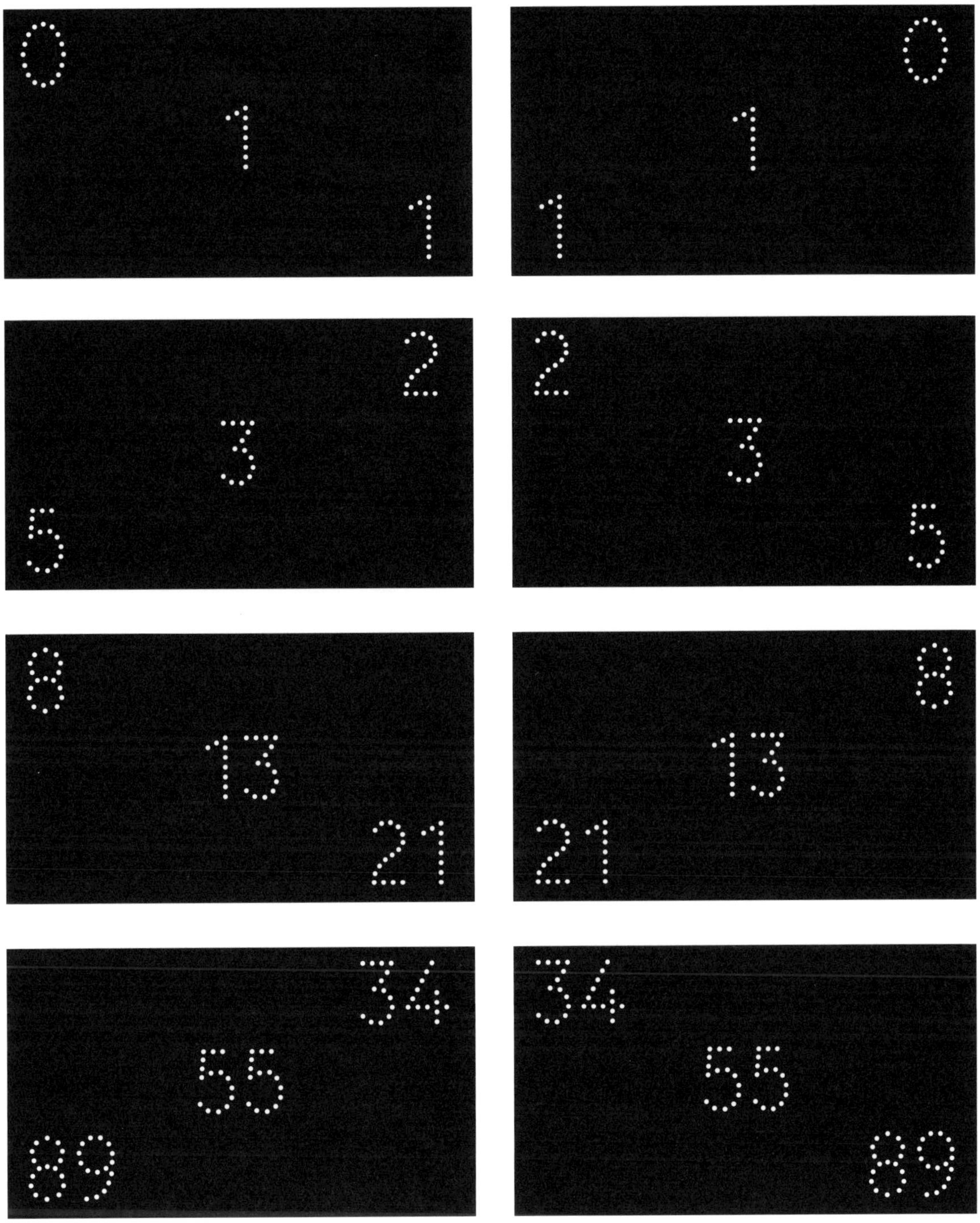

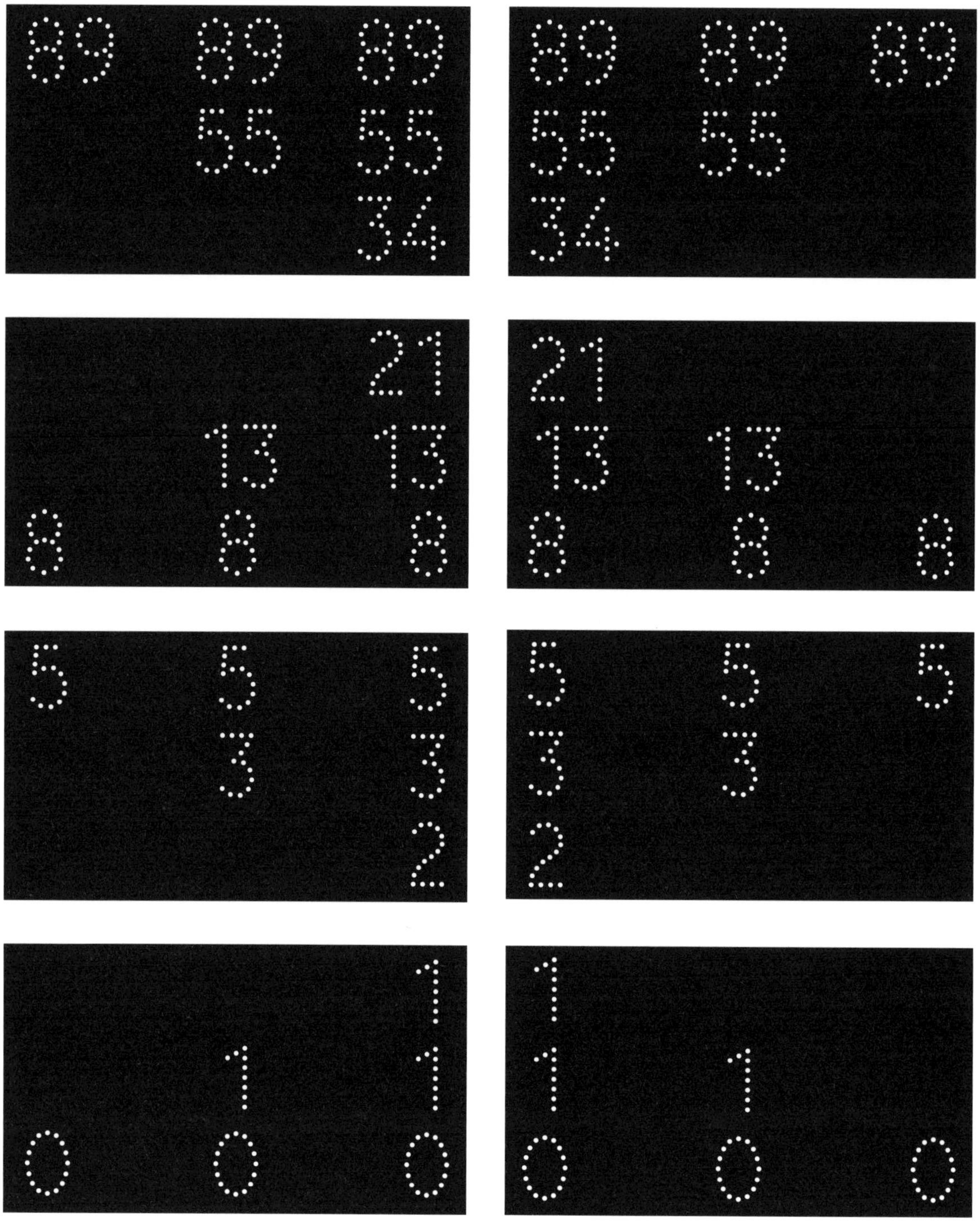
89 89 89
55 55
34
89 89 89
55 55
34
21
13 13
8 8 8
21
13 13
8 8 8
5 5 5
3 3
2
5 5 5
3 3
2
1
1 1
0 0 0
1
1 1
0 0 0

C-R-E-D-I-T-S

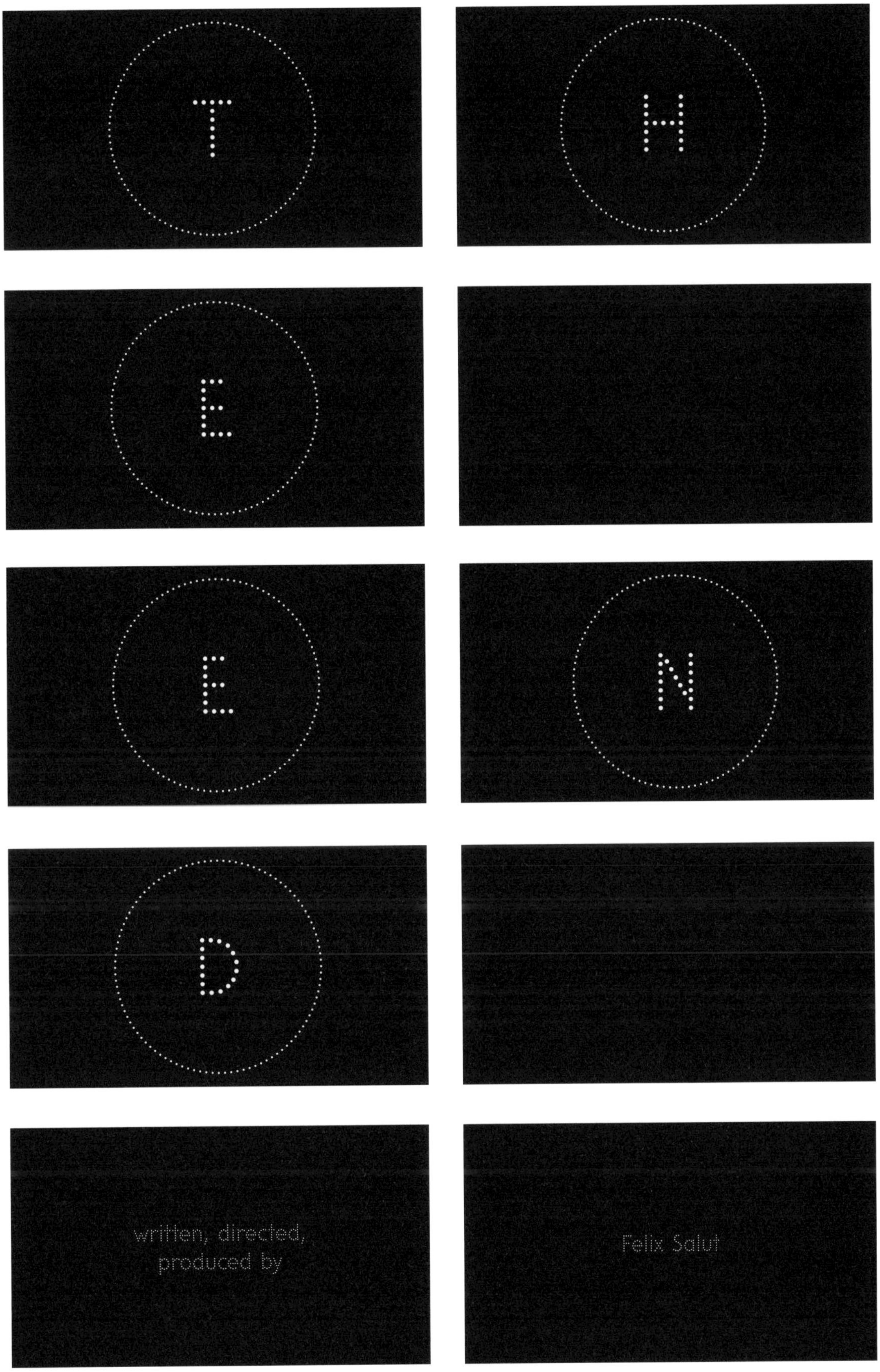

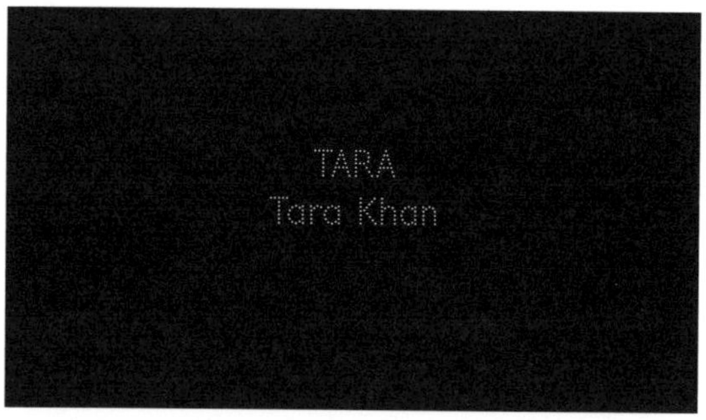
TARA
Tara Khan

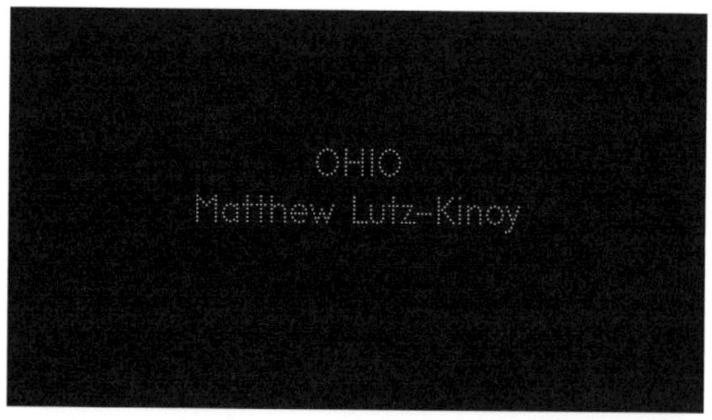
OHIO
Matthew Lutz-Kinoy

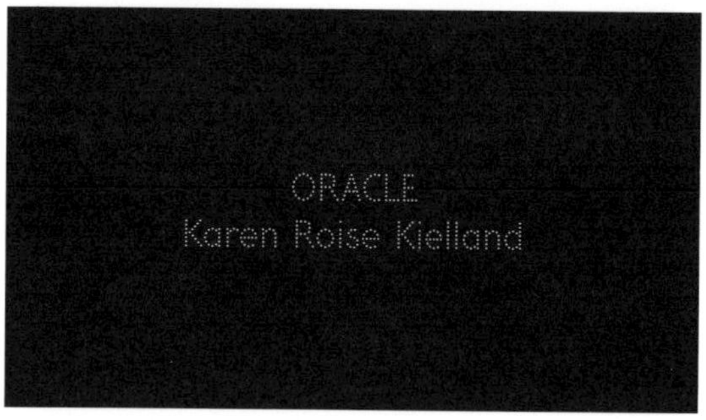
ORACLE
Karen Roise Kielland

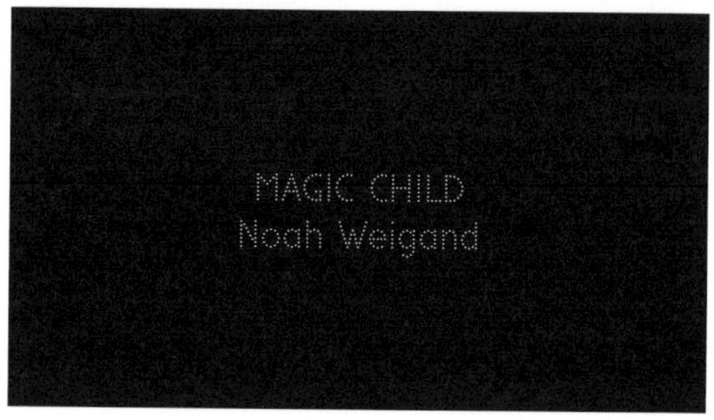
MAGIC CHILD
Noah Weigand

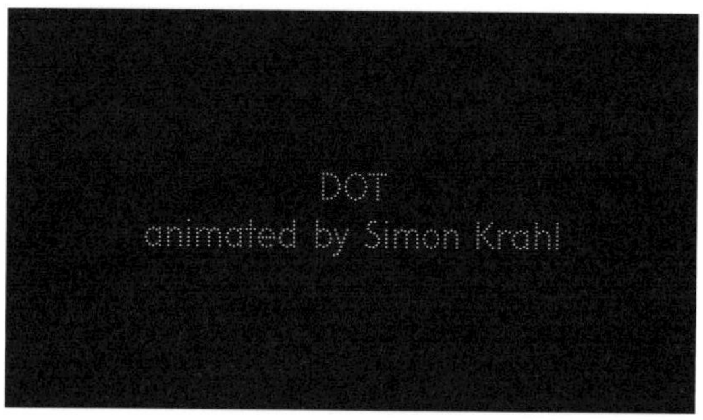
DOT
animated by Simon Krahl

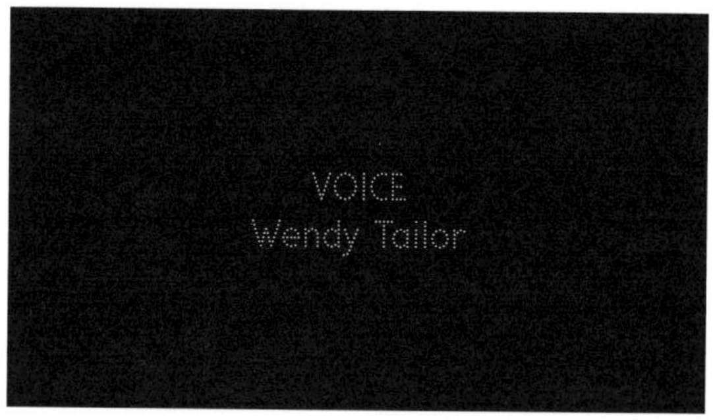
VOICE
Wendy Tailor

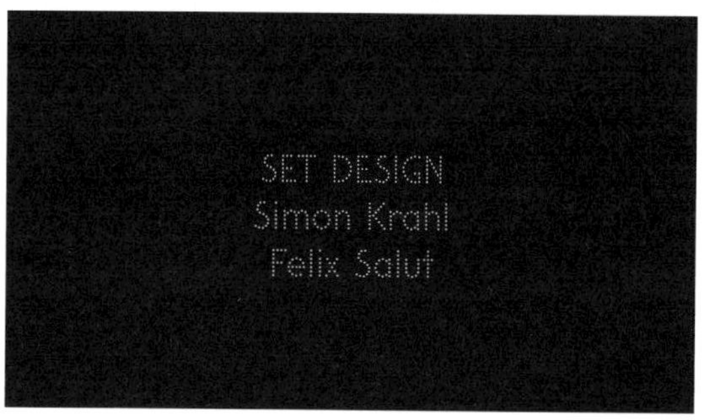
SET DESIGN
Simon Krahl
Felix Salut

EDITING
Simon Krahl
Felix Salut

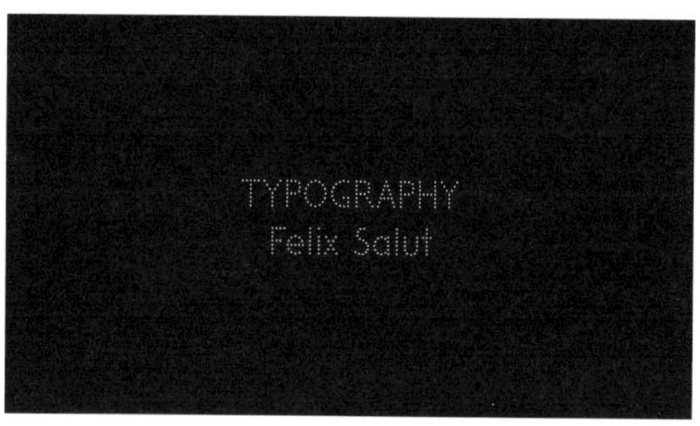
TYPOGRAPHY
Felix Salut

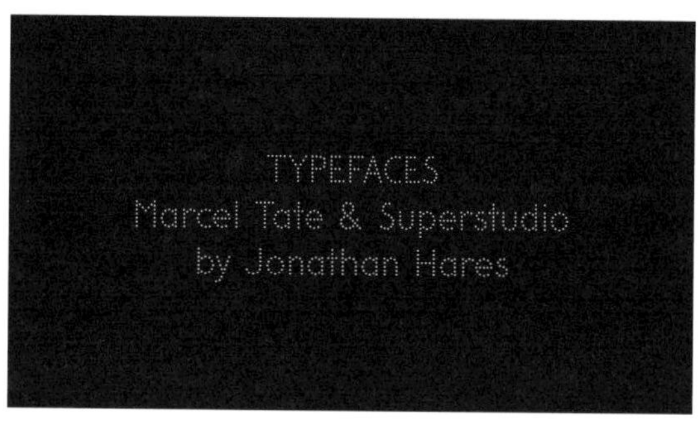
TYPEFACES
Marcel Tate & Superstudio
by Jonathan Hares

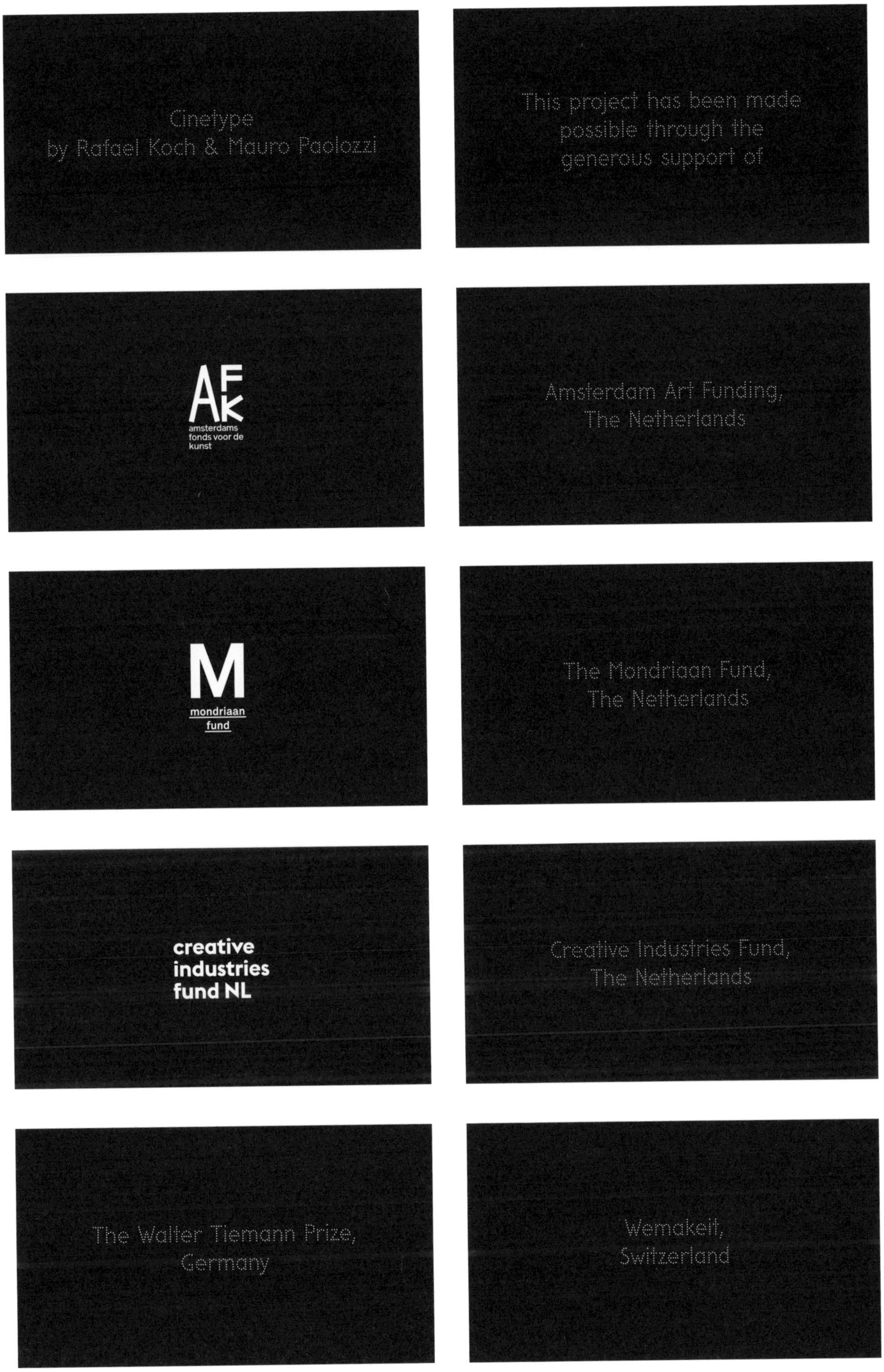
Cinetype
by Rafael Koch & Mauro Paolozzi
This project has been made
possible through the
generous support of
AFK
amsterdams
fonds voor de
kunst
Amsterdam Art Funding,
The Netherlands
M
mondriaan
fund
The Mondriaan Fund,
The Netherlands
creative
industries
fund NL
Creative Industries Fund,
The Netherlands
The Walter Tiemann Prize,
Germany
Wemakeit,
Switzerland

and the following people:

Kasper Andreasen
Anonymous (2x)
Phil Baber
Stuart Bailey

Tom Balm
Irma & Nico Barnas
Maria Barnas
Martijn Barnas

Rudi Berner
Rosa Berner
Remco van Bladel
Julia Born
Laurenz Brunner

Lorenz and Romina Bülow
Sara Cavani
Jean-Marie Courant
Cee Dee

Linda van Deursen
Veronica Ditting
Markus Dressen
Chris Evans

Christian Frey
Roland Früh
Katharina Gaenssler
Lotte van Gelder

Niklas Goldbach
Katja Gretzinger
Voebe de Gruyter
Karl Hedin

Frank Hefner
Anders Hofgaard
Christiane Holzapfel
Xander Karskens

Na Kim
Maxine Kopsa
Markus Lampert
Alon Levin

Alexandra Leykauf
Claudia Mardel
Bele Muff
Petra Noordkamp

Marie Proyart
San Serriffe Bookstore
Annemarie & Hannes Schwaab
Spector Books

Layla Tweedy-Cullen
Marianne & Rudolf Weigand
Werkplaats Typografie
Christine & Andy Wessing

Sean Yendrys

Special Thanks
to:

Aquarium im Zoologischen
Garten Berlin

Spreewaldbad Berlin

Sultan Hamam
Berlin

Medienwerkstatt des
Kulturwerks
des bbk berlin GmbH

Tamilischer Supermarkt
Raamson Berlin

THIS PUBLICATION IS PUBLISHED
BY
SPECTOR BOOKS

www.spectorbooks.com

FIRST EDITION
1200

PROOFREADING
Maxine Kopsa

BOOK DESIGN
Felix Salut

PRINTING
Bendedict Press,
Germany

ISBN
978-3-944669-67-0

BOOK
DISTRIBUTION

USA / Canada:
RAM
Publications+Distribution Inc
www.rampub.com

UK / France /Japan:
Anagram Books Ltd
www.anagrambooks.com

Australia / New Zealand:
Perimeter Distribution
www.perimeterdistribution.com

Germany / Austria:
GVA
Gemeinsame Verlagsauslieferung
Göttingen GmbH&Co. KG
www.gva-verlage.de

Switzerland:
AVA Verlagsauslieferung AG
www.ava.ch

Other Countries:
Motto Distribution
www.mottodistribution.com

FILM
DISTRIBUTION

www.felixsalut.com

Any similarity to persons
living or dead
is not coincidental.